Hawthorne,
Melville,
and the
Novel

WA 1177549 1

Hawthorne,
Melville,
and the
Novel

Richard H. Brodhead

The University of Chicago Press
Chicago and London

For Cindy

RICHARD H. BRODHEAD received his Ph.D.
from Yale University where he is an assistant
professor in the Department of English.

The University of Chicago Press, Chicago
    60637
The University of Chicago Press, Ltd.,
    London

Library of Congress Cataloging in Publication Data

Brodhead, Richard H   1947–
    Hawthorne, Melville, and the novel.

    Includes bibliographical references and index.
    1. Hawthorne, Nathaniel, 1804–1864—Criticism and
interpretation.   2. Melville, Herman, 1819–1891—
Criticism and interpretation.   3. Fiction—19th
century—History and criticism.   I. Title.
PS1888.B7 1976   813'.3'09   75.5071
ISBN 0-226-07522-2

Contents

Acknowledgments

It is a pleasure to acknowledge my indebtedness to the friends and colleagues who have helped and supported me during the writing of this book. In particular I wish to thank R. W. B. Lewis and James McIntosh, whose teaching first introduced me to the study of American literature and whose encouragement and good counsels have guided me through all the stages of this undertaking. I am also very grateful to J. Hillis Miller, for his valuable suggestions and his continuing interest in my work; to Robert Weisbuch, for his unfailing enthusiasm and extraordinary generosity; and to Mark Salkind, for conversations that have deepened my understanding of my subject. My most profound debt is to my wife—"but now alas, / All measure, and all language, I should passe, / Should I tell what a miracle shee was."

New Haven, Connecticut
17 April 1975

A Note on
Abbreviations
and Editions Cited

Quotations from the works of Hawthorne and Melville are followed by abbreviated titles and page numbers in parentheses, except that in chapters dealing with a single novel quotations from that work are followed simply by page numbers. Abbreviations refer to titles and editions as follows:

BR   *The Blithedale Romance and Fanshawe. The Centenary Edition of the Works of Nathaniel Hawthorne.* Edited by William Charvat et al. Vol. 3. Columbus: Ohio State University Press, 1964.

CM   *The Confidence-Man: His Masquerade.* Edited by Elizabeth S. Foster. New York: Hendricks House, 1954.

HSG   *The House of the Seven Gables. Centenary Edition.* Vol. 2. Columbus: Ohio State University Press, 1965.

M   *Mardi: And a Voyage Thither. The Writings of Herman Melville.* Edited by Harrison Hayford, Herschel Parker, and G. Thomas Tanselle. Vol. 3. Evanston and Chicago: Northwestern University Press and the Newberry Library, 1970.

MD   *Moby-Dick: or, The Whale.* Edited by Luther S. Mansfield and Howard P. Vincent. New York: Hendricks House, 1952.

MOM   *Mosses from an Old Manse. Centenary Edition.* Vol. 10. Columbus: Ohio State University Press, 1974.

P   *Pierre: or, The Ambiguities. Writings of Herman Melville.* Vol. 7. Evanston and Chicago: Northwestern University Press and the Newberry Library, 1971.

SI   *The Snow-Image and Uncollected Tales. Centenary Edition.* Vol. 11. Columbus: Ohio State University Press, 1974.

SL   *The Scarlet Letter. Centenary Edition.* Vol. 1. Columbus: Ohio State University Press, 1962.

TTT   *Twice-Told Tales. Centenary Edition.* Vol. 9. Columbus: Ohio State University Press, 1974.

Introduction

The span of six or seven years centering on 1850 stands out as one of the glorious ages in the history of the novel in England. This short period encompasses the creation of all the novels of the Brontë sisters, Thackeray's most permanently interesting and characteristic productions, Mrs. Gaskell's first novel, *Mary Barton,* and Dickens's first carefully structured and consistently controlled works. The coincidences of chronology illustrate the story's outlines well enough: we need only recall that *Dombey and Son, Wuthering Heights, Vanity Fair,* and *Jane Eyre* were all being written at the same time in order to realize what a concentration of creative energy this period includes within it.[1] During these years a literary genre and a body of visions in effect found each other; and the outcome combines all the advantages of a marriage of convenience and a marriage of love. The novel permits these authors to realize themselves as authors; they discover in it a structure, an architecture, within which to articulate their visions. And in doing this they return the favor; they so transform the novel, so extend its possibilities, as to make it available as a responsible and responsive form for later authors.

One of the most interesting facts of transatlantic literary history in the nineteenth century is that this glorious age of English fiction exactly coincides with a period of equally significant fictional achievement in America. This short span also encompasses the most fertile conjunction of large vision and formal craft that the American novel was to experience for at least several decades—the production of the major work of Hawthorne and Melville. Melville's *Mardi* is another novel of 1847–48, an exact contemporary of both *Dombey and Son* and *Vanity Fair.* But the central moment of this great period is even more compressed in time in America than in England. It lasts, really, for little more than two years—from the appearance of *The Scarlet Letter* in 1850 through *The House of the Seven Gables* and *Moby-Dick* in 1851 to *The Blithedale Romance* and *Pierre; or, The Ambiguities* in 1852. Simply to reconstruct

1

the chronology is to recapture part of the excitement of this period. Here again we witness a fearful and wonderful welling up of creative energy, an energy which is given form by being channeled into the production of novels and which, in the process, significantly realizes and extends the potentialities of that genre.

These two golden ages seem to be parallel but not causally related phenomena. Hawthorne read new English novels dutifully, and Melville sporadically, but the work of their English contemporaries was of relatively little importance to them as a direct influence or even as an inspiring example. The example that most helped Melville to clarify his ambitions for the novel, as "Hawthorne and His Mosses" and *Pierre* show, was that of Hawthorne's work; and the friendship of the two authors as neighbors in the Berkshires during these crucial years can be seen as symbolic of the self-containedness of their revolution.

The remarkable outpouring of novels is best understood as the product of the confluence of developments in Hawthorne's and Melville's individual artistic careers. By 1850 Hawthorne had been writing tales and sketches for twenty years, and, after having been for so long, as he says, "the obscurest man of letters in America" (*TTT* 3), he had begun to win a significant measure of recognition for his work. But there are indications that he had also come to find these sorts of productions increasingly unsatisfactory. In "The Custom-House" he imagines the scorn of his Puritan ancestors for his achievements as "a writer of story-books!" (*SL* 10). The similarly felt presence of eight generations of earnest divines recorded in "The Old Manse" again makes him feel ashamed of his "idle stories" (*MOM* 4). Under their shadow he resolves "at least to achieve a novel," a large and serious work "that should evolve some deep lesson, and should possess physical substance enough to stand alone" (*MOM* 5). Hawthorne did not carry out this resolution for four years, but from this point on, the prospect of writing a novel consistently represents for him a self-prescribed antidote to what he feels to be the idleness and insubstantiality of his short fictions. And his protestations in his later prefaces that he is a romancer, not a novelist, should not disguise from us the fact that his work with larger fictional forms is, throughout, the result of an effort to achieve the kind of serious and substantial creation that he envisages in this resolution.

Melville's advent as an ambitiously creative novelist came about more swiftly than Hawthorne's, and with less forethought. His equivalent for Hawthorne's storybooks are his first adventure narratives, *Typee* and *Omoo,* and he needs no mocking ancestors to make him laugh at himself as "H. M. author of 'Peedee' 'Hullabaloo' & 'Pog-Dog.' "[2] His turn toward a new kind of imaginative production can be conveniently located in the letter, at once saucy and totally serious in tone, in which he announces to his publisher what has happened to *Mardi.*

> Well: proceeding in my narrative of *facts* I began to feel an incurible distaste for the same; & a longing to plume my pinions for a flight, & felt irked, cramped & fettered by plodding along with dull common places,— So suddenly standing [abandoning?] the thing alltogether, I went to work heart & soul at a romance which is now in fair progress, since I had worked at it under an earnest ardor.—Shout not, nor exclaim "Pshaw! Puh!" —My romance I assure you is no dish water nor its model borrowed from the Circulating Library. It is something new I assure you, & original if nothing more. But I can give you no adequate idea, of it. You must see it for yourself.—Only forbear to prejudge it.—It opens like a true narrative—like Omoo for example, on ship board—& the romance & poetry of the thing thence grow continually, till it becomes a story wild enough I assure you & with a meaning too.[3]

Melville, unlike Hawthorne, regards his earlier works as being not too imaginative but too solid, too attached to "facts" and "common place." But as he plumes his pinions here he too, like Hawthorne in "The Old Manse," is setting out in search of a large form in which deep meanings can be evolved. In writing *Mardi* Melville initiates himself into a cult of spontaneity, a faith in the imagination's automatic creation of its own valid forms: "instincts," he tells Murray, "are prophetic, & better than acquired wisdom."[4] *Mardi* becomes a "deep book" by throwing over the "shallow nothing" (*P* 305) of its original narrative. Melville does not entirely relinquish his belief in and habit of instinctual writing at least until the time of *Pierre.* But his career as a novelist after *Mardi* is composed of repeated attempts to strike a balance between spontaneity and control, to make room for a deep book within the constraining structure of the novel form.

Hawthorne's hopeful resolution and Melville's de facto announcement stand as the bright dawn of their creative lives as novelists. But if the achievements thus forecast are impressive, it is also remarkable for how short a time these creative lives last. Both *The Blithedale Romance* and *Pierre*—the first in an understated, the second in an overstated way— confess themselves to be at least partial failures to their authors. In the preface to *Blithedale* Hawthorne seems to think that by giving "a more lifelike tint to the fancy-sketch" (*BR* 1) he has inadvertently aroused the kind of expectations of verisimilitude that he had hoped to allay. The orchestration of physical substance and fancy-work, rather than articulating a deep meaning, seems to him to have made the book's compositional features—its "paint and pasteboard" (*BR* 2)—too evident; and he feels that his work with the novel is bound to remain unsatisfactory at least until he can get better readers and more adequate conventional liberties. In *Pierre* the novelist who set out to write a "book of sacred truth" (*P* 107) ends up finding that his book has trapped him in the role of a "canting showman" (*P* 337); he becomes suspicious of the sincerity of his own meanings and he despairs of the possibility that he can communicate truthfully within the novel form. The glorious age of American fiction thus has a terminal point in a way that the English one does not. Its authors, through the very process of making their novels, come to doubt both the adequacy of their form and the validity of their own imaginative procedures.

And when we reconsider the paths that led up to their great works, this premature conclusion becomes less surprising. Hawthorne's wish to write novels is in part a desire to restrain or reharness a kind of fanciful imagination which he recognizes as being genuinely his own. Melville's declaration of independence from the narrative opening of *Mardi* is indicative of his persistent tendency to pursue deep metaphysical truths directly, and thus at the expense of novelistic incarnation. Both men possess imaginations which are in a fundamental way hostile to the kind of formal procedure that the novel's organization requires. As a result— and this is what makes the nature of their glorious age so utterly unlike that of their English contemporaries—all of their work is characterized by a powerful tension between their visions and the nature of the genre they choose to work in. Their careers as novelists are made up of repeated efforts to stabilize this tension, to discipline their imaginations, on the one hand, and on the other to modify and reconstruct the constitutive conventions of their genre in such a way as to make it a more fit vehicle for their peculiar visions. This tension is as central to their best work as it is to their worst, and it is the secret link between the new formal possibilities that they created for the novel and the dead ends that they encountered.

The relation of author to genre in Hawthorne and Melville, then, is best described not as a productive marriage but as a protracted affair, beginning with the experience of new and strange pleasures, continuing through a period of accumulating misunderstandings and mistrust, and culminating in a discovery of mutual betrayal. Their affair with the novel is my subject in the following chapters. Hawthorne's and Melville's artistic tempers, methods, and ambitions differ considerably, so that we must study each of their experiences of this affair in its own terms. At the same time, their separate cases exhibit strikingly similar patterns of development; and their individual productions possess so many shared features as to exemplify, taken together, a distinct mode of formal creation. Their work composes a unified phase of endeavor and achievement, one that eloquently testifies to the possibilities and difficulties attendant upon the domestication of the novel in America.

I

Form

Ah, how dost thou change,
Agnello! See! thou art not double
   now,
Nor only one!
            Dante, *Inferno*, cited by
            Melville in *Pierre*

1 | Hawthorne, Melville, and the Form of the Novel

"It is with fiction as with religion: it should present another world, and yet one to which we feel the tie" (*CM* 207). When we undertake the study of a novel's form we are not abstracting or marking off a detachable feature for independent consideration but rather paying attention to the nature of a fiction's other world and to the way in which it makes us aware of itself, the way in which it makes us feel the tie. Nothing in a novel exists in itself; each included element has its being—its relative massiveness or slightness, its relative significance or insignificance—in its relation to the novel's whole configuration of elements. A novel's form is the system of relations in its created world, the elementary laws of conservation and interaction that structure its behavior and govern the potentialities within it for meaning and for action. To paraphrase Wayne Booth's comment on fictional rhetoric, a novelist may not choose whether or not his work will have a form; his only choice is what kind of form he will achieve for it.

To consider novel form, then, is to consider the whole way in which an author presents his fiction's reality to himself and to us. In such a study nothing in the novel can be exempted from our attention; but at the same time everything must be seen in its relation to the created totality. We must be concerned with plot, with character, with setting, not as discrete entities but as minor structures within the major one: we are, then, less interested in what happens in a plot than in how a plot gathers together and gives direction to the novel's elements as an action; less interested in the nature of characters than in how they are articulated and related, how the novel's energies and concerns are delegated into their beings. Similarly we must be less concerned with themes themselves than with the way in which themes are won from or immersed in the novel's actuality, the degree to which the novel's elements are marshaled into and out of organized patterns of significance. The study of form involves the consideration not so much of what happens as of what sorts of things can happen and how they happen, not so much of what the novel means as of how it has its meaning—but our questions are phrased in this way on the understanding that such a study is not separate from but is rather a precondition for the elucidation of a novel's action and meaning.

The novelist brings his fictional world into existence by telling a story, and whatever else he may succeed in arousing our concern for, it is in the first place *as* a story that his work makes its claims on our interest. In making a novel he must tell one thing after another; and establishing expectations of some sort of satisfaction of curiosity as the story unfolds is one important way in which he capitalizes on the temporal nature of his form. The extent to which novels play upon this future-directed curiosity, of course, varies greatly. In the romance forms which Hawthorne inherits, the reliance on interest in surprising endings is nearly total; the sort of adventure narrative that Melville's work starts from tends to arouse and satisfy curiosity about unusual experiences at each stage of its progress, but this continual dissipation of interest is counteracted by the sense of forward movement through time which the journey itself creates as a plot. Once the novelist succeeds in getting us moving forward, the ends for which he can solicit our curiosity vary equally greatly, as R. S. Crane's useful discrimination among plots of action, character, and thought suggests.[1] But no matter how tactful or shameless an author is in arousing our curiosity, and no matter how elementary or sophisticated the objects toward which he directs this curiosity, in choosing to write a novel he makes a tacit commitment to the premise that the kind of world he wants to create can be articulated through a temporal narration, through an account of the progressive unfolding of sequential experience.

The novels of Hawthorne and Melville are no exceptions to this rule, and their works offer impressive examples of the novelist's ability to regulate primary curiosity and to transmute it into more complex interests. Each chapter in *The Scarlet Letter,* for instance, unfolds a new portion of its characters' lives in such a way as to move us inexorably forward toward their climactic moment. From the point at which Hester resolves to go to Dimmesdale's aid each chapter helps us to envision in a new way the form which that moment of crisis will take; our progress toward that denouement is retarded, however, and our interest in it simply as an event is converted into an acutely discriminating moral and psychological interest in the quality of the characters' experience. *Moby-Dick* both in its quest plot and in its plot of cetological inquiry manages to refine the basic interests of an adventure narrative into what can only be called an epistemological suspense.

But at the same time, Hawthorne's and Melville's commitment to the representation of experience in its unfolding is, in an interesting way, somewhat equivocal: alongside their forward-directed narratives we find evidence of efforts to circumvent temporal communication. Thus at critical moments in *The Scarlet Letter* the story stands still and we are left staring at the scarlet letter itself, at a mute symbol that seems to reabsorb into itself and communicate instantaneously the "tale of human frailty and sorrow" (*SL* 48) that the narrative tells sequentially. To choose a comparable instance in Melville's works, in *Moby-Dick* when Ahab, in "The Grand Armada," sees that the *Pequod* pursuing whales ahead is itself pursued by pirates behind, the sequential narrative opens up to include a momentary vision of the whole action and the whole meaning of Ahab's quest. The action which must be lived through and which can thus form a plot gives place to a vision which takes us outside of plot and allows us to look back on it in its entire outline. Northrop Frye writes in "The Road of Excess," "Narrative in literature may also be seen as theme, and theme *is* narrative, but narrative seen as a simultaneous unity."[2] The epiphanic moments in *The Scarlet Letter* and *Moby-Dick* lead us abruptly from narrative to theme in this sense, and from a temporal to an atemporal vision.

Such moments of vision are, of course, hardly unique to Hawthorne's and Melville's works, but the kind of resistance to sequential narration that they embody is highly characteristic of their novels. We can see this resistance in another form in the way in which their novels frequently articulate strong thematic or conceptual designs which are not at odds with their story's content but which are at odds with its dramatic method.

A particularly interesting example occurs in *The Blithedale Romance.* This novel, like *The Scarlet Letter,* presents a cast of characters who are all intimately linked to one another by strong bonds of love and hate, and its action consists in the dance of approaches and withdrawals, of alliances and estrangements, by which they group and regroup themselves. But alongside its passionate intrigue *Blithedale* contains a second line of suspense, introduced in the first chapter and nurtured with extreme care all through the book, which teases our curiosity about the real relationship between Priscilla and Zenobia. This second line is, in a strange way, muffed. The secret is discovered offstage, it has nothing like the effect on the action which we have been led to anticipate, and none of the characters except Priscilla seems at all interested in dwelling on it after it has been revealed.

The nature of the revelation as it is recast by Miles Coverdale into the tale "Fauntleroy" makes clear what has gone wrong. This tale uses the secret half-sisterhood of Priscilla and Zenobia to place them in a conceptual relationship; it is the means by which they become allegorized as the daughter of shame and the daughter of pride, the daughter of poverty and the daughter of wealth. In these terms they exemplify the two possible conditions of womanhood in an artificial and money-oriented society. They are apparently opposites, but they are secretly sisters, secretly akin as women and as victims. This conceptualized arrangement affords us an important vantage point on the book's drama: it permits us to see the shared power of love in the two women and the overlapping patterns of masculine exploitation—they are both victims first of their father's social station, then of Westervelt, then (nearly) of Hollingsworth—by which their powers of love have become perverted. Blithedale receives these two as a test of whether its new society can transcend false social conditions and restore them to their true selves and to their true relationship.

But Hawthorne's artistic problem is that the secret's worth to his book's meaning and to its plot fail to coincide. When the secret is revealed the characters are already too overextended in the drama of their personal relationships to pause and consider the meaning of their relationships in terms of such an abstract scheme; and the narrative action has already accumulated so much dramatic momentum that it cannot now, if it will, change itself into an allegory. And so the secret is made known hurriedly, then dropped; and the true plot—the plot of passionate lives—resumes.

The attempt to impose a static conceptual design on dynamically actual human relationships fails in *Blithedale;* idealized reorderings are defeated by the energy of unregenerate reality in the book's form just as they are in its utopian community. But the kind of dual perspective that this book thus fails to maintain is a structural possibility that Hawthorne and Melville return to again and again. The dream vision of Enceladus in *Pierre* is analogous in function and procedure to the tale "Fauntleroy" in *Blithedale.* It too serves to make known a secret so well kept that the novel now has little room left in which to include it, and it too makes its revelation by translating the lived relations of its characters into a conceptual schema. In it Mrs. Glendinning and Isabel lose their individual and personal natures to become the double incarnation of Terra, the goddess through whom the original heavenly paternity of the doubly incestuous Enceladus is twice bound down to earth. The complex web of relationships which has transformed Pierre into an impotent Titan is, here, translated from dramatic into mythic terms, such that the temporally revealed characters and their progressive interactions become points in an all-seen pattern.

"Fauntleroy" and the vision of Enceladus are climactic recognition scenes. What makes them instructive as examples, however, is that the modulation from dramatic to thematic organization that they exhibit is not confined to such scenes; it is a persistent feature of Hawthorne's and Melville's presentation of relationships.

Thus in *The House of the Seven Gables* the relationship between Hepzibah and Phoebe Pyncheon is sometimes presented in what could be called its human aspect—each is seen as having her own prejudices, affections, and embarrassments, and their gradual coming to terms with each other is shown dramatically as a function of their personal capacities for relation. But at other times Phoebe and Hepzibah are placed side by side in frozen postures and labeled as exempla of contrasted concepts—May and November, youth and age, plebeian and aristocrat, present and past. When Ahab, Starbuck, Stubb, and Flask are pulling after whales they are related as men engaged in a community of activity and excitement; but when, after the climactic scenes in "The Quarter-Deck" and "The Candles," each of them steps forward in turn to deliver his reaction in a soliloquy, the conspicuous organization of their responses serves to show them related to one another as stages in a hierarchy of modes of being.

Like Cervantes and Fielding, and unlike their English and European contemporaries, Hawthorne and Melville characteristically include within their novels minor narrative forms set off as discrete units of fiction. Their interpolated tales serve as a kind of auxiliary heart for their books, gathering in, purifying, and reenergizing their animating concerns and then pumping these back into the narratives that envelop them. Because the tales always retell the work's larger story in a more highly stylized fictional mode we see in them more nearly face to face what we see elsewhere in the novel more darkly. Isabel's "vague tale of terribleness" in *Pierre* (121) permits us to see the essential nature of that book's sequential drama as an exploration of "humanness among the inhuman-ities" (*P* 123). The "wild, spectral legend" (*BR* 107) Zenobia tells in "The Silvery Veil" is a parable of love illustrating the moral and psychological consequences of commitment and reserve told to a group and a community whose own most essential choice is the same as the one that confronts Theodore in her story. We will see later on how such other interpolations as Holgrave's story "Alice Pyncheon," Ishmael's "The Town-Ho's Story," Coverdale's "Fauntleroy," and Plotinus Plin-limmon's pamphlet "Ei" operate in their specific contexts. What should be noted at this point is that all of these tales produce the same effect as the shifts in focus by which lived relations among the characters come to be seen in terms of conceptual patterns. They force us to step outside the novel's unfolding action and see its whole design in clarified form, to understand in its meaning what is elsewhere articulated as drama.

The kinds of thematic structure we have been examining are evidence of reservations in Hawthorne's and Melville's commitment to the novel as a temporal and dramatic form. What needs to be insisted on now, however, is that that commitment *is* genuinely equivocal. The narrative frame is not, for them, simply an imposed necessity, a hostage offered to a novel-reading public within which they write the kind of fiction they really believe in. It embodies, for them, positive values. However much they are interested in conceptual schemes, they are also interested in experience which must take the form of a story, in dramas of personal self-fulfillment and self-destruction that can be visualized only as they unfold themselves in time. Both interests seem to these authors valid ways of understanding experience but are not, for them, homogeneous. The dual structures in their novels of thematically arranged and individually lived life, of simultaneously seen and sequentially revealed action, are their ways of doing justice both to the texture and to the meaning of experience. Hawthorne and Melville both genuinely *are* and genuinely are *not* interested in plot and character; and this is so because they both do and do not wholly subscribe to the understanding of experience which those constitutive conventions embody in the novel.

Rather than telling several different stories, Hawthorne and Melville usually tell a story in several different ways. The coincidence of chronology that sets *Mardi* beside *Dombey and Son* and *Vanity Fair* offers an instructive example here. These books are all instances of what Barbara Hardy calls the expansive novel, the massive work which attempts to reproduce something like the spacious scale and range of life itself. But while Dickens and Thackeray do this by shuttling back and forth among different lives, Melville's multiple plot is composed of stories that differ from one another in kind as imaginative creations; it moves among adventure narrative and romance quest and allegorical satire, among the visions and modes of discourse of poetry, philosophy, and history. Dickens's and Thackeray's character groups interact with one another both causally and as alternative moral possibilities, and their multiple plots are indexes to their concern with all different sorts of lives; Melville's, by contrast, are indexes to his concern with different ways in which life can be envisioned and understood.

Mardi is an extravaganza, but as a "polysensuum" (*M* 357) it is typical of the novels we are considering. *Moby-Dick,* for instance, is like *Anna Karenina* in that it achieves its structure by counterpointing two plots, each of which belongs to a major character. Ahab and Ishmael might even be tentatively compared to Anna and Levin as paired figures, one of an intensity leading toward self-destruction, and the other of an intensity leading toward self-creation. Tolstoy's stories have antithetical conclusions, but as stories they share a common method of dramatic exposition. But in Melville's novel these different sorts of life-potential come into existence in different kinds of plot, a suspenseful and linear story that leads toward a completion in Ahab's encounter with the white whale and a jerky, digressive, constitutionally incomplete narrative that traces Ishmael's efforts to get to know the whale. Hawthorne does not write in the expansive form—like Jane Austen's or Turgenev's, his work thrives on constriction—but we can observe a somewhat similar interplay among different kinds of plot in his novels. To the double system of suspense in *The Blithedale Romance*, in which one line of interest leads toward a movingly human completion, the other toward an intellectual recognition,³ may be compared the coexistence in *The Scarlet Letter* of suspense about what choice Dimmesdale will make and what effect this will have on the others with the—again, more intellectual—suspense engendered by Hawthorne's frequent references to a mysterious presence on Dimmesdale's bosom. In *The House of the Seven Gables* the plot of the present-day Pyncheons moves toward its completion in Jaffrey's death, Clifford's revival, and Holgrave's and Phoebe's marriage; but intertwined with this is a historical plot, the story of seven generations of pyschic warfare, which has its own culmination in the recovery of the deed and in the revelation of Holgrave's identity as the modern Maule. None of these supplementary lines is as fully independently realized as Melville's multiple plots usually are, but they do make us pay a kind of attention to the unfolding action distinctly different from that of the main plot. And in this respect they do function as Melville's plots do: they represent not so much different sorts of life as different ways of imaginatively arranging life into significant actions.

W. J. Harvey is surely right in seeing the novel as a form defined by its liberality, its openness to "the partial, the limited, the relative, the imperfect"⁴ in its multiplicity rather than in its unity; the novel's world is, if not always unruly, at least attentive to what Melville calls "ragged edges." But it remains for the novelist to decide what kind of multiplicity, or multiplicity in what direction, he will seek to include. Hawthorne's and Melville's common tendency to tell a story in several ways is symptomatic of their characteristic decision on this point. They achieve what Yeats calls an "emotion of multitude"⁵ less by representing a large variety of individual lives, or by giving a small number of characters a large variety of occasions or relations or attitudes or feelings, than by *seeing* their subjects in a large variety of ways.

A comparison may be helpful here. The first paragraph of *Mansfield*

Park shows how Jane Austen makes her small world dense. In presenting the marital fates and fortunes of the three Misses Ward she surrounds their choices, by a ventriloquist's art, with a wealth of evaluative words illustrating the overlapping and conflicting claims of legal, societal, financial, and familial considerations. The paragraph itself thus becomes a verbal microcosm of the novel's community, of the complex system of relationships in which the individual is defined and defines herself; and the narrator's voice, sliding into and out of different value systems and playing these against one another, exemplifies the maximal lucidity which the heroine will need to achieve in order to live within her world without simply submitting to it.

We can put beside this the brief first chapter of *The Scarlet Letter*, "The Prison-Door." It too has a confined subject—the static scene of the prison—and it too moves around its subject in such a way as to sketch in the rudimentary outlines of a world. The narrator finds in his scene occasion for meditations on the antithesis of liberty and restraint, of utopia and prisons, of life and death, of nature and civilization. He combines and recombines his scenic elements, interweaving as he does so an antiquarian's interest in historical fact with a willingness to let things create a mood, a sociological commentary with a symbolic organization. Finally, he comes to rest on the red rose bush, which becomes, as he puzzles over it, first a locus of natural sympathy, then a token of the survival into a civilized state of the energy of precivilized wild life, then a relic of a miracle of integrity, a heretical emblem of the sainthood of Anne Hutchinson, and finally a symbol of the book's own prospective "sweet moral blossom" (*SL* 48). What we see, here, is a mind playing across its objects, allowing them to enkindle reflections and projecting onto them its own thoughts and feelings. The process ends up by giving us, as the opening of *Mansfield Park* does, a picture of the conflicting and coinciding exigencies of the individual's life in a community; but here in addition we watch that sense being made, we watch a mind calling that system of multiple life into being by making use of all the resources of its own imagination.

The multiplicity in "The Prison-Door" is, then, a function not of the reality it addresses itself to but of the ways in which it brings that reality into existence. And in this respect the chapter is typical both of *The Scarlet Letter* and of the other novels under consideration here. We need only think of all the different kinds of mental activity—of fancy, sentimentalizing, symbol-seeing, allegorization, and so on—in *The House of the Seven Gables* to see the extent to which imagination makes much of a paucity of compositional elements in that book. *Moby-Dick*, by contrast, is a novel full of things, but its hugeness is achieved finally less through the length of its inventory than through the sheer variety of suggestions which Ishmael finds in things and of mental stances, sciences, and languages through which he tries to grasp things. In a sense the most characteristic sentence in *Moby-Dick* is Ishmael's: "I have another idea for you" (*MD* 347). The emotion of multitude in these novels attaches itself not so much to the life they represent as to the liveliness with which they go about their representations. It exists not in the novel's created world but between the reader and that world; or, more accurately, it comes into existence in the author's act, joined in by the reader, of calling that world into being, of sending to his objects different sorts of what Keats calls greetings of the spirit in order to constitute them to himself as real and meaningful.

This helps to explain the sort of cast of characters that Hawthorne and Melville create. The novels of Dickens or Thackeray or Eliot or Tolstoy require casts of hundreds, and the edges of their novels' worlds are inhabited by minor characters whose existences can either dimly adumbrate alternative life-possibilities or simply serve to fill out those worlds with redundant life. There are many fewer minor characters in Hawthorne and Melville, and the ones they do create are usually rather centrally related to thematic concerns—Uncle Venner seems to exemplify the possibility of mental health through anti-possessiveness in *The House of the Seven Gables;* Charlie Millthorpe in *Pierre*, a rather uninspired imitation of such Dickensian good-natured lame-brains as Tom Pinch and Mr. Toots, is repeatedly called upon to stand for a variation on the theme of head and heart. The web of alternative possibilities in their novels is realized not through a large society but through the kinds of meaning they attach to different settings, through overlapping systems of allusions, through modulations of voice and verbal style, through the plurality of surmises by which multivalent symbols are read—in short, through local intensities and variations in the novel's imagined surface itself.

And the characters they do create reinforce this sense of multiplicity of surface. In *Pierre* each character is presented in a mode of fiction appropriate to the mental world he inhabits. Melville's style takes on the crisp ironic tone, the attention to intonation and gesture, of a novelist of manners as he approaches Mrs. Glendinning and Reverend Falsgrave, the characters who think of themselves and others in terms of social forms; Isabel is rendered in a lurid gothic style appropriate to this partial prisoner of the unconscious; Lucy, the novel's good angel, is fashioned according to the idealizing conventions of sentimental romance. It is as if the author so highly respects the individual nature of each character that he can only envision them in the terms in which they envision themselves; or, to put it another way, it is as if in imagining characters the author conceives of a personality and of a fictional mode at the same time. We will have occasion to examine the workings of a similar art of character in other novels later. Hester Prynne and Roger Chillingworth, Ahab and Stubb are like characters from different kinds of books; they differ from one another not just as variations on a common human nature but as different ways of imagining the contents of human nature. We can even find such differences of kind within the mode of being of single characters. The social theme of *The Blithedale Romance* requires Priscilla to be sickly, the spiritual theme requires her to be clairvoyant, and the novelist never allows us to decide, and apparently never decides himself, whether she is a creature of urban naturalism or of spectral romance.[6] Barbara Hardy speaks of minor characters in George Eliot's novels who exist "on the margin of someone else's excitement";[7] the cases of Pearl and Fedallah, both of whom are sometimes seen as individuals but sometimes as projections of the psychic lives of Hester and Ahab, show how much more literally her phrase can apply to the characters of Hawthorne and Melville. Their characters seem to have been greeted into being in different ways, created and ushered into the novel's house by different kinds of imagination.

The variety of ways in which characters are conceived and presented in Hawthorne's and Melville's novels can be understood as a special case of a more general phenomenon, the coexistence in these works of distinctly different representational modes. The first chapter of *The Scarlet Letter* illustrates this in little: in it things are seen now simply as objects, now as suggestive segments of a social reality, now as emblems of a supersensual natural power, now as symbols of an order of moral truth. As the focus of vision changes, the mode of existence of the objects changes too. They become less and less indifferent or "free," more and more laden with urgent meaning. All these novels make use of this sort of shift in focus in coordinating their larger units.

Hawthorne and Melville are not customarily thought of as sharing the concerns of nineteenth-century realists, but in their novels they do experiment with the methods of realism with considerable care. The barroom in *The Blithedale Romance* in which Coverdale corners Old Moodie is, as a seamy underside of city life, a subject worthy of Balzac. And Hawthorne's descriptive technique here is also somewhat Balzacian: Coverdale's minute attention to the observable details of the scene—its seedy clientele, its decor of fountains and paintings of idealized dinners

—creates a solidly factual image which also gradually reveals, in its debased luxury, the aspirations and failures of a segment of society. Melville's extended description of the Church of the Apostles in *Pierre* similarly focuses on an image of inverted urban community, a spiritual center which, abandoned by its newly prosperous congregation, has become the haunt of downtown lawyers and displaced intellectuals. Here again a patient and self-effacing record of a place and its human activities gradually comes to suggest the workings of a larger society, and explicitly the workings of larger processes of social change.

But in these two books this style of vision is one among many. The city at night in *Pierre* is less an objective environment than an externalized nightmare, its details arranging themselves into a self-terrifying vision of evil's assaults on innocence. If things constitute a solid social setting in the barroom, when Coverdale returns to Blithedale he sees the features of the scene he passes through as charged with portentous significance: a riverbank and a moldering woodpile conjure up intimations of mysterious deaths. In *The House of the Seven Gables* things outside the house—in the railroad car, in the street and shop—are mostly seen as solid and present actuality, while everything in the house and its garden is seen as symbolic of something else; chickens and chairs repeat the story of ancestral sin and decline. In *Moby-Dick* a line can be at one moment a functional physical object and at another an emblem for the human condition in a world in which "all men live enveloped in whale-lines" (*MD* 281); a comic vision of purposeful present activity in a world of solid but slippery surfaces such as we find in "Cisterns and Buckets" can instantaneously change into a transcendent vision of miraculous rebirth. The alternation of large movements in which things are seen as things and in which they take on enormous meanings or open up to reveal the interlinked wonders and terrors of a more supernatural world is what gives *Moby-Dick* its distinctive rhythm; but the alternation conducted on such a large scale in this book is present in and characteristic of all of the novels we are considering.

Hawthorne and Melville do not try to merge the representational modes they use, nor do they try to efface their differences by moving among them gradually and transitionally. If anything, they enlarge the differences; they allow each mode to write its own chapters, to bring its own kind of world into existence. And this is true of their art of character as well. Other novelists who share with them the rich confusion of a double legacy from an analytic or realistic and a projective or romance tradition— Dickens is a prime instance—include characters different in kind just as Hawthorne and Melville do. Thus in *Dombey and Son* Mr. Dombey is considered with the psychological attentiveness of an analytic novelist, Florence Dombey is seen as a fairy-tale princess, and Good Mrs. Brown has about her the supernatural aura of a romance witch.[8] Dickens does not try to minimize these discrepancies of fictional kind, but his novel is so full of partially overlapping character kinds that the differences of mode among them become less prominent. Hawthorne and Melville include few of such modal mediators; nor do they attempt, in articulating their characters, to make them more homogeneous. Melville's effort is to make Ahab and Stubb less, not more, alike; one becomes a figure of comic realism, the other is decked out as "a mighty pageant creature, formed for noble tragedies" (*MD* 73). Similarly in *The Scarlet Letter* Hester takes on more and more moral and psychological complexity, while Chillingworth progressively recedes into the role of the Black Man of pure romance. Hawthorne and Melville enlarge and emphasize the differences of vision out of which their characters are being formed.

The multiplicity of imagined surface we have been observing in these novels is symptomatic of a more fundamental formal principle. The interpolated tales, all of which are written in fictional modes asymmetrical to that of the main narrative; the multiple plots and lines of suspense which are related not just as different stories but as different ways of putting a story together; characters who seem to come out of different kinds of books; representational modes which envision and achieve meaning for parts of worlds in radically different ways—all these characteristic features testify to the fact that Hawthorne's and Melville's novel form is insistently a mixed medium. Instead of trying to subsume varied material into a unifying and homogeneous narrative mode they compose novels by bringing together and placing alongside of one another different kinds of fiction. These authors are fundamentally unwilling to delegate to any one style of vision or organization the exclusive right to represent their world. As a result they generate in their works a conflict of fictions, and the reality of their imagined world, rather than lying in any one of these fictions, comes into existence in their interaction.

This realization helps us to see how we should take the claim both of the novelists themselves and of their modern critics that the distinctive feature of their work is, in Richard Chase's words, its "assumed freedom from the ordinary novelistic requirements of verisimilitude, development, and continuity"[9]—its reliance on the vision and method of romance. This claim should initiate, not terminate, discussion. After all, when we call to mind *Jane Eyre* or *Great Expectations* or *Jude the Obscure* we recognize at once that the heritage of romance is not exclusively American property. The now traditional either/or that pairs European and American fiction as exempla of antithetical fictional modes ignores complicated similarities among these bodies of literature; further, it implies too simple and absolute a distinction between "novel" (or "realism") and "romance."

What is most helpful about the work of Northrop Frye is his recognition of a body of basic fables present in all fiction. What distinguishes one book's version of such a fable from another's, for Frye, is its degree of displacement, the canon of plausibility to which an author adapts it.[10] This view enables us to understand realistic fiction not as a faithful imitation of real life but as a group of stories seeking to cloak their fabulous nature within the illusion of such an imitation. A realistic novel moves to turn the fairy precinct, the unlocalized psychic space, of romance into an actual historical and geographical province; it strives to individuate and "humanize" the shadowy figures of romance by giving them complex personalities and by situating them in a complex web of social relations; it works to supply for the motions of romance plot the causality of well-motivated and probable events of actual life. Frye's view sees all fiction except pure myth as combining romance elements and realistic displacements, so that these two terms can stand for not stable and mutually exclusive categories but rather tendencies each individual work combines in its own way.

Frye's discussion of displacement makes it clear that what is distinctive about Hawthorne's and Melville's work must be a function less of the fact that they make use of romance than of the way they make use of it. And it is in these terms that Chase's generalizations become genuinely helpful. In Eliot's *The Mill on the Floss* Lucy Dean and Maggie Tulliver are paired as the light and dark ladies of romance, and Maggie's reflections on the heroines of Sir Walter Scott bring the presence of this archetypal formulation into the novel's consciousness. But if her thoughts clarify its presence, they also have the effect of making us see how much the archetype has been displaced, how much less romantic and more socially complicated the world of *The Mill* is than the worlds of *Waverley* or *Ivanhoe*. However suggestive hair color may be, the real relation of Eliot's cousins is also a function of personal affection and rivalry, of family ties, of the economic dependence of the Tullivers on the Deans, and so on. The Lucy of Melville's *Pierre* is also paired with a dark-haired antithesis, the mysterious Isabel, but rather than presenting this as one facet of their complicated relationship Melville insists over and over on the pure fact of the schematic formulation. He reverses Eliot's customary displacement to seize the archetypal formulation in its pure form.

And Melville's practice here is typical. Hawthorne looks at Roger Chillingworth in such a way as to see the diabolical villain of romance within the more realistic character of a seventeenth-century physician-scholar. In *Moby-Dick* Melville looks through the whaling cruise in such a way as to see its "secret part" (*MD* 241), the romance action of the dragon-slayer's quest. Hawthorne and Melville are bent on discovering romance in its rawest and most primary forms, romance as romance.

This urge is one distinctive feature of their art; what we have said about their mixed medium permits us to see another. Different kinds of fiction compete with one another in their novels because they contain within them romance forms displaced to several different degrees. If Ahab's quest is authentically mythic in its dimensions, in the greater part of *Moby-Dick* Ahab is out of sight, the white leviathan slips the mind of both narrator and reader, and the cruise becomes a busy occupational venture with occasional opportunities for scientific inquiry; the romance plot fades into the light of common day. In *The Scarlet Letter* the plot suspense about a grimly magical manifestation of a symbol in physical form and the suspense about complicated moral actions play against each other as a more primitively romantic and a more realistic kind of psychological fiction. The differences in kind among the Veiled Lady, Priscilla, and Zenobia or Fedallah, Ahab, and Ishmael reproduce the varying degrees to which characters have emerged from a spectral state into one marked by greater complexity of present being. Because tales like "Alice Pyncheon" and "The Silvery Veil" translate the central situations of their novels into a more ghostly romance, these novels permit us to see the same action represented in the different versions of alternative fictional modes. Hawthorne's and Melville's effort to recover raw romance is not an end in itself but part of a larger design: the authors construct their novels by exploring and exploiting the differences of imaginative potential of disparate genres of fiction.

All of this supports Chase's contention that Hawthorne's and Melville's fiction is marked by "its perpetual reassessment and reconstitution of romance within the novel form."[11] But I think we should insist more than Chase does on the way in which this reassessment is carried out within the novels themselves. A tale within a tale makes us conscious of both tales as fictions; and the difference between the worlds the smaller and larger units bring into being makes us aware of the different kinds of imaginative selectivity and activity out of which they have been created. The conflict of fictional mode among different kinds of character and plot has the same effect. Hawthorne and Melville do not simply include different literary modes in their works; they play them off against each other, and they do so in such a way that each mode reveals the imaginative basis of the others' fictions and tests their capacities as vehicles of truth.

This suggests that whatever kinship Hawthorne and Melville may have with authors like James Fenimore Cooper and Charles Brockden Brown as American romancers, their work also bears an authentic family resemblance to that of an earlier generation of reassessors and reconstitutors of romance—to *The Faerie Queene*, to *Don Quixote*, to *As You Like It* and *King Lear* and *The Tempest*. Hawthorne and Melville create a homegrown version of the constant formal practice in Renaissance romance of gathering together different kinds of literary expression and orchestrating them into a complex harmony in which each measures itself against the others as a mode of vision. This composite form comes into existence not as a consistent representation of either an exterior or an interior reality but as a ring of concentric circles of illusion, arranged such that what is real in any one circle is seen to be imagined and imaginative at another. And for both the Renaissance authors and their American descendants this artistic structure is a formal correlative to an understanding of reality not as something given but as a range of possibilities, each of which requires a specific sort of human perception for its realization.[12]

This leads us to recognize a final feature of Hawthorne's and Melville's art—its self-consciousness. Rather than trying to pass themselves off as reflections of a preexisting real world their works call attention to themselves as fictions. They do this not to discredit themselves but to heighten our consciousness of the imaginative processes through which their images of reality come into being. By making us aware of their own art of illusion they engage us in a consideration of a larger subject, the nature of the mental activities through which the fictions of literature, among others, are created. Hawthorne's and Melville's mixed medium is the record of their own adventures in exploring the imaginative creation of reality, and to the extent that it makes us self-conscious of our own activity as readers it is their invitation to us to join them in this adventure.

In invoking Spenser, Cervantes, and Shakespeare as godparents for Hawthorne's and Melville's mixed form I do not mean to assign to them the authority of a primary model. Hawthorne's continuing interest in Spenser is well known, and Melville's debt to Shakespeare is so extensive that it is hard to imagine how the tragical histories of Ahab and Pierre could have been conceived without the examples of *Macbeth*, *King Lear*, and *Hamlet*. But there is little to indicate that Hawthorne and Melville were either chiefly interested in or even particularly conscious of the formal procedures of Renaissance romance as such. Indeed the recurring formal features of their novels described in this chapter seem to be only partly the result of a deliberate artistic intention. There is evidence of their desire to create a mixed and self-exploratory kind of fiction, but in addition in some of their novels they seem to produce such a form in spite of their intentions, not because of them. In any case Hawthorne and Melville do not start out with a well-defined aesthetic program and then seek to enact it in an individual work. They are, rather, true experimenters: what this chapter has presented as an accomplished formal design is better understood as something they achieve in response to their own specific imaginative needs while they write. If the products of their experiments bear a genuine resemblance to the self-conscious forms of Renaissance romance, what is most interesting is that they come to reinvent such forms by encountering problems and possibilities of their own.

I suggested earlier that the mixed medium of Renaissance romance is the artistic coordinate to a sense of reality as a set of imaginative possibilities. Hawthorne's and Melville's fiction proceeds from such a sense as well; their self-consciousness about the nature of literary fictions is closely related to their intuition that the structures of human reality—social, moral, cosmological—are in some sense also mental creations. But again, just as they do not start out with a program or a model for their art, so too their work is not a controlled enactment of anything coherent or conscious enough to be called a philosophy of reality. The overt interest in experience as a set of imaginative structures in such later works as *The Blithedale Romance* and *The Confidence-Man* would seem to suggest that they take fictions as their subjects more and more consciously as they proceed, and thus that they become interested in the nature of fictions by making them. The imaginative basis of reality is, like their form, something they discover, explore, extend, and evolve in the very process of writing their novels.

It seems to me that the final interest of Hawthorne and Melville lies less in any message they have to deliver than in their energetically inquisitive habits of mind, and that the permanent value of their work has less to do with the fully developed images of life that it unfolds than with its investigation of how the mind envisions and makes sense of experience. Their persistent artistic experimentation is in the service of a larger process of exploration carried forward in new directions in book after book. After finishing his greatest work Melville looks not backward but forward: ''So, now, let us add Moby Dick to our blessing, and step from that. Leviathan is not the biggest fish;—I have heard of Krakens.''[13] We get closest to their novels by approaching them in Melville's spirit, by considering them not as a unified and finished achievement but as a series of tentative formulations, each of which realizes certain possibilities and also opens up new ones. Thus now that we have uncovered some of the shared formal features of Hawthorne's and Melville's books by considering them synoptically, we must now examine their novels dramatically, as the unfolding records of their attempts to find an appropriate form for their imaginations.

II|

Hawthorne

"The House of the Seven Gables:
A Romance. By Nathaniel Hawthorne. One vol. 16mo, pp. 344."
The contents of this book do not
belie its rich, clustering, romantic
title. With great enjoyment we
spent almost an hour in each separate gable. This book is like a fine
old chamber, abundantly, but still
judiciously, furnished with precisely that sort of furniture best
fitted to furnish it. There are rich
hangings, wherein are braided
scenes from tragedies! There is old
china with rare devices, set out on
the carved buffet; there are long
and indolent lounges to throw
yourself upon; there is an admi-
rable sideboard, plentifully stored
with good viands; there is a smell
as of old wine in the pantry; and
finally, in one corner, there is a
dark little black-letter volume in
golden clasps, entitled "Hawthorne: A Problem."

Melville to Hawthorne,
16? April? 1851

2 | Hawthorne
by Moonlight

Whatever may have been Hawthorne's private lot, he has the importance of being the most beautiful and most eminent representative of a literature.... He is the writer to whom his countrymen most confidently point when they wish to make a claim to have enriched the mother-tongue, and, judging from present appearances, he will long occupy this honourable position.[1]

Henry James's claim for the value of his subject at the opening of his critical essay *Hawthorne* is interesting in that he presents it not as a personal opinion but as an authoritative statement of a self-evident truth. As such these lines reflect a curious feature of the history of Hawthorne's reputation. If there is some justice to Hawthorne's own claim to have been for many years the obscurest man of letters in America, it is remarkable how quickly and how generally he came to be seen, starting about the time he was publishing his major novels, as one of the most illustrious—as a writer whose achievement was of such an order as to offer a shining example of what an American author could do. Hawthorne no longer stands quite so alone as an eminent case as he did for James, but he retains a special place in the tradition of American fiction as a master and originator. However interesting the works of Cooper and Poe may be, *The Scarlet Letter* is the first genuine masterpiece among American novels, and it is as well the first American novel that other novelists have continued to regard as suggesting possibilities for their own art. The admiration of figures like Melville, James, Howells, and Faulkner, as well as George Eliot and D. H. Lawrence, is a finer tribute than that of popular reputation, for it is the tribute of fellow artists to the power of Hawthorne's vision and to his command of their common craft.

In view of Hawthorne's stature as a novelist it always comes as something of a surprise to recall that writing novels was a belated second career for him. After the abortive *Fanshawe* he confined himself to the shorter forms of fiction for twenty years. And his eventual turn to the novel was not, really, the result of his work's accumulated momentum. As he himself recognized, the direction of his most mature work is better indicated by his earliest tales than by the sketches of the 1840s. Certainly it is his whole literary achievement, and not just his novels, that qualifies him for James's "honourable position." But Hawthorne tended to consider story-writing and novel-writing as separate endeavors in his artistic life. His attitude toward his shorter works is a complex one, worth considering for a moment for the light it sheds on the crucial transition in his career.

If we can trust his word in the prefaces to *Twice-Told Tales* and *Mosses from an Old Manse,* what strikes Hawthorne as he reviews the accumulated production of two decades is its perpetual failure to amount to anything worthwhile. He presents these collections to us as bedraggled and faded bouquets. His twice-told tales have, to him, "the pale tint of flowers that blossomed in too retired a shade" (*TTT* 5); the new pieces in *Mosses* are "idle weeds and withering blossoms," while the older ones are "faded things, reminding me of flowers pressed between the leaves of a book" (*MOM* 34). This note of self-deprecation is, of course, characteristic of all Hawthorne's public presentations of himself, and it is not always to be taken at face value. But his evaluations of his short works are cast in terms of imaginative patterns of such urgency in his thought that they must be taken seriously, if not literally. When he sees his ancestors scoffing at his career in "The Custom-House"—" 'A writer of story-books! What kind of business in life,—what mode of glorifying God, or being serviceable to mankind in his day and generation,— may that be?' " (*SL* 10)—Hawthorne has no ready answer with which to meet them, and his problem is made all the harder by his own partial allegiance to the standard they invoke against him, his own belief in the value of sharing in "the united effort of mankind" (*SL* 38). When he writes that the pictures of life in *Twice-Told Tales* are "not always so warmly dressed in its habiliments of flesh and blood, as to be taken into the reader's mind without a shiver" (*TTT* 5), and when he calls the contents of *Mosses* "fitful sketches, with so little of external life about them, yet claiming no profundity of purpose" (*MOM* 34), he links his work to the chill shadow worlds, devoid of human warmth and reality, that stand as a peculiarly horrible sort of death-in-life all through his fiction.

Hawthorne shows the position of the creator of such airy nothings in "The Devil in Manuscript." "By aping the realities of life" Oberon succeeds only in emptying that life of its reality and "surrounding myself with shadows." And his preoccupation with his imagined creatures leads him "into a strange sort of solitude—a solitude in the midst of men—where nobody wishes for what I do, nor thinks nor feels as I do" (*SI* 172). Not only is he not serviceable to mankind; his art has severed him from sustaining contact with the vital chain of human concern. Obviously Hawthorne's position as an author is not simply identical to Oberon's. But his insistence in each preface that "I have done enough in this kind" (*MOM* 34) indicates an abiding discontent with his shorter works, and to the extent that his deprecations of them are sincere they are based on a revulsion from the sense of unreality and isolation of which "The Devil in Manuscript" presents the extreme instance.

Hawthorne records a particularly interesting fit of this revulsion in "The Old Manse." As he approaches his new home in Concord, the manse's former occupants, its eight generations of saintly divines, seem almost physically present to him. The sense of the holy and strenuously thoughtful work to which this spot is consecrated has the effect of making its first lay inhabitant pause to reconsider the direction of his own career. The first stage of this reassessment is simply negative. In the presence of the manse's spirit of high seriousness "I took shame to myself for having been so long a writer of idle stories" (*MOM* 4). But he immediately discovers that the spirit of this place also enables him to form more positive conceptions of new vocational possibilities. Completely yielding his own claims and imagining an identity for himself in terms of the strong tradition of the place, he sees that he might write books in the divines' own vein, "profound treatises of morality." Or—and here he gradually begins to distance himself from the divines—he might retain their matter but treat it from his own more secular point of view, writing "a layman's unprofessional, and therefore unprejudiced views of religion." Or he might transfer their habit of serious meditation to a secular subject matter and produce "histories . . . bright with picture, gleaming over a depth of philosophic thought." And finally: "I resolved at least to achieve a novel, that should evolve some deep lesson, and should possess physical substance enough to stand alone" (*MOM* 5).

At this critical juncture Hawthorne works his way through the manse's forcefully presented ideal to a point at which the role of artist once more seems valid to him. What enables him to come full circle in this way is his ability to conceive of a new form for his art. To win his own self-approval here he needs to feel that he too is capable of undertaking a large and serious treatment of the nature of human existence; and he locates the capacity for this sort of treatment in the novel. As a novelist he will be dealing with physical substance, not shadows; as he evolves deep lessons he will be able to claim a profundity of purpose; if he will not be directly engaged in the united struggle of mankind, his solitude will now have the character not of sterile isolation but rather of the "accessible seclusion" of the divines themselves, who step apart from the everyday life of humanity only to the end of serving as its source of self-comprehension. By rejecting the idle story and embracing the novel he will be changing not just the genre but the whole nature and value of his art. And although the novels he was later to write are not quite of the kind that he envisions in his last resolution, Hawthorne's gravitation toward the larger genres of fiction must be understood as a function of the commitment to an earnest imaginative address to human experience that he dramatizes here.

Hawthorne did not carry out his resolution at the Old Manse. To observe his actual emergence as a novelist we must turn from "The Old Manse" to the next chapter of his spiritual autobiography, "The Custom-House." In accepting the position of Salem's customs inspector Hawthorne seems to have found a more efficient way of releasing himself from the prison of mental solitude and joining in the real life of men. Reacting against the excessive imaginativeness and intellectuality of Concord life he welcomes his new duties as a chance for him to "exercise other faculties of my nature, and nourish myself with food for which I had hitherto had little appetite" (*SL* 25). But he quickly sees that his apparent involvement with actual experience here is delusory; this existence threatens to become even more inauthentic than his previous one. As he contemplates the enervating effect that public life has had on the officers of the Custom House he comes to wonder whether the private imaginative resources he had been content to let lie suspended may not be in danger of permanent destruction.

The central action of "The Custom-House" shows how Hawthorne enters into this "unnatural state" (*SL* 42) and how he gains release from it. The essay's movement repeats his own: it begins outside the Custom House and slowly moves up to and into the building, until finally, in its innermost corner, Hawthorne makes a discovery that brings about a rebirth of his imaginative powers, a discovery that permits him to come forth from the building and his false life there—and to come forth a novelist. "The Custom-House" purports to prove the authenticity of the materials of *The Scarlet Letter,* but what it actually testifies to is the authenticity of the creative energy of *The Scarlet Letter*'s author. Its climactic episode shows how the scarlet letter that Hawthorne finds, like the lady in "Drowne's Wooden Image," "first created the artist who afterwards created her image" (*MOM* 319).

Hawthorne's account of the discovery of the scarlet letter is extremely deliberate in its pace. We are told how he found the bundle of old documents in an upper room, how he recalled the history of Surveyor Pue, and then how he came upon "a certain affair of fine red cloth, much worn and faded" (*SL* 31). The discovery of materials goes along with a slow kindling of interest. At first Hawthorne notes that he is affected with pleasure; then a chance discovery "quickened an instinctive curiosity" (*SL* 29); and finally he finds his attention "most drawn" by the letter. Even after he is thus drawn to it the process of perception continues slowly, step by step: he examines its needlework; then he perceives that the rag is a letter; he measures its sides; he makes surmises about its possible uses as an article of apparel. But in the midst of this investigation he is seized by the letter, fascinated, held fast; the slow process of discovery quickens to a climactic response.

> My eyes fastened themselves upon the old scarlet letter, and would not be turned aside. Certainly, there was some deep meaning in it, most worthy of interpretation, and which, as it were, streamed forth from the mystic symbol, subtly communicating itself to my sensibilities, but evading the analysis of my mind.
>
> (*SL* 31)

And this climax, rather than terminating Hawthorne's discovery, ensures that it will continue. Having engaged the letter with his understanding, and having then felt it engaging his sensibilities, he now comes—again by an accident which is almost like fate—to yet another kind of knowledge and response, this time a physical one: holding the letter to his chest while he muses, he feels it exuding a burning heat.

At this point the tone of excitement modulates, first into a more matter-of-fact one, as Hawthorne tells of finding "a small roll of dingy paper . . . containing many particulars respecting the life and conversation of one Hester Prynne" (*SL* 32), and then into a rather comic one, as Hawthorne gives his pseudo-gothic account of meeting Surveyor Pue's ghost. In this meeting, having been in effect chosen by the symbol, he accepts the responsibility of telling its story. The surviving past that has reawakened his own powers of imagination now requires from him a commitment to the task of imaginatively reconstructing that past. Pue comes to him as his "official ancestor" (*SL* 33), but the office that this encounter forces him to undertake is that of an inspector of customs with a difference; he is to become simultaneously a student of antiquities and an inventor of fictions.

Hawthorne's celebrated description of the moonlit room provides the one crucial account in his works of how his vision becomes transformed into fiction. The passage has a logic and a rhythm of its own, so that it must be cited in full.

The same torpor, as regarded the capacity for intellectual effort, accompanied me home, and weighed upon me in the chamber which I most absurdly termed my study. Nor did it quit me, when, late at night, I sat in the deserted parlour, lighted only by the glimmering coal-fire and the moon, striving to picture forth imaginary scenes, which, the next day, might flow out on the brightening page in many-hued description.

If the imaginative faculty refused to act at such an hour, it might well be deemed a hopeless case. Moonlight, in a familiar room, falling so white upon the carpet, and showing all its figures so distinctly,—making every object so minutely visible, yet so unlike a morning or noontide visibility,—is a medium the most suitable for a romance-writer to get acquainted with his illusive guests. There is the little domestic scenery of the well-known apartment; the chairs, with each its separate individuality; the centre-table, sustaining a work-basket, a volume or two, and an extinguished lamp; the sofa; the book-case; the picture on the wall;—all these details, so completely seen, are so spiritualized by the unusual light, that they seem to lose their actual substance, and become things of intellect. Nothing is too small or too trifling to undergo this change, and acquire dignity thereby. A child's shoe; the doll, seated in her little wicker carriage; the hobby-horse;—whatever, in a word, has been used or played with, during the day, is now invested with a quality of strangeness and remoteness, though still almost as vividly present as by daylight. Thus, therefore, the floor of our familiar room has become a neutral territory, somewhere between the real world and fairy-land, where the Actual and the Imaginary may meet, and each imbue itself with the nature of the other. Ghosts might enter here, without affrighting us. It would be too much in keeping with the scene to excite surprise, were we to look about us and discover a form, beloved, but gone hence, now sitting quietly in a streak of this magic moonshine, with an aspect that would make us doubt whether it had returned from afar, or had never once stirred from our fireside.

The somewhat dim coal-fire has an essential influence in producing the effect which I would describe. It throws its unobtrusive tinge throughout the room, with a faint ruddiness upon the walls and ceiling, and a reflected gleam from the polish of the furniture. This warmer light mingles itself with the cold spirituality of the moonbeams, and communicates, as it were, a heart and sensibilities of human tenderness to the forms which fancy summons up. It converts them from snow-images into men and women. Glancing at the looking-glass, we behold— deep within its haunted verge—the smouldering glow of the half-extinguished anthracite, the white moonbeams on the floor, and a repetition of all the gleam and shadow of the picture, with one remove farther from the actual, and nearer to the imaginative. Then, at such an hour, and with this scene before him, if a man, sitting all alone, cannot dream strange things, and make them look like truth, he need never try to write romances.

(*SL* 35–36)

In the moonlit parlor nature meets imagination halfway. The moonlight illumines the individual outlines of things but at the same time breaks down the boundaries between thing and thought, transforming everything into "things of intellect." It functions therefore as an analogy for the imagination; and, by thus setting a good example, it also functions as a stimulus to the imagination. When he observes the moonlight spiritualizing the furniture, Hawthorne's mind begins to realize its own creatures. The natural process of moonlight initiates an imaginative process that works in exactly the opposite direction, giving actuality and substance to things of intellect, but in such a way that the two can seem to meet and mingle before the author in a vivid interaction pattern.

This passage has such a brilliant metaphorical vitality that it is easy to lose sight of its immediate occasion. Hawthorne goes to the parlor and cultivates the experience of magic moonshine there in response to his specific needs and difficulties as a creator of fiction. After he discovers the scarlet letter, the continuing routine of his official life makes his imagination "a tarnished mirror" that "would not reflect, or only with miserable dimness, the figures with which I did my best to people it" (*SL* 34). He resorts to the natural magic of the moonlit room in an effort to liberate his creative fancy. He wants to get acquainted with his "illusive guests," to make them available to him as characters for his fiction; he wants to "picture forth imaginary scenes" which, when written out the next day, will compose his fiction's action and plot.

Hawthorne's problem is not just that his imagination is torpid; it is that the kind of imaginative energy the symbol ignited in him does not, at this stage, lend itself to fictional creation. The letter overwhelms him with an epiphanic revelation, communicating an impression of total meaningfulness to his sensibilities but refusing to yield up its meaning to his analytical understanding. The symbol's communication is instantaneous; it has nothing to do with the sort of sequential experience that a narrative could be composed of. As Hawthorne's eyes fasten themselves on the letter the tremendous meaning that streams forth from it is not even a human meaning. And the ingredients for a story, the potential characters and actions outlined in the roll of dingy paper, are at this point separate from his source of inspiration.

The symbol burns Hawthorne with its heat, but "the characters of the narrative would not be warmed and rendered malleable, by any heat that I could kindle at my intellectual forge" (*SL* 34). In the terms of this metaphor Hawthorne's task in the moonlit room is to get the symbol to animate his characters with its warm life. To do so he induces in himself a reverie state like that described in "The Haunted Mind," a state in which

> the mind has a passive sensibility, but no active strength; when the imagination is a mirror, imparting vividness to all ideas, without the power of selecting or controlling them. . . . You sink down in a flowery spot, on the borders of sleep and wakefulness, while your thoughts rise before you in pictures. . . .
> (*TTT* 306, 308)

In his reverie he relinquishes his powers of selection and control, and he relinquishes the kind of sense that his conscious mind can make of his corpselike characters, in order to have them come before him on their own terms as the creatures of his fantasy. He allows them to present to him his own thoughts, the processes of his own buried mind, dramatically and pictorially. In this way the part of his mind that communed with the mystic symbol can come before him in the form of a potential narrative. The symbol's deep meaning is metamorphosed into characters and their action. And by analyzing the "motives and modes of passion" (*SL* 33) of these characters later on he can thus make articulate and comprehensible the meaning that in the first place evaded "the analysis of my mind." Of all the things that meet and mingle in the moonlit room the crucial coalescence for the author is that of symbol and story; in its light we can understand Hawthorne's whole experience in the room as a kind of rite by which he courts the muse of narrative fiction.

Hawthorne's account of the discovery of the scarlet letter is itself an invention, but as a presentation of his process of inspiration this account seems accurate enough. "Endicott and the Red Cross" and an entry in his *American Notebooks*[2] demonstrate that Hawthorne was fascinated by the scarlet letter as a symbol long before he attempted to work out its implications in the form of a dramatic tale. And "The Custom-House" also seems accurate in its suggestion of the place of narrative in Hawthorne's process of creation. Its pattern can be detected over and over in his works. As he leads his readers down to the monument to the Battle of Concord in "The Old Manse" he tells of how he heard about the boy who killed the wounded British soldier with his ax, and then he adds, "the story comes home to me like truth" (*MOM* 10). His own response, like his response to the letter, transcends the linear and specifically human dimensions of the story. Then, to get at the "truth" that comes home to him, he has to go on to imagine more of the story; he undertakes "as an intellectual and moral exercise" to envision the rest of the boy's life. The germ of "Wakefield" is a remembered report of a strange episode of marital dereliction that fills Hawthorne with "wonder, but with a sense that the story must be true" (*TTT* 131). And again, to discover the content of this felt revelation, he proceeds to invent a narrative action. For Hawthorne creation characteristically begins with an arresting response, an encounter in which his whole mind gathers to receive an intimation of inarticulate truth. To make these truths comprehensible he must reverse his mind's initial centripetal motion and, by resorting to conventions of character, scene, and plot, translate them into an image of unfolding human experience.[3]

Telling a story is in this way necessary for Hawthorne; it is only through his narrative embodiment that he can unpack the truths that come home to him. But it should also be noted that Hawthorne does not begin with plot and character, and that even as he gives himself to the task of imagining his characters' lives he retains an interest in exploring, through them, a "deep meaning" that is of a different order from the experiential one. Because of this there is always a potential gap in his fiction between the meaning that is his characters' experience and the meaning that their experience can be seen as symbolizing. Hawthorne is an intensely dramatic novelist without ever becoming a completely dramatic novelist; and the tendency of his work to include structures of meaning somewhat distinct from that of their human interactions can be understood as the product of this initial doubleness within his creative process.

As a model for the operation of the imagination Hawthorne's moonlit room suggests the basis for another tension within his fictional forms as well. In the room the moon, by making the actual seem strange and spiritual, encourages the author to project his ghostly guests before him, and the red tinge of the coal fire then makes these guests seem warm and substantial. The room's lighting makes discontinuous orders of reality seem continuous, so that the mirror can repeat back the whole scene without marking differences between the imaginary and the actual. By analogy the author is able to imagine scenes which he can write out the next day because in this haunted place images of actuality become malleable to him, capable of imaginative reordering, and at the same time the figures of his reverie seem to become human and to live out actual lives. And, like the mirror, his mind can receive back the mixed world he has created as if it were uniformly real and as if it existed independent of him.

Because the presence of so many of Hawthorne's own favorite images gives this passage a highly personal cast, it is necessary to stress the fact that the imaginative activity he is describing is not his and his alone. In a discussion of Balzac, Albert Béguin writes:

> A fictional society, when it is the work of a great artist, arises at the point where two different projections meet: the projection into the imaginary of a real world which the novelist has recorded to the best of his ability; and the projection into reality of a personal myth, expressing his self-knowledge, his knowledge of fate, his notion of the material and spiritual forces whose field is the human being.[4]

Béguin's terms and emphases are obviously not as well suited to Hawthorne's work as they are to Balzac's, but in their comprehensiveness his comments help to show the more general implication of what goes on in the moonlit room. Clearly Béguin's system of double projections is exactly analogous to what Hawthorne describes; his point where two projections meet is Hawthorne's neutral territory. The novelist creates that territory for himself when he is capable of giving his imagination's order to the actual as its logic and of giving the actual's texture to his imaginings as their body. Hawthorne's description figures forth the process by which any novelist conceives a fictional world, a world whose reality is neither simply subjective nor simply objective but which synthesizes elements chosen from both.

But what is peculiar about Hawthorne is that the two processes shown as blending in "The Custom-House" seem more often than not separate to him. Later in this essay he does not seem convinced by his own testimony that the imaginative act of creating a fictional world transcends the dualism of Actual and Imaginary. To choose to write *The Scarlet Letter,* he says, is "to insist on creating the semblance of a world out of airy matter"; but the

> wiser effort would have been, to diffuse thought and imagination through the opaque substance of to-day, and thus to make it a bright transparency; to spiritualize the burden that began to

weigh so heavily; to seek, resolutely, the true and indestructible
value that lay hidden in the petty and wearisome incidents, and
ordinary characters, with which I was now conversant.

(*SL* 37)

He should have done something like what the moonlight does; but—
and this is what should be emphasized—the work of the moonlight and
of the coal fire now seem to him antithetical, not complementary. He can
choose either to give substance to his fancies or to attend imaginatively to
the solid world around him, but he cannot do both. And even though,
given the nature of the daily life that ''The Custom-House'' depicts, it is
hard to agree with him that this second way would have been the wiser
effort, it is highly characteristic that Hawthorne thinks so. Charles
Feidelson notes that ''Hawthorne had enormous respect for the material
world and for common-sense reality.''[5] To this it can be added that one
of the defining features of that reality is its dullness. Its incidents are petty
and wearisome, its characters ordinary. Miles Coverdale seems to be
expressing a tenet of his creator's metaphysics when he says of Blithedale,
''when the reality comes, it will wear the every-day, common-place,
dusty, and rather homely garb, that reality always does put on'' (*BR*
130-31). And if his respect for the everyday world is partly based on an
''indestructible value'' that lurks in its homely appearance, it is also
partly based on that world's sheer opacity, its brute actuality. As his turn
against his tales in ''The Old Manse'' suggests, physical substance in its
very physicality is of value to a man who dreads the emptiness of shadow
worlds.

Given the sort of allegiance that he pays to commonsense reality,
Hawthorne cannot help being hyperconscious of the gap between fact
and fiction; thus in the face of his actual life in the Custom House *The
Scarlet Letter* seems to him only an airy semblance, not a real world. But,
paradoxically, it is only after he has created this world of airy matter that
his daily life comes to seem so full of value to him. By his own confession,
he had found that existence deadening; it was only by withdrawing from
its oppression of his senses that he freed his sensibilities to respond so
powerfully to the scarlet letter's revelation. Because his inspiration
proceeds in this way a part of Hawthorne is as hostile to the material
world as another part of him is devoted to it. The sketches in *Mosses*
illustrate this most clearly. It is not as if Hawthorne had aimed to endow
them with richly observed external life and missed. He makes them as
fantastic as possible, and he does so in order to enable them to reveal
what the appearances of actual life conceal. The device of the moral lost-
and-found in ''The Intelligence Office'' is designed to show something

"truer ... than is the living drama of action, as it evolves around us" (*MOM* 333); it dispenses with verisimilitude in order to study the essential determinant of character as a power of wish. The post-millennial tour through the relics of civilization in "A New Adam and Eve" permits him to burst "those iron fetters, which we call truth and reality" (*MOM* 247) and to explore instead the psychological foundations of civil institutions. A line from "Rappaccini's Daughter" can be taken as the implicit motto of Hawthorne's anti-realistic works: "there is something truer and more real, than what we can see with the eyes, and touch with the finger" (*MOM* 120). This is the truth of hidden processes, psychological and imaginative, that underlie and give shape to the apparent world; and for Hawthorne this truth is to be discovered not by trying to see into the actual but by exploring the contents of his own sensibilities.

But this position is one pole in the continuing oscillation of Hawthorne's thought, not a permanent stance. In the presence of brute actuality he comes to believe in a reality concealed by appearances and thus accessible only to the imagination; but as soon as he commits himself to the imaginative articulation of what he sees, his work comes to seem shadowy and he comes once more to consider the visible and tangible as what is really real.[6] The conflict between these two conceptions of and approaches to reality is recapitulated in Hawthorne's theory of genres. In his definition the novelist takes as his subject "the probable and ordinary course of man's experience" (*HSG* 1). He sits himself down before this reality and carefully records it; or he picks up chunks of it and puts them between the covers of a book—in an image that shows how literally he takes the connection of the novel to physical substance Hawthorne describes Trollope's books as being "just as real as if some giant had hewn a great lump out of the earth and put it under a glass case, with all its inhabitants going about their daily business and not suspecting that they were being made a show of."[7] The contents of the novel have their meaning by referring outward to "the actual events of real lives" (*BR* 1), by faithfully mirroring aspects of the realm of experience visible and knowable to us all. To the extent that the novel allows itself to be imaginative, and not merely a faithful record, it does so only in order to reveal a value that is seen as inhering in this experience, lying just inside its opaque substance.

By contrast romance declares its independence from the surface texture and causal order of actual life. The romance writer turns away from the world given by the senses and allows his own fantasies to come before his eyes. The world he envisions is frankly a subjective projection, but by being fully subjective it ceases to have a validity that is merely personal. By pursuing "his researches in that dusky region"—his own buried life—he can observe the operations of deep psychological forces that give shape to "our common nature" (*SI* 4). In this way romance too can claim to deal with experiential truth—not the truth of actual events but "the truth of the human heart" (*HSG* 1).[8]

How useful is this theory of genres? It seems to me that Hawthorne's strong defense of romance is achieved at the expense of an impoverished conception of the novel. He tends to forget that in the act of telling a story even the most realistic of novels organizes its presented reality into imaginative patterns of coherence and significance. His adherence to an idea of the novel as a strictly mimetic form makes him overlook its essentially fictive nature. Further, his presentation of novel and romance as antitheses implies too clear-cut a division of prose fiction into two distinct camps. Certainly his own works exemplify neither genre in a pure form. In the light of Frye's discussion of displacement it might be more helpful to understand Hawthorne's "novel" and "romance" as indicating two tendencies present and synthesized in every work of fiction, or as the end points of a whole spectrum of fictional options. Thus to the extent that a work submerges its imagined design into representations of the textures and processes of actual experience it is closer to the pole of the novel; to the extent that it orders its images of actuality into a conspicuously imagined design it is closer to the pole of romance.

But if it hampers the general theoretical validity of his definitions, Hawthorne's presentation of the novel's imaginative recording of ordinary life and romance's actualization of fantasies as mutually exclusive alternatives is in accord with the nature of his own imagination. His mind is capable of proceeding powerfully in both these directions, but it tends to work in them separately, not to merge them or mediate between them. The practical result of this habitually divided vision can be seen in the coexistence, in his novels, of solidly verisimilar and dreamily emblematic settings, of characters endowed with the large variety of overlapping attributes that compose a whole personality and spectral characters who have the reality of archetypical figures of good and evil, of actions that flow from fully dramatized relationships and actions governed by a more ghostly logic of violation and revenge. And his vision's dividedness is reinforced by his divided artistic aspirations. However much he defends romance in his prefaces, with another part of his mind he wants to achieve the novel's sort of substantiality—his description of Trollope's great lumps of earth is written with envious admiration. Hawthorne is bound to produce a mixed medium in his fiction becomes he will not choose one of these fictional modes at the expense of the other and he cannot see them as anything but antithetical.

But if he does not transcend or neutralize this tension within his imagination, he does, in his best work, convert this tension into an artistic asset. The way of the novel and the way of romance are not, for him, simply two methods to pick and choose between. As his theoretical statements show, he thinks of each of them as corresponding to a particular conception of the nature of reality and as being capable of rendering a particular sort of experiential truth. And although it might seem from the preface to *The House of the Seven Gables* that he is content to settle back and accept both these modes as valid in their own ways, this should be understood as a temporary stance, not Hawthorne's last word. What we have seen of his habitual oscillation between them suggests that it is more characteristic for him to see the claims of these modes as conflicting and competing; the nature of their validity is a subject of constant and anxious reformulation, not of settled opinion. Within his novels this question is emphatically an open one. All of them are experiments in which he allows each kind of vision to create its own fictional reality and explores, in the context of the specific experience that is the work's subject, the sort of truth that each of them can articulate.

Hawthorne's unwillingness or inability to abjure the rough magic of romance keeps his novels from fully achieving the "physical substance enough to stand alone" that he had at first desired for them. But by bringing his own discontinuous modes of vision into meaningful relationships he is able to keep the spirit of his resolution at the Old Manse even as he violates its letter. By this means as he undertakes his large and serious treatment of human experience his fictional form acts out a drama appropriate to that subject. It holds open court on the question of how experience is best visualized and understood.

3 | New and Old Tales: *The Scarlet Letter*

This news, which is called true, is so like an old tale that the verity of it is in strong suspicion.

The Winter's Tale

The Scarlet Letter is at the same time Hawthorne's debut in a new artistic medium and a kind of retrospective exhibit of his work. No other of his novels is so close to the preoccupations of his tales. His choice of chronological setting aligns the book with all his studies of the historical past, and in particular with his explorations of the energetic restrictiveness of the Puritans in tales like "The Maypole of Merry Mount" and "Endicott and the Red Cross." The dramas that Hawthorne enacts in this setting are also familiar ones. Dimmesdale's experience exhibits the self-destructive operations of concealed guilt and the obsession with sin portrayed in "Roger Malvin's Burial" and "Young Goodman Brown"; Roger Chillingworth's passionate intellectual curiosity looks back to Ethan Brand's, and he shares Brand's experience of willed violation of others and the unwilled dehumanization of the self. In composing *The Scarlet Letter* Hawthorne seems purposely to gather together the themes—historical, moral, psychological—that have given his work its distinct identity; then, by integrating them and projecting them onto a larger canvas, he manages to eclipse his earlier achievements exactly by fully realizing their subjects' interest and potential.

When *The Scarlet Letter* is approached through Hawthorne's tales its status as an almost self-conscious culmination of his artistic career is the first thing that is striking; the second is the confidence with which Hawthorne proceeds to execute his larger design. The rightness of the opening scene as a suggestive introduction to the novel's major concerns; the gradual but steady unfolding of its action, in which Hawthorne unobtrusively scores in part after part; the firm balance of continuing action and authorial exposition—all demonstrate his assured artistry as a novelist and serve to announce, in an understated way, his mastery of his new craft.

The first scene of *The Scarlet Letter* involves the punishment of the convicted adulteress, Hester Prynne, by public exposure on the scaffold in the Boston marketplace. The scene unfolds with a slow and deliberate pace. Before he allows Hester to appear, Hawthorne focuses our attention on the prison door, meditating on it in such a way as both to localize it in a specific time and place and to see in it a dark exigency, a "black flower of civilized society" (48). Then he allows the point of view to pass over to other observers of this scene, a group of Puritan women. In their comments—ranging from a legalistic, punitive desire to brand or execute the adulteress to a softer voice that recognizes the anguish of the victim of punishment—Hawthorne affords us a series of vantage points by which to frame our own initial response to Hester. But in offering possible attitudes in this way the women do not cease to be participants in a specific scene. They are part of the audience before which Hester is to be exposed, and by surrounding Hester's emergence with their reactions Hawthorne makes us see the experience of his main characters from the first as being bounded by, as well as the affair of, a larger society. His own commentary emphasizes the nature of the community the women represent. By placing them near the age of "man-like Elizabeth" (50) and contrasting them with the paler women of his own day he sees their coarseness of body and speech in relation to a specific moment in a historical evolution. Their sentiments are understood historically as well, as exemplifications of "the early severity of the Puritan character" (49). In their concern with the rigid administration of punishment to a criminal and sinner they exhibit the special outlook of "a people amongst whom religion and law were almost identical" (50). Through them we recognize the values by which their society defines itself and also the quality of private feeling that upholds those values, "the general sentiment which gives law its vitality" (231).

By choosing the punishment of Hester as his first scene Hawthorne is able to reveal the Puritan community in what seems to him its most essential aspect, enacting its deepest social and religious values. The scene is typical of his handling of the Puritans in *The Scarlet Letter* in its focus on their celebration of their community's own special nature and its bonds of authority. We see this again in the Election Day scene which balances this one at the book's conclusion. In both cases he is unusually attentive to what he calls "the forms of authority" (64), the ceremonious behavior through which they act out their values. The comments of the chorus of women end when the prison door opens and the town beadle emerges, "with a sword by his side and his staff of office in his hand."

> This personage prefigured and represented in his aspect the whole dismal severity of the Puritanic code of law, which it was his business to administer in its final and closest application to the offender. Stretching forth the official staff in his left hand,

he laid his right upon the shoulder of a young woman, whom he
thus drew forward.

(52)

The action here has the stylization of a ritual. The beadle submerges his
individual personality into his role as agent of justice, identified by
appropriate emblems. He acts out that role in his ceremonious gesture,
converting Hester's emergence into a carefully contrived visual allegory of
civil and spiritual righteousness: "A blessing on the righteous Colony of
Massachusetts, where iniquity is dragged out into the sunshine!" (54).

But his ritual is disrupted. Hester pushes his staff aside and walks
forward "as if by her own free-will" (52). This is Hester's first act, and its
resonance is amplified by the next detail Hawthorne presents: "On the
breast of her gown, in fine red cloth, surrounded with an elaborate
embroidery and fantastic flourishes of gold thread, appeared the letter
A" (53). The Puritan pageant casts Hester as Iniquity; the A they impose
on her is the symbolic badge of her office, that of Adulteress. Their strict
symbolism moves to rigidify experience into formal categories of virtue
and sin, and they conceive of their symbols as having sanction for their
meaning in divine principles of good and evil. As Hester rejects their
pageant she also rejects the code on which it is based. She converts the
spectacle of "iniquity dragged forth" into an act proceeding from her
own free choice. She accepts the designation of adulteress, but on her
own terms; her embroidery of the scarlet letter turns it into a more
complex symbol, one that does justice to the inseparable conjunction of
something guilty and something vital and fertile in her passionate nature.
And while the art of the Puritans' A has the sanction of divine truth, her
personalized letter is presented as an act of creative self-expression, a
product of her own imagination that has its meaning in terms of her own
knowledge of herself.

Hester's rejection or modification of the pageant prefigures the conflict
between her and her society, but it also suggests a larger conflict in *The
Scarlet Letter* of which this is only one version, a strife between two modes
of experience and understanding: one that tends toward restriction,
fixity, and orthodoxy, and one that tends toward a freer expression and
recognition of the self's desires, needs, and powers. The moment marks,
as well, a turning point in the scene from a social and historical
perspective to an individual and psychological one. As Hester mounts the
scaffold Hawthorne adopts her point of view, measuring the nature of the
assembled crowd now by registering its presence to her consciousness. As
he notes her urge to reckless defiance, her anguished shame, and her
peculiar defenselessness against the solemnity of the occasion, he quali-

fies her initial assertion of freedom, enabling us to see the power the community holds over her emotional life. The freedom she does attain here comes through the reveries of her past life that intervene between her and the crowd's awful gaze. At the same time, her daydream finally destroys its own value as a means of escape; as she watches her life unfold she is led back inexorably to the present moment and the present scene.

In presenting Hester's reverie Hawthorne skillfully observes both her psyche's instinctive mechanism of self-protection and her own coming to an awareness that her position on the scaffold is the inevitable outcome of the whole course of her life. His observation here gives us our first glimpse of the exquisite shorthand by which he records the processes of consciousness throughout the novel. In addition to demonstrating his skill as a psychological analyst Hester's reverie also illustrates Hawthorne's more basic craft as a storyteller. *The Scarlet Letter* emphatically opens in the middle of an action, and through this vision he is able to sketch in, in two paragraphs, the past that has led up to this action. Further, Hester's momentary recollection of her husband, "a man well stricken in years, a pale, thin, scholar-like visage ... with the left shoulder a trifle higher than the right" (58), serves to prepare us for the immediate future. Exactly as Hester's reverie comes to a close we look back out at the scene and recognize, at the edge of the crowd, the figure whom Hester has just seen.

As Hester recognizes her husband her relation to the crowd changes. Their gaze now becomes a "shelter" (63) from the intenser gaze of Chillingworth and from the more specific shame and guilt that she feels before him. The appearance of Chillingworth marks a subtle shift in the action of the scene. The dramatic conflict between Hester and the Puritans gives way to a more private drama involving the characters most intimately connected with the fact of adultery. Thus it is appropriate that in the next scenic transition, to the injunctions of the Puritan magistrates and ministers, what is ostensibly a cut back to the Puritans is actually the occasion for Hawthorne's first introduction of Dimmesdale. The role that Dimmesdale must play in this scene, again, implicitly suggests the whole ambiguity of the position of this "remorseful hypocrite" (144). In urging Hester to reveal the name of her child's father he speaks as the voice of community authority and righteousness. At the same time, the combination of his equivocation—"If thou feelest it to be for thy soul's peace" (67)—and his impassioned appeal that she ease her accomplice of the burden of his secrecy hints at his own part in the plot, reflecting his dread of being, as well as his desperate longing to be, revealed in his true position.

The characters who belong together are now assembled, placed in the suggestive grouping around the scaffold that they will form again in "The Minister's Vigil" and once again when the true relations that that grouping embodies are revealed in the book's final scene. And as it gathers together the characters of this private drama, so too this scene engenders the energies of that drama. Dimmesdale, poised with his hand upon his heart, is seen protecting his secret; Chillingworth's resolution—"He will be known!" (63)—already incarnates his fierce purpose to expose that secret.

A consideration of this much of *The Scarlet Letter* may be enough to demonstrate the remarkable skill of Hawthorne's narrative exposition. Everything that he tells us contributes to our understanding and visualization of this highly charged scene. And without ever going outside that scene in these chapters he manages to establish all the characters, motives, and thematic conflicts that will animate the rest of the book. These chapters serve as well as any others to reveal a persistent feature of Hawthorne's art of the novel, his strict economy.

If the first scene is typical of Hawthorne's artistry, it also exemplifies the sort of fictional world he creates in *The Scarlet Letter*. This world possesses, first, a dense social and historical reality. The feelings and forms of behavior of the Puritan characters are linked to the outlook of a particular group set in a particular moment in time. The prison and the scaffold, located in accordance with the actual topography of early Boston, are also understood as extensions of the Puritans' care for lawful authority and punishment. Hawthorne's concern for accuracy of historical detail is evident throughout the book,[1] but his interest is never merely antiquarian; all his descriptions of physical settings work to exhibit the nature of the society that creates them. This is true even of his minute account of the architecture, furnishings, and garden of Governor Bellingham's hall in the seventh chapter, which seems at first like the one point in the book where he aims at a purely factual description of place. The overbearing defensive outer wall and Bellingham's suit of armor suggest once again the stern militance of the Puritans. The glass of ale on the table, the comfortable furnishings, and the evidences of a failed attempt to create an English garden show a kind of counterimpulse, an inclination toward a more pleasurable way of life out of which these men of iron try to re-create what they can of the more commodious civilization they have left behind. By the time he finishes his description of the hall Hawthorne has revealed, through the details of the scene, a complex image both of the Puritans' temperament and of the historical situation that gives rise to that temperament, their situation between Elizabethan England and America's hostile and barren strand.

In addition Hawthorne's world possesses a dense psychological reality.

He endows his characters with their own individuating tempers and desires, then watches their peculiar consciousnesses responding to their situations and to one another. If he describes the interior of a house in "The Governor's Hall," much more often he turns to sift the contents of "the interior of a heart" (139). His brief account of Hester's feelings on the scaffold prepares the way for chapters like "Hester at Her Needle," "The Interior of a Heart," "Another View of Hester," and "The Minister in a Maze," chapters which have as their only actions Hawthorne's minute dissections of his characters' inner worlds—their responses to their daily positions before the community, their continuing desires, and the new forms that their desires take under the pressure of their circumstances.

The first chapters also illustrate how Hawthorne animates the social and psychological realities he creates and gives them the forward motion of an action. There are three levels of interaction here, the public one involving the Puritan community, the internal one of feeling, thought, and psychic struggle, and the private drama of interaction among the main characters. Hawthorne's subtle modulations among them prefigure the larger movements of his narrative, which alternates in the same way among communal scenes, introspections of characters seen in isolation, and dramatizations of their personal encounters. Each level generates its own conflicts, such that the initiative of the action can pass back and forth among them. Thus for example the public exposure of Hester rebounds on the nature of Chillingworth in such a way as to generate the jealous and revengeful passion to know that governs his action throughout the story; Dimmesdale's private obsession with penance leads him onto the scaffold at night, and Hester's recognition of his feebleness in their encounter here in turn generates her desire to make Chillingworth known to him and to propose their mutual escape.

The world Hawthorne creates in *The Scarlet Letter* is the final product of the inspiration that he dramatized in "The Custom-House," and the nature of this world enables us now to understand more precisely the relation of his inspiration to his process of fictional creation. The scarlet letter comes to him streaming with revelation. But this revelation is peculiarly inarticulate; the "deep meaning in it, most worthy of interpretation" communicates itself to his sensibilities, but it evades "the analysis of my mind" (31). Further, while the letter itself is full of fixating power, the story that accompanies it—the dingy roll of paper pertaining to Hester Prynne—is at this point lifeless and uninteresting to him. In the moonlit room he attempts to spread out his intuited revelation into imagined characters and scenes, to transfer the burning heat of the symbol into a warmth that will animate the participants in his story.

The Scarlet Letter illustrates how Hawthorne does this. He converts the isolated symbol into a badge fashioned by a historical community. The A becomes the Puritans' A, the emblem through which they impose their judgment on a violator of their communal values. The letter thus brings the book's social and historical stratum into being, and by meditating on their use of the symbol Hawthorne can analyze the peculiar nature of the Puritans—their devotion to law and religion, their addiction to formalized behavior, the imaginative outlook inherent in their orthodox symbolism. At the same time the A is a badge for individuals, a token of their act of adultery and the passions that have led to that act, and a mark as well of the complex system of guilt and responsibility that ensues from that act. In this aspect the scarlet letter becomes the focal point of the characters' daily experience and the center of their attention. Chillingworth's vengeful inquiry reaches its first climax when he discovers the letter on Dimmesdale's chest. Dimmesdale's obsession with his guilt is most clearly revealed in his compulsive visions of the letter in the world outside his mind. Hawthorne presents Hester's life as an outcast by recording the variety of responses she feels as others look at her scarlet letter, and he measures her efforts at creative resistance by showing her various modifications of the letter into tentative expressions of a complex truth. He passes his own experience of fixation before the scarlet letter on to his characters; their need, like his own, is to find out or express the meaning of the symbol even as they live out that meaning, if they are to free themselves from its purely obsessive power.[2] As he grounds the letter in his characters' experience and observes their motives and modes of passion before it, the symbol evolves into the dense web of psychological and dramatic relationships in his novel.

By composing a narrative in this way Hawthorne overcomes the tensions within his own creative vision. The symbol and the ingredients of a story come together in a seamless unity in which each manifestation of the letter illuminates an aspect of the characters' or the community's evolving experience. He overcomes, as well, the initial gap between what he calls his sensibilities and his conscious mind. By calling forth dramatic scenes and then analyzing the implications of their actions he achieves a synthesis in which imagining and understanding are continually changing into each other. And there is no sense of a gap here between what he calls the Actual and the Imaginary. He freely draws on both social history and psychic activity, creating his novel's world by engaging the two in a process of dynamic interchange.

The reconciliation of opposites is what gives *The Scarlet Letter* its singular intensity and its consistent formal poise. It also helps to account for some of the characteristics that set this novel apart from the other books I will be discussing. The world of *The Scarlet Letter* has, for all its complexity, a more uniform reality than do the other novels. It is more generous in the amount of individual life with which it endows its characters, and it adheres more closely to the texture of their experience of themselves and their world. Hawthorne and Melville wrote other books that are as powerfully tragic as this one, but none that has its interest so simply as a moving human drama—"a tale of human frailty and sorrow" (48). One reason for this is that the position of author and reader as imaginative creators is less pronounced and problematic here. In telling his story Hawthorne assumes the role of a concerned yet dispassionate observer, one whose knowledge of the past and skill in the science of the heart enable him to follow the implications of his drama's turns of events with maximum lucidity. He implicitly invites us as readers to join him in accepting his imagined world as real and in bringing to bear on that world a concerned yet finely discriminating attention. Another, related reason is that *The Scarlet Letter* has a more coherent and uniform narrative manner than the other novels. It is significant, for example, that this novel alone does not contain a tale within a tale. Coming to *The Scarlet Letter* from Hawthorne's next two books, with their curious mixtures of modes, or from Melville's fragmented and fictively exuberant novels, we must be struck by its sustained style and tone, its symmetrical structure, and its spare, linear plot. Henry James is right to ascribe to *The Scarlet Letter* "a sort of straightness and naturalness of execution."[3] This is the one case in which the author seems to feel able to do everything he wants to do by embracing the storytelling procedures of the novel in a straightforward way.

These are some of the features that make *The Scarlet Letter* seem to belong, as no other novel of the American Renaissance does, to the mainstream of nineteenth-century fiction in England and Europe. The resemblances go beyond formal practice to include as well the vision of life that form is in the service of. The central place that Hawthorne gives to the presentation of individual life as lived within the context of a particular social group and historical moment and to the dramatization of a struggle between social restraint and the impulse toward self-fulfillment links *The Scarlet Letter* to such far-flung cousins as *The Red and the Black*, *The Mill on the Floss*, and *Anna Karenina*. Nicolaus Mills has demonstrated its especially close thematic affinities with *Adam Bede*. Both books use a sexual transgression as a center from which to study the conflict between community morality and individual desire. Both focus not on the act of transgression but on the movements of remorse, repentance, and revenge that are its consequences. And they do so because both Hawthorne and Eliot are interested in social and psychological phenomena from a point of view that is finally ethical.[4]

The links that make *The Scarlet Letter* seem closer in form and theme to a work like *Adam Bede* than to a work like *Moby-Dick* are genuine and important. At the same time, as soon as it is compared to a novel in the European realistic tradition its own peculiar features come into high relief. Eliot's novel has a plenitude next to which *The Scarlet Letter* seems compact or even niggardly in its presented life. Eliot is willing to give such minor characters as Reverend Irvine, the Poysers, Lisbeth Bede, and Bartle Massey a fullness of realization beyond what their function for the plot requires. Because her world is so densely peopled her main characters are always seen within a large web of relations, and their actions are seen as having consequences not just in their own lives but in the lives of many others as well. By contrast Hawthorne confines his lesser characters to walk-on parts, reserving a fuller dramatization exclusively for his major characters. This has the effect of making them seem detached from and larger than the figures of the background, and of focusing attention not on the whole round of their lives but on their urgent reactions to the fact of adultery. Eliot also works against a sense of central effect by enveloping her main action in a multitude of scenes of more leisurely and ordinary life. Hawthorne concentrates instead on scenes of crisis and major encounter. What makes the descriptive sketch in ''The Governor's Hall'' stand out from the rest of *The Scarlet Letter* is that it is the only point at which Hawthorne seems to be describing daily life simply for its own sake. But even here description gives way to significant action, to Hester's defense against the Puritans' desire to take Pearl, the product of her sin, away from her. Where Eliot's novel seems to overflow with a fullness of represented life Hawthorne's has an intense and almost exclusive preoccupation with the conflicts directly embodied in the scarlet letter. He himself notes the sort of tautness and single-mindedness his work possesses when, in a letter, he describes *The Scarlet Letter* as ''keeping so close to its point ... and diversified no otherwise than by turning different sides of the same dark idea to the reader's eye.''[5]

This phrase suggests another way of accounting for the singular intensity of *The Scarlet Letter*. It is not just that Hawthorne does not include an abundant record of variegated life, but that the details he does include are so intimately bound together as ''sides of the same dark idea.'' Part of what works against a sense of openness and free life in the novel is its marshaling of its components into strong patterns of interrelation. Thus we see the scaffold as a physical object, and also as a social creation; but our sense of its meaning is also shaped by its appearance in Hawthorne's figurative language. He says of Dimmesdale:

> it would always be essential to his peace to feel the pressure of a faith about him, supporting, while it confined him within its iron framework.
>
> (123)

He uses a related image to describe Hester's emotions on the scaffold:

> The very law that condemned her—a giant of stern features, but with vigor to support, as well as to annihilate, in its iron arm—had held her up, through the terrible ordeal of her ignominy.
>
> (78)

The framework that both supports and confines recalls the actual pillory on the scaffold, and the resonance between the object and these images suggests a complex relation between things and inner experience. It links the actual forms the Puritans construct as instruments of their law on the one hand to the individual psychic needs that make law strong and on the other to the individual psychic experience produced by the law's implementation. The sort of complex link between public and private that this cluster of images establishes is a recurrent feature of *The Scarlet Letter*. To choose another example, Hawthorne tells us in "The Prison-Door" that every community contains a prison and a graveyard. The novel begins outside an actual prison and ends in contemplation of an actual grave. But between these points we see them in other forms: the Dimmesdale who keeps the truth of his life secret is called a "prisoner" in the "dungeon of his own heart" (201); when Hester allows her continuing love for Dimmesdale to surface into her conscious mind she hastens "to bar it in its dungeon" (80). Both the town and the mind contain dungeons, and both the Puritans and the main characters are jailers; their private and psychic acts of repression repeat the public and social one. What makes Hawthorne's dramatization of the conflict between untamed desire and repressive restraint interesting is his sense that the self contains its own version of the parties to this conflict within itself. Some of the most moving passages of analysis in the whole novel are those in which he shows how his characters, under the burden of their situation, come to dehumanize themselves even more thoroughly than their oppressors do. His images of the dungeon are the means by which he shows the dynamic interaction between the external and the internal versions of this conflict.

The cross-linking of things and images that these two examples illustrate takes place constantly in *The Scarlet Letter*. The novel's world obeys a rigid law of conservation, such that whatever appears in its physical world is bound to reappear, before long, in the figurative language describing its mental world. This rule holds true for its obvious symbolic objects—the red rose and the black flower that appear in the first scene reappear as metaphors by which Pearl is linked to the wild vitality of nature and by which Chillingworth expresses his dark determinism. But it holds true as well for relatively less significant objects. Chillingworth's freethinking is as a "window . . . thrown open" (123) to Dimmesdale, and shortly after this is said the two men look out of an actual open window and see Hester and Pearl. Hester embroiders robes for occasions of state, and official ceremonies like the Election Day pageant are called the "brilliant embroidery to the great robe of state" (230). It is all but impossible to isolate an item in *The Scarlet Letter* that does not make both physical and metaphorical appearances.

The system of cross-reference that this kind of repetition establishes is obviously one of the major ways in which Hawthorne suggests and controls meaning in *The Scarlet Letter*. But what is more important for our discussion here is the effect that this system has on the texture of reality in the novel. It makes that texture an insistently patterned one; and the participation of each of the novel's details in such larger configurations of elements works against their functions as simply aspects of a representation of actual life. Further, it works against a clear distinction between mental and physical reality. The supportive framework and the area of repressive confinement float between the two, making themselves manifest now as parts of an actual scene, now as features of the mind. The forest in which Hester meets Dimmesdale is both a topographical fact and an image of "the moral wilderness in which she had been so long wandering" (183); the sunshine that brightens and fades in strict accordance with their emotions of joy and despair makes the forest appear both as a natural place and as an externalization of their mental states, a product of the process Harry Berger describes in *The Faerie Queene* by which "psyche is . . . unfolded into an environment."[6] Our experience in the world of this novel is akin to Hawthorne's own in the moonlit room. Ordinary boundaries become fluid, such that things are both seen as things and felt as thoughts. Above all Hawthorne's world is governed by the moonlit room's sense of haunted interconnectedness. It is not enough to describe it as economical or compact; its fluid interrelatedness of parts and its supersaturation with significant patterns give it the quality of overdetermination that Freud ascribes to dreams.[7]

This double sense of distinctness of individual outline and dreamlike

interconnectedness is exactly the effect produced by the item that
reappears most insistently in the book, the scarlet letter itself. Hester's A
is almost always before us, and it has a curious power to replicate itself in
a series of visual variants. It is reflected in suits of armor, pools, brooks,
and eyes; it is repeated in Pearl's clothing and in her seaweed creations;
it shines forth in the midnight sky; it burns itself onto Dimmesdale's
chest. In each of its manifestations the letter has an analyzable meaning
in terms of the characters' and the community's experience. But at the
same time the various letters keep returning our attention to something
prior to its specific embodiments, to the fact of the scarlet letter itself. Its
continual presence makes us feel in reading the novel as Miles Coverdale
does during his troubled dream on his first night at Blithedale:

> During the greater part of it, I was in that vilest of states when a
> fixed idea remains in the mind, like the nail in Sisera's brain,
> while innumerable other ideas go and come, and flutter to-and-
> fro, combining constant transition with intolerable sameness.
>
> (BR 38)

Images combine, separate, and recombine, the action accelerates and
slows down, the characters come together and move apart—but while all
of this is happening, infusing it and linking its parts to one another and
to itself is the scarlet letter.

I noted earlier that *The Scarlet Letter* differs from *Adam Bede* in its
single-minded focus on its characters' experience of the consequences of
adultery. This is a difference of emphasis; but the features we have just
been considering point to a more fundamental difference, to something
that distinguishes this novel from the rest of its European relatives as well.
In none of these is the drama so pervasively haunted by an autonomous
symbol. As Hawthorne turns his symbol into a story he gives its revelation
a specific human content, grounding it in the reality of his characters'
and their society's experience. But as he does so the symbol does not
evaporate; its insistent presence within the novel indicates that it retains a
residue of its original power. The effect of this can be seen in the
existence in the novel of narrative structures somewhat separate from the
dramatic one, structures by which Hawthorne encourages us to perceive
the letter more nearly in its original form *as* a symbol.

An illustration of this can be found at the end of "The Governor's
Hall." Hester has come to challenge the community's right to deprive
her of Pearl, and Hawthorne painstakingly sketches in the furnishings of
the room in which she waits. But suddenly the furniture yields up a
revelation: Hester sees herself mirrored in the suit of armor, and on its

curved surface she is reflected in such a way that her badge of sin becomes disproportionately large, and her human figure disproportionately small. The meaning of this revelation is enacted dramatically in the ensuing scene, in which she must struggle to defend her own human desires and needs against the reductive and distorted view of her as "a scarlet woman, and a worthy type of her of Babylon" (110) that the Puritan men of iron assume. Indeed the conflict is so fully realized within the dramatized interaction of Hester and the Puritan leaders that the moment of reflection in the armor is in a strict sense unnecessary to the scene's significance. What it enables us to do is to perceive the outlines of the scene's conflict in advance, in a static and symbolic, rather than dynamic and dramatic, form.

The kind of double presentation that takes place here is a common feature in *The Scarlet Letter*. Curiously, Hawthorne follows this procedure even in the midst of his book's most intense encounters. The nineteenth chapter, "The Child at the Brook-Side," offers an example of this. Hester has just made the identity of Chillingworth known to Dimmesdale, and the two have resolved to flee together. In the surge of joy with which they cast aside, for a moment, the perplexity and pain of their seven years' suffering, they turn their attention to the third member of their family, little Pearl. The scene that follows is a beautiful instance of Hawthorne's dramatic art. He circles among his characters, briefly noting their reactions in this tense moment: Dimmesdale's timid hopes and his nervous dread of exclusion; Pearl's anger and jealousy at seeing Dimmesdale usurp her place at her mother's side, and her incomprehension of her mother divested of her letter; Hester's feelings of estrangement from Pearl, and the troubled sense of shame and resentment with which she resumes her badge. But, strangely, planted in the middle of this dramatic moment is another version of the scene, an intricate visual tableau. Pearl, dressed as the scarlet letter, stands beside the brook, and her reflection in it is said to be a "more refined and spiritualized" version of her "reality," which "seemed to communicate somewhat of its own shadowy and intangible quality to the child herself" (208). On the other side of the brook is the discarded scarlet letter, and it too is reflected in the brook, so that as Pearl points at Hester her reflection points at the letter.

Why does Hawthorne insist on doubling and redoubling in this way? It is obvious that, as in "The Governor's Hall," the scene could function effectively enough without this complication. To see what it would look like without reflections, as a simple presentation of a child's jealous and insecure response to her mother's lover, we can turn to the scene in *The*

Rainbow in which D. H. Lawrence, apparently drawing on Hawthorne, shows Anna Lensky's reaction to Tom Brangwen. Hawthorne's treatment at the dramatic level is, if anything, subtler than Lawrence's; the problem, then, is not that he cannot render psychological drama, but that even as he does so he insists on including another articulation of his scene as well. In the fourfold reflection the scarlet letter itself becomes, in effect, a character, insisting upon itself as the reality of the characters' lives and the condition of their relationships. Hawthorne's technique forces us to observe the action from a double perspective. At one level we are involved with the characters, sympathetically observing their experience of the letter and of one another; at another level we are distanced from them, watching the letter itself express as meaning what they are experiencing as action. Here again an interaction of complex characters and an exercise in symbolic perception meet and mingle without quite coalescing.

The modulation between symbolic and dramatic in "The Child at the Brook-Side" is in part a function of the peculiar status of Pearl in the novel; and a look at Pearl shows that the tension between two kinds of vision and realization in Hawthorne's scenic art extends to his art of character as well. Some of the details of Pearl's wild and wayward playfulness are taken from Hawthorne's notebook observations of his daughter Una, and this illustrates the sort of fidelity to life that he aims at in creating his elf-child. In both the notebook and the novel he is particularly interested in the succession of games by which the child both acts out her imaginative freedom and, unconsciously, prepares herself for a mature life. Some of the finest passages in *The Scarlet Letter* are those in which Hawthorne describes the imaginative counterworld Pearl establishes in her play, in an effort to gain control over her hostile and baffling environment—her savage uprooting of the weeds that represent the Puritan children to her, for instance, or her re-creation of the mysterious scarlet letter in seaweed. These serve as well to show forth the modification of her nature by her specific situation. Her alternate moods of hostility and affection, of perverse glee and anxious brooding over her origin and separateness, mark her as the child who has grown up in the shadow of her mother's isolation, rebelliousness, and despair.

Hawthorne thus presents Pearl as having a complex psychological nature with its own origins in her environment, but this is only one version of her character in the novel. At other points she is seen not just as Hester's child but as an externalization of her repressed character; thus in the Election Day scene Pearl acts out the impulses that her mother stifles in herself. Her "trait of passion" (90), her luxuriance of imagination, the natural wildness in her that refuses to comply with rules and restraints link her to the aspect of Hester that has found expression in her crime. These qualities are what lead Hester to identify Pearl with the scarlet letter; and to a surprising extent Hawthorne accepts the simile she creates as indicating a true identity: Pearl *is* the scarlet letter. She is, thus, the "emblem and product of sin" (93), a "living hieroglyphic" (207), now acting like a perverse or bewildered child, now serving an allegorical office of embodying the complex of traits that the letter stands for or reminding others of the power of the symbol when they try to ignore it.

The problem that Pearl presents to us as readers is that these two roles coincide at so many points without ever coalescing. And again, it is not as if Hawthorne were incapable of rendering her compellingly in one or the other of these modes of being; nor is he simply confused in his perception of her. With the character of Pearl as with the drama of his scenes he deliberately chooses to adopt the procedures both of a realistic fiction and of a frankly symbolic mode. In doing so he chooses in effect to exploit the tension between his symbol and his story, and he does so for the sake of producing a specific effect. He complicates our relation to his presented materials, making us succumb to his illusion and accept his world as a complex reality unfolding itself dramatically but at the same time holding us back and encouraging us to understand his drama's emerging meaning through the clearer exposition of a symbolic design.

One of the most interesting moments of symbolic experience in *The Scarlet Letter,* and one that best shows how Hawthorne complicates our relation to his fiction, is found in "The Minister's Vigil." In this chapter Dimmesdale goes to the scaffold at midnight to do public penance for his sin. But even as he does so he is half-aware that his act, like the rest of his rituals of self-scrutiny and self-torture, is a "vain show of expiation" (148). By going through the forms of penitence without actually revealing his guilt Dimmesdale only succeeds in renewing his sin of concealment. Each renewal reinforces his imaginative allegiance to the law that condemns him—thus Hawthorne notes that his sin has the effect of binding him more tightly to the categories of Puritan orthodoxy—so that the fact of his own untruth becomes his only reality and his only identity.[8] "The Minister's Vigil" provides an extreme close-up of the processes of Dimmesdale's mind. Its noting of his masochistic fantasies of exposure before the townspeople, of his involuntary and perverse attempts to betray himself by laughing and shrieking, and of his recoils of dread from the prospect of discovery gives us the book's richest realization of the compulsive fantasy life in which Dimmesdale's obsession with

his guilt imprisons him. In the midst of these fantasies he gains for a
moment an opportunity to escape from his unreal world. He stops Hester
and Pearl as they pass through the marketplace, making them stand with
him on the scaffold. As he joins hands with them he feels "a tumultuous
rush of new life, other life than his own," an "electric chain" (153) of
vital relatedness. But he refuses to embrace the possibility for release that
this moment offers. When Pearl asks him when he will stand with them
publicly he replies: "At the great judgment day!" (153). And exactly as
he states his refusal a version of the judgment day takes place: the sky is
illuminated as if by "the light that is to reveal all secrets" (154).

At this point Hawthorne does not trouble us unduly about the nature
of this light, allowing us to accept, if we like, the plausible explanation
that it is "doubtless caused by one of those meteors" (153–54).
Doubtless. But to Dimmesdale the light looks like a scarlet A, and in the
brief scene that concludes the chapter the sexton informs us that many of
the townspeople saw the same thing. The scarlet letter makes, here, its
most audacious appearance. And its appearance works here, as in "The
Governor's Hall" and "The Child at the Brook-Side," to reverse the
direction of our perception. We have been reading a psychological novel,
observing the course of a character's perceptions and emotions; even
when we watch Dimmesdale seeing the portent we are still considering
the symbol in terms of a character's mental experience of it. But with the
sexton's second sighting Hawthorne gives the symbol an independent
reality and makes us observe the characters under its aspect as it
announces itself as an imperious necessity. Under its aspect the relationships that the characters must live through in the book's dramatic plot are
revealed, in an instantaneous vision, in their essential nature. Dimmesdale, Hester, and Pearl stand joined together in the place of punishment,
and Chillingworth, looking like the "arch-fiend" (156), looks on. And
above them, including them all in its light, is the scarlet letter.

Was it a vision, or a waking dream? Hawthorne does everything he can
to make his letter in the sky unsettling for his readers, but correspondingly he does everything he can to afford us ways of coping with it. We
might take it as a naturalistic fact, a somewhat oddly shaped and colored
meteor. Or we might treat its apparent supernaturalism as really a psychic
projection of Dimmesdale's guilty mind; by refusing to pass judgment on
himself he compulsively sees that judgment as being passed on him by
the world. Or we might join the Puritans, who unblinkingly accept the
supernaturalism of the A and read it as a divine message to their
community, announcing the accession of Governor Winthrop to the
status of Angel. The inclusion of the Puritans' interpretation here

clarifies the peculiarity of Dimmesdale's own. He shares their habit of finding symbols latent with divine meaning in nature, but he perverts that practice by finding "a revelation, addressed to himself alone" rather than to the whole of God's chosen community. In the morbid egotism of his guilt he assumes that "the firmament itself should appear no more than a fitting page for his soul's history and fate" (155). His is a further way in which we might read the celestial sign.

As the last paragraph indicates, "The Minister's Vigil" concludes with a drama of interpretation. We see how the characters understand the letter, and we see their understandings as proceeding from a whole way of making sense of experience. But what is most interesting about this drama is that we are implicated in it. For finally, when the characters are done with it, we have the fact of the A in the sky left over, unexplained. Hawthorne in effect withdraws his narrative's mediating veil and makes us undergo his own and his characters' central experience of direct and unaided encounter with the flaming symbol. And as we are forced to decide what to make of it the characters' modes of vision become the matter not of detached observation but of our own urgent choice. We are left alone to complete the episode's reality and meaning as we may, and as we do so, Hawthorne's demonstration of the implications of the available options ensures that we will be highly self-conscious about our own procedure as an imaginative act of a certain sort. A final purpose of the symbolic mode of *The Scarlet Letter,* therefore, is to complicate our perception of the story in such a way as to turn it in on itself.

An episode like this one illustrates the most important difference between *The Scarlet Letter* and the realistic novels with which it shares some features. Hawthorne includes all the interacting facets of individual and social life that compose their presented reality, but he refuses to exclude from his novel the presence of a magical or supernatural order. This order is seldom entirely absent even in more strictly realistic fiction. Adam Bede's premonition of his father's death and Anna Karenina's prophetic dream of the train are incidents marvelous enough from the point of view of everyday causality. But Hawthorne is unique in the central place he gives to this mode of experience and in the way he engages his readers' perception of it. He strives to make the celestial A not plausible but as spooky as possible; and at the same time, he uses it to worry us, to render the nature of reality problematic and to make us aware of our own assumptions about that nature.

Supernatural magic plays a role throughout *The Scarlet Letter.* The novel contains within it the materials for another novel, the Puritans' version of its characters, events, and significance. Their version is a lurid romance. Pearl is, to them, a demon offspring; Hester's letter emits an infernal light and heat; Dimmesdale is an angel, and Chillingworth a "diabolical agent" who, like Satan in the Book of Job, "had the Divine permission, for a season, to burrow into the clergyman's intimacy, and plot against his soul" (128). The phrases "there was a rumor" and "some averred" with which Hawthorne introduces these details are reminiscent of the "some will say" and "some maintain" in Wordsworth poems like "The Thorn" and "Lucy Gray." Both authors include the ghostly surmises of superstitious rumor in their narratives as a way of regaining access to a suppressed stratum of imaginative experience. Hawthorne's surmises help him to show the workings of the Puritan imagination from within. They see their world as a strife between supernatural and subterranean powers of good and evil, and they see this strife as governed by a providential order. At the same time, Hawthorne consciously distances himself from their raw magic, accepting it as indicative of a psychological, not theological, truth. Rather than rejecting outright the notion that the A burns Hester with infernal fire, he notes that it does indeed sear her bosom, with shame. Similarly he suggests that Mistress Hibbins, rather than being an actual witch, may simply be mad, and at another point he speculates that insanity may be the psychological equivalent of damnation, "that eternal alienation from the Good and True" (193).

Hawthorne's invocations of the magical formulas of a more primitive and archaic sort of fiction and his conversion of their significance into psychological terms is part of a larger effort in *The Scarlet Letter,* an effort to resuscitate something like the Puritans' ideas of evil, sin, and damnation as serious concepts that can be used in a more secular treatment of human experience. His extremely self-conscious experiments in qualified credulity illustrate the feature Geoffrey Hartman describes in the Miltonic and Romantic revival of romance, a "freer attitude of the mind toward the fictions its entertains."[9] Hartman's description of "L'Allegro" fits *The Scarlet Letter* perfectly:

> Thus psyche emerges from the spooky larvae of masques and moralities like a free-ranging butterfly. Though still in contact with the world of spirits, it is no longer coerced or compelled.[10]

But, as "The Minister's Vigil" shows, Hawthorne does not always make the demystification of the supernatural so easy for himself and his readers, nor does he always maintain the same self-conscious distance from the extravagant romance of the Puritans.

Consider, for a moment, the character of Chillingworth. The Puritans

believe that the fire in his laboratory is brought from hell, and just after
he records this rumor Hawthorne himself adopts a closely related image.

> Sometimes, a light glimmered out of the physician's eyes,
> burning blue and ominous, like the reflection of a furnace, or,
> let us say, like one of those gleams of ghastly fire that darted
> from Bunyan's awful door-way in the hill-side, and quivered on
> the pilgrim's face.
>
> (129)

The "let us say" implies a degree of detachment in this invocation of the
Puritans' demonic imagery. But what is curious about the characterization of Chillingworth is the extent to which Hawthorne makes use of
the Puritans' imaginative mode in presenting him. When he meets
Hester at the seaside "there came a glare of red light out of his eyes; as if
the old man's soul were on fire" (169). The vulgar are not alone in seeing
him as Satan's emissary; Hester, Pearl, and Dimmesdale all associate
with the Black Man, and he appears as the arch-fiend in the last two
scaffold scenes.

There is, of course, a psychological truth contained in this diabolical
imagery. "In a word, old Roger Chillingworth was a striking evidence of a
man's faculty of transforming himself into a devil, if he will only, for a
reasonable space of time, undertake a devil's office" (170). Giving
himself up completely to his one evil purpose, Chillingworth brings
about his own dehumanization and makes himself "more wretched than
his victim" (141). And his malignity is not motiveless. His character has,
as have the others, a psychological complexity and etiology of its own.
Frederick Crews insists on this:

> We cannot conscientiously say that Chillingworth *is* a devil . . .
> when Hawthorne takes such care to show us how his devilishness
> has proceeded from his physical deformity, his sense of inferior-
> ity and impotence, his sexual jealousy, and his perverted craving
> for knowledge.[11]

But the real question is not whether Chillingworth is plausibly moti-
vated, as he surely is, but whether or not he is offered to us as a character
possessing the sort of realistic psychological density that Crews's insistence
on motive implies. And in this respect we must conscientiously say that
he is a devil. As with some other villains—Richard III or Iago or Milton's
Satan—what pass as his motives seem at times results rather than causes;
his deformity, for instance, is seen steadily developing as his evil intent
strengthens, as an outward expression of his inner condition. As the novel
progresses his dark face, his disfigured body, the hideous glares in his

eyes, his lurid satanic speech—these become the central features of his character. Whereas a novelist like Eliot, in dealing with a similar figure—Casaubon, in *Middlemarch*, is another impotent scholar-husband, one who has so completely channeled his vital energies into his intellectual researches that his belated marriage can be only a betrayal of a passionate woman's "budding youth into a false and unnatural relation with my decay" (75)—fills out her type with an abundance of detail and many-sided analysis, Hawthorne purposely makes his character less and less complex, more and more the rigidified villain of raw romance.[12] In presenting Chillingworth, rather than distancing himself from it, Hawthorne adopts the sort of fiction that he associates with the Puritans and allows it to bring a part of his created world into being.

Leslie Fiedler notes that "one of the major problems involved in reading *The Scarlet Letter* is determining the ontological status of the characters, the sense in which we are being asked to believe in them."[13] The characterization of Chillingworth shows why this is so: ontology is a problem because the characters in the novel are endowed with radically different sorts of reality. Hester's mode of existence is at the furthest extreme from Chillingworth's. We have already seen some examples of her ability to attenuate or complicate the implications of the forms the Puritans seek to impose on her. When she does accept Puritan designations she does so out of a process of mind that belies their meaning. Thus in the beautiful chapter "Hester at Her Needle" Hawthorne observes with fine tact the process by which she comes to reject the pleasures of her art as sinful. She senses that her art might be a way of expressing, and thus of soothing, her repressed passion, and in order to protect her love she rejects—and labels as sin—whatever might help her to sublimate it. Here she employs Puritan terminology in a most un-Puritan strategy of consciousness, using it to perpetuate an inner need which she is unable to act out and unwilling to relinquish. Her effort to retain her passion intact leads her, in the chapter "Hester and Pearl," to commit a conscious deception. In the face of Pearl's earnest questionings Hester senses that Pearl might be capable of becoming a confidante, a friend, and thus of helping her to "overcome the passion, once so wild, and even yet neither dead nor asleep" (180). In telling Pearl that she wears the scarlet letter for the sake of its gold thread she is not true, to Pearl, to her badge, or to herself. But her falseness here is another strategy by which she attempts to maintain all the elements of her true self in suspension. She cannot achieve in her life the full expression of her complex self that she has wrought into her symbol, but she instinctively and covertly moves to keep this alive as a possibility.

Hawthorne writes that "the tendency of her fate and fortunes had been to set her free" (199). Her freedom is a mixed state of lucidity and self-deception, integrity and falsehood, love and hate: she experiences herself as being, like her letter, a "mesh of good and evil" (64). What is most exciting about Hester is her openness to all the varieties of experience—intellectual, imaginative, emotional—that the continuing emergency of her life brings to her. When she meets Chillingworth at the seaside she has a clear vision of what he has become; she perceives her own share of the responsibility for his transformation; she desperately insists on the possibility of a free act of forgiveness; and she recoils with bitterness from his grim refusal. No other character in the book is capable of this range of feeling. When she decides to go to Dimmesdale's aid she is prompted by her love, by her perception of his weakness, and by her recognition of the responsibility she has incurred for his destruction by promising to keep Chillingworth's identity secret. In defining a duty for herself she generates an ethical imperative out of a clear insight into the whole range of contradictory desires and obligations that confront her. Again, no other character in the book is capable of the adventure of free ethical choice that Hester undertakes here.

Hawthorne lavishes on Hester all of the psychological analysis that he deliberately withholds from Chillingworth. He endows her with the complex reality of a whole self as he becomes increasingly content simply to present Chillingworth's diabolical face. This is what creates the discrepancy between their ontological statuses, and it should be obvious by now that this discrepancy is neither careless nor purposeless. The way in which we are asked to believe in them as characters is a function of the way in which they believe in themselves. Chillingworth relinquishes his own freedom and adopts, in a perverted because atheistic way, the deterministic outlook of the Puritans. A dark necessity, he tells Hester, rules their fates: "Let the black flower blossom as it may!" (174). As he does so he gives up his complexity of being and becomes a rigidified figure of diabolical evil, a character in the sort of providential romance that the Puritans imagine. Hester is allowed the freedom and variegated selfhood of a character in a more realistic mode because she first opens herself to the full complexity of her existence. It is as if in deciding how they will understand themselves and their world the characters also get to decide what sort of literary reality their author will let them acquire; the different fictional modes in which they are realized become explicit reflections of their own imaginative outlooks.

Charles Feidelson notes that Hawthorne carefully sets *The Scarlet Letter* at the historical watershed between the medieval and the modern, and that the novel presents the interaction of these ages as a conflict between two ways of creating and perceiving meaning.[14] One of these sees experience as having meaning within a context of divine truth; within this context its symbolism tends toward fixity of significance, and its moral perception similarly moves to fix the value of characters and acts within rigidly separated categories of good and evil. The other is more secular and indeterminate. It sees meaning and value as generated from within human experience itself, so that its symbolic expressions and moral discriminations are valid to the extent that they emerge from a recognition of the whole complexity of life, including its inseparable mixture of good and evil. The contrast between Chillingworth's determinism and Hester's openness is only one version of this conflict; we see it again in the contrast between the A the Puritans impose on Hester and the A she creates, and between the sense of duty implicit in the Puritan's legal and religious forms and the sense of duty that leads Hester to go to Dimmesdale's rescue.

In its use of different fictional modes *The Scarlet Letter* also reenacts this conflict in its form. By using in his own right the romance form he associates with the Puritans Hawthorne makes us experience Chillingworth as fixed to his role in a drama of angels and devils; his inclusion of magic throughout the novel encourages us to participate in the imaginative experience of a supernatural conflict between good and evil. The more realistic—in Hawthorne's terms, novelistic—mode of the bulk of his narrative forces us to make sense of the novel's world in another way. Here our understanding emerges gradually, from a careful observation of the twists of motive, thought, and emotion that make up the characters' lives. And our judgments here must always be tentative and open-ended, coming nearer to truth to the extent that they are faithfully responsive to the quality of the characters' whole experience. In effect the book itself illustrates a newer way of imaginatively conceiving of human existence emerging from an older way.

The inclusion of radically incommensurate fictional modes in *The Scarlet Letter* is a final way in which Hawthorne complicates his book's world and our relation to it. Like the inclusion of symbolic and dramatic articulations, it makes us perceive that world alternately under different aspects; and here again Hawthorne's double procedure also works to heighten our awareness of our own activity of perception. As they play against each other in the novel we become aware of each mode as a kind of fiction, as a specific form of imaginative representation. Hawthorne draws our attention to his own art of illusion, and he does so in order that we will be aware of the views of experience we are subscribing to as we accept his illusion as reality.[15] In doing this he does not destroy the illusion his fiction creates or undermine its value; but he does keep its validity from being assumed too readily. Having understood the Puritans' sense of reality as a function of their scheme of perception, Hawthorne cannot but be aware that whatever he creates must be a function of another such scheme. This does not mean that he sees all representations of reality as simply illusory. But it means that their validity is conditional on a clear awareness of the outlook through which we make sense of reality. Thus he allows us to participate in both versions of his novel's experience, and also frankly to recognize each *as* a version, so that we may decide within the context of that recognition in which terms that experience is better understood.

The peculiarities of fictive form that I have been discussing are all present in the last scene of *The Scarlet Letter*. The chapters leading up to "The Revelation of the Scarlet Letter" are superb examples of Hawthorne's narrative art. Everything that has appeared in the book is gathered together in preparation for a fateful climax. The descriptions of the crowd, of the procession, and of Dimmesdale's sermon and its effects are among the most beautiful and thorough passages of social observation in the book, and at the same time we never forget that this public spectacle is postponing a critical event in the book's private drama. As the ministers and the magistrates leave the church the action becomes genuinely suspenseful. Everything is done in slow motion. Dimmesdale totters; he rejects Reverend Wilson's aid; he advances to the scaffold; Bellingham comes forward to assist him, but he is warned back by Dimmesdale's look. The martial music plays on, but Dimmesdale pauses. And now, with grim theatricality, he stages a ceremonious spectacle of his own, the spectacle of exposure of sin that he has acted out in his mind and on the scaffold at night. Supported by Hester, and with Pearl between them, he acts out a scene in which he is both avenger and sinner, exposer and concealer, agent and victim of God's wrath.

In this scene a dogmatic and theological and a secular and humanistic imagination come into passionate conflict one last time. Dimmesdale's outlook here is that of the Puritans raised to a ghastly pitch. He sees Chillingworth as the tempter and fiend; he speaks of the lurid gleam of Hester's letter; he sees the drama of his own life as a strife between God and the Devil, and his revelation as a "plea of guilty at the bar of Eternal Justice" (254). Set against his grim exultation and the narrow fixity of his orthodox interpretation are Hester's despair and her desperate attempts to broaden and thus deny the categories of his thought: "Shall we not

spend our immortal life together? Surely, surely we have ransomed one
another, with all this woe!" (256). Their debate is fully dramatic. Behind
each of their claims we are aware of the personal psychic processes that
inform their attitudes. We realize that Dimmesdale's orthodoxy, here as
before, is perverted in the image of his own guilt-obsessed mind. He is as
masochistically obsessed with passing a self-destructive judgment on
himself as he was in "The Minister's Vigil." And his is here, as it was
there, an egotistical interpretation of the providential design: "behold
me here, the one sinner of the world!" (254). We also realize that Hester
is giving expression to her own guilty fantasy of a heavenly consummation, and that her affirmation that human love provides its own
sanctifications and ransoms, like her bold claim in the forest that their
love had a consecration of its own, is a desperate one, and one that does
not square with the full complexity of the aftermath of their adultery.
Each one's version of what their experience means is qualified by our
awareness of his character, but these versions are allowed to stand side by
side, without further comment. The narrator refuses to press the question
of the truth or falsity of their statements beyond what they themselves
have attained. If we try to do so we must return to Hester's answer: "I
know not! I know not!" (254).

Dimmesdale concludes his confession with a fierce shriek:

> "He bids you look again at Hester's scarlet letter! He tells you,
> that, with all its mysterious horror, it is but the shadow of what
> he bears on his own breast, and that even this, his own red
> stigma, is no more than the type of what has seared his inmost
> heart! Stand any here that question God's judgment on a
> sinner? Behold! Behold! a dreadful witness of it!"
>   With a convulsive motion he tore away the ministerial band
> from before his breast. It was revealed!
>
>   (255)

But no sooner does he make his revelation than the author draws the
curtain before our eyes: "But it were irreverent to describe that revelation." And, having dismissed the ghastly miracle, he continues with his
narration of the scene.

By now we have grown accustomed to seeing the scarlet letter announce
itself as a symbol in the middle of a fully dramatic scene. But this
demurrer on Hawthorne's part is nonetheless startling. It is hard to say
which is more surprising: the fact that he insists on including as the
climax of his scene such a strange and wondrous revelation, or the fact
that, having done so, he then refuses to show it forth. Why should he so

carefully arouse the sort of curiosity that he does here and then so pointedly cheat it out of its gratification? This final scene brings to a head a conflict of narrative methods that has run all through the book. Dimmesdale's uncovering of his red stigma stands as the culmination of a carefully cultivated line of suspense—Hawthorne has teased and teased us with allusions to this mystery. In constructing his plot around the concealed presence of this physical sign he gives his book the shape of a ghostly romance; it operates by a magical order of causal determinism in which internal conditions are externalized as physical appearances. This line of suspense is the narrative's equivalent to the fictional mode in which Chillingworth is envisioned, and again Hawthorne associates this mode with Puritan mental fictions. As Dimmesdale presents it the symbol is fraught with providential significance, a wonder-working token of God's justice to sinners. And just as Chillingworth's fictional mode plays against Hester's, so too another kind of suspense is set against that of Hawthorne's romance plot. This interests us not in supernatural manifestations, or in what God has wrought, or in anything that admits of a determinate meaning, but rather in what choice Dimmesdale will make, what role his decision will play in his own psychic life, and what effect his choice will have on the other characters. This is the suspense of a more realistic novel; it invites us to see the story's meaning in its drama, in the texture of the characters' experience and in their exercise of their human freedom.

Hawthorne can and does give us the sort of scene that the latter kind of interest demands, but he insists on including a more mysterious and magical drama as well, and he refuses to make it easy for us to ignore it. As in "The Minister's Vigil," when the dramatic scene is completed the appearance of the scarlet letter is still to be explained, and here again Hawthorne uses its problematic status to engage us in a self-conscious act of interpretation. In returning to Dimmesdale's revelation in his last chapter he offers no explanation of his own for his story's omitted climax. Instead he reports the explanations of various spectators—that the letter on Dimmesdale's chest was the result of self-inflicted penitential torture, that it was magically produced by Chillingworth's potent necromancy, that it was the work of "the ever active tooth of remorse, gnawing from the inmost heart outwardly" (258). There is a fourth account as well, that of certain "highly respectable witnesses," according to whom there was no scarlet letter and Dimmesdale had no hidden personal guilt to conceal. To these witnesses Dimmesdale stood on the scaffold with the adulteress and her child to express in parabolic form the lesson that "in the view of Infinite Purity, we are all sinners alike" (259).

Hawthorne releases us from his narrative authority and allows us to choose among these, or to adopt whatever other explanation we like. And while at first his multiple choice seems simply to make the meaning and even the factuality of Dimmesdale's revelation ambiguous, the dimensions and the point of the ambiguity are not at all imprecise. Each of these choices gives the scene significance in terms of an implicit view of the nature of human guilt and evil. By absconding with his book's climax and providing these alternate versions of it instead, he allows us to construct our own conclusion, to see something or nothing on Dimmesdale's chest, but either one on the condition that we be aware of the nature of the vision that will make what we see meaningful to us. Our final moment of direct confrontation with the scarlet letter has the same purpose as the earlier ones did, but now that purpose is more obvious: it leaves us alone to complete the novel by determining its reality and its meaning as we think best, and to be conscious of our imaginative procedure as we do so.

Finally Hawthorne's multiple choices provide one last clue to the purpose of his use of romance in *The Scarlet Letter*. From what we have seen of the Puritans in the novel the fourth choice sounds less like their reaction than like that of highly respectable readers of a later age. In its unwillingness to admit mysteries like Dimmesdale's letter to its consciousness it partakes of what Hawthorne calls "our modern incredulity" (88). And in ceasing to believe in any form of magic it also ceases to adhere to a concept of sin as anything more than a comfortably universal phenomenon, lacking individual manifestations. In its light we see what the first three views have in common. They are all willing to accept the mysterious letter as a reality, and they all accept as a reality the "deep life-matter" (254) of guilt or evil from which they see it as springing. Hawthorne's own willingness to enter into the enchantments of romance and his eagerness to make us experience romance's magic all through *The Scarlet Letter* is a form of resistance to the trivializations latent in the secularism of an age that places "gilded volumes on the centre-table" (105) where the Puritans placed more serious literature and an age that makes adultery a matter of "mocking infamy and ridicule" (50). It is his way of regaining access to the mysteries of the psychic life, the reality of which both the Puritans and his own more secular fiction attest to in their own ways.

4| Double Exposure: *The House of the Seven Gables*

As soon as histories are properly told there will be no more need of romances.

Whitman, 1855 Preface
to *Leaves of Grass*

Few novels realize their own potential so completely as does *The Scarlet Letter*. It seems inevitable; it is inconceivable that anything could be added to it, or anything taken away. At the same time, this very success inspires reservations in Hawthorne. Toward the end of "The Custom-House" he says of this book:

> it wears, to my eye, a stern and sombre aspect; too much ungladdened by genial sunshine; too little relieved by the tender and familiar influences which soften almost every scene of nature and real life, and, undoubtedly, should soften every picture of them.
>
> (*SL* 43)

Certainly a great part of the power of *The Scarlet Letter* comes from its continual awareness of the forces that make its characters incapable of escaping from their own self-divisions and defeats, however magnificently they may live through their suffering. But Hawthorne is uncomfortable with the starkness of his own tragic vision. What bothers him is not so much the inclusion of the stern and somber in the book's atmosphere as the exclusion of everything else. It seems to him one-sided, too uniform in its tone and its sense of life.

The Scarlet Letter itself helps to explain the reasons for this anxiety. One of its major subjects is the way in which characters forge the varied powers of their selves into a grim unity of concern and thus sever themselves from the richness of experience. In his last chapter Hawthorne hints that he has become as much a victim of the scarlet letter's compulsive power as Dimmesdale—he would, he says, "gladly . . . erase its deep print out of our own brain; where long meditation has fixed it in very undesirable distinctness" (*SL* 259). He may be speaking playfully, but the suggestion that the author shares the experience of obsession with his characters corresponds to real features of the book. In its rigidly exclusive preoccupation with one symbol and one action, and in its

69

haunting sense that every item it observes bears on the meaning of that action, the novel's fictional mode partakes of the constriction of outlook that it associates, in its drama, with a mental disease. Hawthorne's wish to let the genial sunshine into his work expresses not merely a taste for a cheerier sort of novel; diversity of tone and an open inclusiveness of subject are necessary to lead his fiction from sickness into health.

Hawthorne's comments on *The Scarlet Letter* indicate the direction his next experiment with the novel will take. *The House of the Seven Gables* has as its center another tale of guilt and sorrow, but this time that tale ends with a vision of expiation and renewal. Like Shakespeare's romances, *The House of the Seven Gables* includes and transcends a tragedy. Throughout the book Hawthorne also distances and softens his drama's somberness by sketching in a spacious foreground of homely and familiar life. This foreground is the product of his effort to write a new sort of realistic fiction, a fiction more faithful, as he sees it, to nature and real life. As he begins this second work he in effect renews his pledge in "The Old Manse" "at least to achieve a novel," arming himself with a deep lesson and setting off in a new direction in pursuit of "physical substance enough to stand alone."

Hawthorne's effort to endow this book's world with a new kind of reality is most readily evident in the pains he takes to record what he calls its exterior life. He extensively notes each character's physical appearance —his clothing, manner, and facial expression. And he is so careful to fill in the physical environment around them that long passages—the description of the shop's contents, for instance, or of the garden's produce—take on the air of itemized inventories. Having once recorded all the comings and goings of an ordinary day in Pyncheon Street, he repeats this round again and again. In *The Scarlet Letter* a descriptive chapter like "The Governor's Hall" seems to be the product of a conscious effort to slow the action down and make the narrative more circumstantial; in this novel Hawthorne's tendency to linger in a scene and patiently describe the life it contains is so pronounced that more than once he has to remind himself to move along. "Many passages of the book," Hawthorne wrote to James T. Fields while at work on *The House of the Seven Gables,* "ought to be finished with the minuteness of a Dutch picture, in order to give them their proper effect."[1]

On the basis of these instances and this expressed intention it would seem that Hawthorne's remedy for infidelities to nature and real life in *The Scarlet Letter* is simply to inundate us with lifelike and lively detail. Hester and Pearl seem never to eat; in *The House of the Seven Gables* we know not only what the inmates of the Pyncheon house eat but also how

the food is procured, prepared, and served. But the real difference
between the representational procedures is not so much that such
information is more plentiful here as that the details that compose its
world are more neutral. The features of its settings usually lack the
supersuggestive quality that characterizes the world of *The Scarlet Letter:*
its spilled marbles, garden vegetables, and scissor-grinders are included
not because they belong to larger patterns of significance but simply
because they belong to the actual world in which the characters live.
The characters in *The Scarlet Letter* are observed in moments of conflict
and crisis; even in the chapters that show their lives between crises—those
that show Hester sewing, or Pearl at play—Hawthorne's interest is in the
psychological effects of Hester's crime and passion on their ordinary lives.
But in *The House of the Seven Gables* he focuses on characters during
lulls of action; the sort of minute attention to the unfolding course of
experience that he gives to Dimmesdales's act of self-exposure in "The
Minister's Vigil" is applied, here, to such events as Hepzibah's first day
behind the counter or Clifford's day in the garden. Instead of exhibiting
facets of one dark idea, Hawthorne presents us with the varied occurrences
of ordinary days. He dispels *The Scarlet Letter's* haunted atmosphere of
total relevance to provide a clean and quiet picture of normal life.

   This change in the treatment of his subject matter goes along with a
change in the nature of that matter. Compare the first narrative chapters
of the two books, "The Market-Place" and "The Little Shop-Window."
Both chapters have a door as their focus; both have as their actions a crisis
of emergence in which the heroine is compelled to leave a place of privacy
and protection and step forth to a position of public exposure. We
encounter Hester's pain and shame at the public gaze again in Hepzibah,
whose greatest dread in opening her shop is of the power she will give
others to stare at her and judge her. But the amount these chapters have
in common serves to underline their differences. Hester is beautiful and
majestic; Hepzibah is a "time-stricken virgin" (34) with creaky joints, a
scowling face, and an absurd turban. Hester's emergence takes the form
of a solemn legal ceremony, and the stare of the crowd has, in her case,
the moral sanction of punishment by shame. Hepzibah emerges in the
role of "the hucksteress of a cent-shop" (38), and the stare she
encounters is simply the gape of idle curiosity. In *The House of the Seven
Gables* Hawthorne abandons the grandeurs of high tragedy for the sake
of engaging his fiction with a plainer and more mundane life.

   A scowling old maid going into business in a small way is not, on the
surface of it, a very promising start for a novel, and rather than concealing
this fact Hawthorne conducts his narration in "The Little Shop-Window"

in such a way as to insist upon it. By positioning himself as a "disembodied listener" (30) who cannot see Hepzibah until she opens her chamber door and crosses "the threshold of our story" (31) he builds up a rather arch suspense about her, a suspense that makes her actual emergence, "feeling her way toward the stairs like a near-sighted person, as in truth she is" (32), seem devastatingly disappointing. By pretending to know only what he can see and hear of Hepzibah he directs our attention to the grotesque and ludicrous exterior of her person.

Of course this is not all that we see of Hepzibah. The cruel humor of this jaunty listener is supplemented by another voice, that of a more omniscient narrator who is privileged to know the interior of Hepzibah's heart and who can thus see her as an object worthy of compassion. Hawthorne oscillates wildly between these two positions throughout the chapter, and if at first they seem to indicate his personal inability to take a balanced view of his character, as the chapter continues their purpose becomes clearer. For at the end the tone, the attitude to be taken toward Hepzibah, itself becomes his subject.

It is a heavy annoyance to a writer, who endeavors to represent nature, its various attitudes and circumstances, in a reasonably correct outline and true coloring, that so much of the mean and ludicrous should be hopelessly mixed up with the purest pathos which life anywhere supplies to him. What tragic dignity, for example, can be wrought into a scene like this! How can we elevate our history of retribution for the sin of long ago, when, as one of our most prominent figures, we are compelled to intro-duce—not a young and lovely woman, nor even the stately remains of beauty, storm-shattered by affliction—but a gaunt, sallow, rusty-jointed maiden, in a long-waisted silk gown, and with the strange horror of a turban on her head! Her visage is not even ugly. It is redeemed from insignificance only by the contraction of her eyebrows into a near-sighted scowl. And, finally, her great life-trial seems to be, that, after sixty years of idleness, she finds it convenient to earn comfortable bread by setting up a shop, in a small way. Nevertheless, if we look through all the heroic fortunes of mankind, we shall find this same entanglement of something mean and trivial with whatever is noblest in joy or sorrow. Life is made up of marble and mud. And, without all the deeper trust in a comprehensive sympathy above us, we might hence be led to suspect the insult of a sneer, as well as an immitigable frown, on the iron countenance of fate. What is called poetic insight is the gift of discerning in this sphere of strangely mingled elements, the beauty and the majesty which are compelled to assume a garb so sordid.
(40–41)

This passage urges us to recognize the chapter's double view of Hepzibah as a function of its author's commitment to a truthful representation of the complexity of actual life. The voice of the disembodied listener insists that we see everything mean and ludicrous in Hepzibah and her position, everything that makes her less dignified and heroic than Hester is. This is the sordid garb, the mud of common existence, and Hawthorne dwells on it as a way of demonstrating that what he is presenting *is* real life, not an author's falsifying dressing up of the human condition. At the same time, by seeing more of Hepzibah than her scowl, by understanding the quality of her devotion to Clifford and the pain and bravery involved in opening a shop, he dramatizes his own gift of what he calls poetic insight, a gift of compassionate recognition of the beauty and human worth that reside in humble circumstances.

Hawthorne's discussion of his relation to his materials here indicates that the realism of *The House of the Seven Gables* is more than a matter of minute and neutral fidelity to surface detail: it addresses a certain sort of life, and it approaches this life in a certain way. Minuteness is not an end in itself for Hawthorne any more than it is for George Eliot, who in the seventeenth chapter of *Adam Bede* also finds a model for her art in "Dutch paintings . . . of a monotonous homely existence."[2] Both of them raise the image of a more elevated art form only to dismiss it, and for both of them the choice of a less sublime pictorial style goes along with a principled choice of a more lowly matter as art's truest subject. They dismiss the "great world" (159) in order to embrace what Wordsworth, in a phrase Eliot cites as her epigraph in *Adam Bede,* calls "nature's unambitious underwood." They seek to present "the well-worn track of ordinary life" (142), and to present it in its prosaic and muddy ordinariness. But they do not just show it naked. Eliot finds in the very attentiveness to humble life in Dutch paintings a testimony to the author's "delicious sympathy" as well as a capacity to awaken such fellow feeling with the common lot in the viewer. If Hawthorne does not possess in quite the same measure Eliot's feeling for the beauty of humanity in its common fellowship, he does share her conception of fidelity to the everyday as an act of love. "The author needs great faith in his reader's sympathy," he writes in "The Pyncheon-Garden," "else he must hesitate to give details so minute, and incidents apparently so trifling" (150)—the minute details and the trifling incidents are the record of his own sympathetic attention, and they require a parallel emotional commitment on our part. Like Eliot's, Hawthorne's comments on the method of his fiction work not to make his book's world seem imagined but exactly to underline its reality; and they clarify the value of his method as a mode of sympathetic insight into commonplace actuality.

The bond between realism and love helps to explain the sorts of details and scenes Hawthorne chooses to present in *The House of the Seven Gables*. We know so much about its characters' eating habits not because the narrator is uniformly more informative here than in *The Scarlet Letter* but because such events as breakfasts and picnics enable him to dramatize at length everyday community, the small acts of love and sharing that fill out daily relationships. This same concern with unobtrusive kindness and sharing explains the almost boundless patience with which Hawthorne records Hepzibah's and Phoebe's attempts to alleviate the torpid monotony of Clifford's day. This bond also helps to account for the narrator's relation to his characters in *The House of the Seven Gables*. This relation includes, I think, what is most annoying and unsuccessful in the book. In the scene in "The Little Shop-Window" the narrator giggles over Hepzibah so vigorously that his assertions of compassion sound insincere, and in any case both his giggles and his sighs are dramatized at such length that it is difficult even to see Hepzibah, let alone to tell what emotion she arouses. Throughout the book Hawthorne has a dismaying habit of chuckling and weeping over his characters, and all too often he is, as here, quicker to tender his feelings and beg us to join in them than to show in his characters the sort of experience that would warrant such feelings. This quantity of asserted emotion in excess of its occasion is a flaw that should not be explained away, but we can at least see why this particular fault should be so prevalent in *The House of the Seven Gables*. Phoebe, who is repeatedly associated with the commonplace, makes the world seem real, warm, and substantial to Clifford, "and no longer a delusion"; and in feeling this Clifford also feels that his "place was good in the whole sympathetic chain of human nature" (141). Hawthorne wants his own realism to have the same effect as Phoebe's reality. Just as his domestic scenes work to knit up a loving community among his characters, so too his effusions are an attempt to extend that sympathetic chain from the characters to their author and his readers.

When, having refused to give her the dignity of a tragic heroine, Hawthorne provides Hepzibah with a sort of dignity commensurate with her ludicrousness, he does this partly by appreciating the quality of her heart, but also partly by placing her act in its social context. The force that compels Hepzibah to leave her solitude is an economic one—"She must earn her own food, or starve!" (38). And the shape that her emergence takes is to be understood, as well, in terms of the economic options—opening a shop or teaching school—available to women in Hepzibah's society. The source of her resistance to such external defini-tion, and thus of the pain with which she submits to it, is her pretension to exalted rank. And again Hawthorne asks us to understand her personal pretension in larger social terms, in terms of the special strength of the attachment to rank in a republican country, where it must be grounded not on titles but on "the grosser substance of wealth and a splendid establishment" (38). If Hawthorne's realism is a way of seeing feelingly, it is also a way of seeing socially; in this instance his analysis partakes of the sense of life Georg Lukács associates with the realism of Balzac and Tolstoy, a sense that "every action, thought, and emotion of human beings is inseparably bound up with the life and struggles of a community . . . whether the humans themselves are conscious of this, unconscious of it or even trying to escape from it."[3]

Lukács says that "the central category and criterion of realist literature is the type, a peculiar synthesis which organically binds together the general and the particular, both in characters and situations,"[4] and it is this sort of synthesis that Hawthorne aims for in his analysis of Hepzibah. By locating her act in relation to economic pressures and class sentiments he both explains the social forces at work in her individual case and enables that case to take on a representative cast. Hepzibah's pain and courage are her own, but as she lives through her crisis she comes to stand for all those "at the drowning point" in a "republican country" (38), to figure as the heroine of a national tragedy. Hawthorne uses the language of typicality throughout *The House of the Seven Gables*. He refers, for example, to Phoebe and Holgrave as "characters proper to New England life" (175). Phoebe exhibits the "genial activity" which is "one of the most valuable traits of the true New England woman" (74–75); Holgrave, whose persistently sanguine temper is the only link between his randomly adopted trades and roles, is "the representative of many compeers in his native land" (181). Hawthorne's fidelity to the humble and domestic precludes the portrayal of the whole web of a society, but the characters in his homely foreground have a remarkable power to suggest the life possibilities of a larger world; thus Phoebe brings along with her the virtues and limitations of the New England village, and Holgrave's social life permits Hawthorne to suggest the presence of a radical fringe of "reformers, temperance lecturers, and all manner of cross-looking philanthropists" (84). This power is particularly acute in the case of Jaffrey Pyncheon, whose association with cold official charities, the speculative capitalism of State Street, and the politics of smoke-filled rooms enables him to indicate the institutions of wealth and power that surround the book's island of domestic tranquility.[5]

Comparisons of *The House of the Seven Gables* with Lukács's preferred forms of realism should not be pressed too far. If Hawthorne sees some of his characters as representative cases, when he analyzes Clifford in terms of a type it is a psychological one, that of the lover of the beautiful, not a social one. And if he sometimes hints at the presence of larger social forces, his predominant concern is with a ragtag band of social outsiders and the quality of their private lives. But even his depiction of a "paltry rivulet of life" (153) rather than its grander currents serves to articulate a social critique. His garden group of kindly but also rather incomplete souls stands in the same relation to Jaffrey and the dehumanizing world of wealth and power as the group gathered around Sleary's Horseriders does to the world of Bounderby and Gradgrind in Dickens's *Hard Times,* or as the characters associated with Solomon Gills's old-fashioned shop do to those associated with the cold and competitive firm of Dombey and Son. Hawthorne's sympathy with his defective crew is as whole-hearted as Dickens's. And like Dickens, he uses that crew to measure both the evil of the public life it has dropped out of and the sort of incompleteness of self that such a society necessitates in its opponents. If Clifford's emotions are those of a lover of beauty, it is nonetheless true that his ruined condition is the product of Jaffrey's greed, the law, and the prison.

The sympathetic method of Hawthorne's realism in *The House of the Seven Gables* exhibits its characters in their private community of affection. The social method of that realism supplements and extends this; it links the characters to the community of a larger society. It should be stressed here that this larger context is specifically a contemporary one, or one at any rate "not very remote from the present day" (6). Holgrave's is "the experience of many individuals among us" (176); if you would see him, Hawthorne says in effect, look about you! The details of exterior life that he specifies are, similarly, often explicitly contemporary—the prominent place given to the railroad, the daguerreotype, and the telegraph are obvious examples. The new fictional method of *The House of the Seven Gables,* with its attention to the appearances, activities, characters, and forces that make up "the opaque substance of to-day" (*SL* 37), indicates the presence of a new fictional goal. Hawthorne is here, to a limited but genuine extent, using the novel to make a record of and to make imaginative sense of contemporary social life.

The novel itself clarifies the value of this goal. When Hepzibah opens her shop she ceases to be a prisoner of the past and joins in the life of the present; she leaves her sterile isolation to lend her strength, in Holgrave's overstatement, to "the united struggle of mankind" (45). Her move resembles Hawthorne's own. Moving away from *The Scarlet Letter,* he takes his fiction forward in time, to engage it with the present world. And the method through which he links individual cases with a larger social community is the imaginative correlative to the sort of involvement with the life of men and women that he values so highly in his heroine. I have dwelled so long on the realism of *The House of the Seven Gables* for two reasons. This is the method Hawthorne associates with the novel, and it is necessary to note the extraordinary care with which he works at it in order to see the direction in which he is trying to steer his fiction. Further, *The House of the Seven Gables* illuminates with unusual clarity the group of values—substantiality, sympathy, presentness, involvement —that cluster around his conception of the novel and form the basis of his imaginative allegiance to this form. At the same time, however much its technique and vision may have in common with those of an author like Dickens, the book's deep lesson—"that the wrong-doing of one generation lives into the successive ones" (2)—marks its place in another tradition, in a direct line of descent from Walpole's *The Castle of Otranto.* Like *The Scarlet Letter,* in the sort of fictional reality it creates *The House* has genuine resemblances to the novels that are its European contemporaries; but it finally parts ways with them in its simultaneous inclusion of the marvelous methods of a primitive mode of romance. And if the realism of *The House* possesses in Hawthorne's eyes a closer relation to nature and real life, its hereditary curses and magical portraits constitute a romance mode that is even more wild and extravagant than that of *The Scarlet Letter.*

Hawthorne himself is fully conscious of the doubleness of his intention and of the artistic problems it poses. "The 'House of the Seven Gables' is, in my opinion, better than 'The Scarlet Letter,' " he tells Horatio Bridge, "but I should not wonder . . . if the romance of the book should be found somewhat at odds with the humble and familiar scenery in which I invest it."[6] Here again he faces a gap between two sorts of imaginative articulation, between the symbolic and fantastic design of romance and the fidelity to the texture and order of actual experience of the novel. In constructing this book he widens the gap between these incommensurate modes of fiction, and he exploits the tension between them even more self-consciously and calculatingly than in *The Scarlet Letter.* To complete our discussion of this work's form we must now consider the function of its romance elements and then go on to see how Hawthorne regulates the odds between his conflicting fictions.

The House of the Seven Gables, like *The Scarlet Letter,* begins with what Leslie Fiedler calls a "prehistoric" act.[7] Colonel Pyncheon's dispossession of the Maules, like Hester's adultery, is completed before the story proper begins, and in both cases this act establishes the conflict that provides the story with its occasion. What the characters of *The Scarlet*

Letter experience as the consequence of their own acts the characters of
The House of the Seven Gables experience as a problem of inheritance
and heredity. Here the prehistoric act spreads its consequences down
through seven generations, and Hawthorne uses the devices of gothic
romance to show that past prolonging itself into the present.

In Colonel Pyncheon the stolid unimaginativeness of the Puritans of
The Scarlet Letter has degenerated into a "common-sense, as massive and
hard as blocks of granite" (9); the militant moral rigor with which the
Puritans impose their community's values on others survives in the
Colonel's "iron energy of purpose" (7), but now that energy is a purely
selfish one. The Colonel treats others as the objects of this energetically
selfish will. The overbearing masculine aggressiveness that rumor records
in his sexual life is the private version of the grasping greed he exhibits in
his public life. By treating others in this way the Colonel transforms them
into reverse images of himself; thus the Maules, who are at first simply
ordinary settlers, after their dispossession become associated with poverty,
plebeianism, supernatural magic, and the subconscious. And he renders
this counterforce as inhuman as himself. He commits the Maules to the
logic of vengeance, so that their power becomes not creative but
destructive. At the same time he puts himself in this force's power. His
act of expropriation mysteriously confers upon the Maules control over
both the deed to the tract of Maine wilderness and the wilderness of his
own mind, his "topsyturvy commonwealth of sleep" (26). The spirit of
Pyncheon and the spirit of Maule thus become, like Dimmesdale and
Chillingworth, "mutual victims" (*SL* 261). The magical operation of
Maule's curse figures forth the cycle of victimization. Each new incarnation of the Colonel's spirit and each repetition of his act gives new
destructive power to the Maules, each new victory breeds its own defeat,
and then, as at the end of Blake's "The Mental Traveller," the cycle starts
all over again.

The cyclical struggle of the Pyncheon spirit and the Maule spirit,
established by Hawthorne's sifting of wild legends and rumors in the first
chapter and extended by Holgrave's romance narration, "Alice Pyncheon," is the central myth of *The House of the Seven Gables,* and as a
myth it lends itself as a structure to many possible contexts. The story of a
family feud can be read, as well, as a story of internal psychic conflict.
The association of the Maules with the commonwealth of sleep suggests
that the Colonel's act may be like the event that starts Blake's myth in his
Prophetic Books, an act in which one aspect of an integrated personality
separates itself and strives to dominate the others. His self-assertion as a
force of sense and will calls into being a subconscious that is separate and

bound to vie with him. By committing a guilty act he both robs himself of the potential riches of the more untamed part of himself and endows that part with the power to keep him from enjoying what his will can accumulate.

If the Colonel's act divides the mind against itself, it also represents a primal act of social division. He makes himself wealthy by making the Maules poor, and he makes his family aristocrats by making the Maules plebeians. The mutual victimization of Pyncheon and Maule becomes in this context a model of class warfare. The Pyncheons reject a natural society of human interdependence to set themselves over others. But in doing so they incur an involuntary dependence on the Maules, a dependence that can only be, for them, a source of frustration. At the same time, their claims to higher rank ensure that the plebeian class they call into being will feel its relation to them only as one of enmity. This process is most clearly shown in "Alice Pyncheon," where Alice's aristocratic manner turns the bristlingly proud plebeian Matthew Maule's love into a desire for revenge and domination. Once again an original act of self-assertion touches off a chain of strife, defeat, and self-defeat.

The method through which this cyclical struggle is realized is an anti-realistic one—to see its operation we must leave aside the canons of ordinary plausibility and enter into the supernatural causal order by which curses work—but it provides a crucial complement to Hawthorne's more realistic foreground. In that foreground he can observe the play upon contemporary individual lives of larger forces of economics and class, but it is only through his legendary background that he can exhibit the historical origin and the psychological dynamics of those forces in society. At the realistic level he can display a social split between Jaffrey's sphere of wealth and power and the Pyncheon garden, a place that gives shelter to sympathy and imagination, love of nature, poetry, and fiction, as well as imbecility and radicalism. But it is only through the romance device of the hereditary curse, which envisions the Establishments of different ages—Pyncheon is a colonel in the late seventeenth century, an Anglophile merchant in the eighteenth, a judge and congressman in the mid-nineteenth—as linked together by a persisting spirit of grasping practical energy, that he can suggest why public life now takes the shape it does; and it is only through the romance vision of psychic strife that he can understand the specific forms of social withdrawal he shows in the present as the antithesis that grasping spirit itself generates. Hawthorne's myth permits him to supplement his record of contemporary society with a kind of psychohistory of New England. And the myth gives his book its moral center as well. However much general value he can assign to love and affection in his portrait of everyday life, it is the myth's depiction of the dialectic of assertion and retribution that clarifies the ultimate value of love as a refusal to victimize others.

These are some of the large contributions that Hawthorne's romance art makes to his more realistic art in *The House of the Seven Gables*. But how do these two modes of vision meet and mingle in the work's less legendary chapters? All through *The House of the Seven Gables* Hawthorne's double intention makes itself felt as a series of modulations in the texture of his narrative. If parts of his canvas are filled in with the minuteness of a Dutch picture, other parts are achieved in a radically different representational style. Thus Hawthorne records with neutral precision the events in the street that Clifford watches for amusement, but at times these events suddenly take on a life and interest of their own: the organ-grinder's monkey, ostensibly included to illustrate Clifford's instinctive revulsion from all that is not beautiful, becomes a full-fledged allegorical figure, "the Mammon of copper coin" (164). He enumerates at great length the flora and fauna that make the garden a pleasant retreat, but at moments this comfortable world of natural things realigns itself into a revelation: flowers and vegetables pair off as aristocratic and plebeian; the chickens, which are seen as containing the whole accumulated past of their race within them, and which have, as a result, grown increasingly shrunken and infertile, become a "feathered riddle," a "symbol of the life of the old house; embodying its interpretation, likewise" (152).

By modulating between a mimetic and a more acutely symbolic visual style Hawthorne adjusts and readjusts the angle of our involvement with his material. He goes to such lengths to record the contents of the garden because "they had the earth-smell in them, and they contributed to give [Clifford] health and substance" (153). The meaning of these details is their actuality, and their actuality to Clifford: they are antidotes, as Phoebe is, to his chilly ideality. By contrast Hawthorne's symbolic insets take us back to something more like the overdetermined landscape of *The Scarlet Letter*. The humorously uncanny physical resemblance of the chickens to Hepzibah and Clifford urges us to cross-reference physical things and psychic facts, and to understand that the characters too have been rendered impotent by the accumulation of generations. Hawthorne's Dutch picture realism makes us attend to his characters' unfolding experience of their present world; his symbolic tableaux make us see that experience against the larger background of patterns prolonged through time. These tableaux show the terms and tensions of

Pyncheon history as being present in things, and in this book symbolism as a visual mode is a correlative to the persistence of that history.

The same sort of alternation between close-ups and long views is characteristic of Hawthorne's dramatic method in *The House of the Seven Gables*. The scenes of everyday sharing that, as I noted earlier, he works so patiently to record have a curious tendency to turn into ideological duets. Over the counter Holgrave and Hepzibah discuss aristocracy and involvement with the united struggle of mankind; Phoebe and Uncle Venner debate the evils of accumulating wealth and the possible pleasures of having a home; Phoebe and Holgrave argue about continuity, change, and the giant Past. The characters have a remarkable freedom to discuss the book's central concerns, a freedom like that which enables Perdita and Polixenes to debate the relation of art to nature in *The Winter's Tale*. Hawthorne is always careful to touch down again after these duets, to return to the humble details of daily personal interactions —Hepzibah terminates the discussion of private property in "The Pyncheon-Garden" by reminding Phoebe that "it is time to bring the currants" (156). But before he does so he shows the characters arranged in a strong thematic structure, related to one another as points in the large web of overlapping issues that is the legacy of Pyncheon history.

A similar duality of vision governs Hawthorne's presentation of character here. Careful as he is to fill in the appearances and manners of his characters, he seems to have curiously little faith in the revelatory value of such exterior details. His book exhibits the attitude to these that he expresses in the preface to *The Snow-Image*, written in the same year: such "matters entirely upon the surface" as "his external habits, his abode, his casual associates," he says there, "hide the man, instead of displaying him" (*SI* 4). Accordingly he tends to present exterior and interior separately, and to see them as contradictory. The ludicrous appearance of Hepzibah exactly belies her true tenderness of heart. Every time that Jaffrey enters the shop the narrator notes his unctuous manners and sultry smile; but when Jaffrey frowns and "a red fire" kindles "in his eyes" (129), revealing a romance devil like Chillingworth within this man of the world, the narrator cuts from the observed scene to extensive passages of interior surmise that clarify the true man concealed within the palace of his publicly presented selfhood. We see alternately what Holgrave calls the "merest surface" and the "secret character" (91), and, like the modulations between realistic and symbolic descriptions and between dramatic and thematic scenes, these double exposures alternately exhibit the characters' present beings and the historical determinants of their beings. Thus the sympathetic narrator who sees Hepzibah as a beleaguered maiden also views her as a figure in "our history of retribution for the sin of long ago" (41), and the inner views of Jaffrey also study him as "the Pyncheon of to-day" (115), this generation's avatar of the hereditary spirit.

As revelations of secret and historical character the book's inner views are supplemented by its portraits. The portrait of the Colonel, Malbone's miniature of Clifford, and Holgrave's daguerreotype of Jaffrey, each of which has a magical power to capture the true nature of its subject's character, are the most conspicuous romance devices within the body of Hawthorne's narrative. Whenever one of these is mentioned it evokes the other two, and the narrator and his characters repeatedly observe the startling similarities and contrasts among them. Because of this the pictures come to form a complex in the book, and as a complex they also exemplify the true nature of their subjects' relationships. The daguerreotype which records not Jaffrey's smile but the same hard, ruthless masculine spirit that the portrait exhibits establishes him as a new incarnation of his grasping ancestor. In Hawthorne's analyses of Clifford his feminine traits, his tendency toward imagination rather than common sense, and his amoral devotion to sensuous pleasure seem to be merely individual attributes. But the portraits' vivid contrast of Clifford with Jaffrey and the Colonel enables us to recognize Clifford's position as the antithesis created by the Pyncheon spirit and as the most recent victim of that spirit. The strife between Pyncheon and Maule has become, in a later generation, a strife among Pyncheons.

Like the moment in which the scarlet letter shines forth above the scaffold, the passages in which the related portraits are discussed are, in effect, epiphanies of their book; they offer a momentary static and iconic image of the terms of its persisting conflict. And like the paired portraits in the tale "The Prophetic Pictures," the truth they figure forth in visual form both reflects upon and depends upon the story, the progressive present lives of the characters. The portraits show the essences of relationships, but these relationships must act themselves out in order for the portraits' prophecies to be ratified. Jaffrey's portrait shows him as identical to the Colonel, but the truth suggested by the resemblance comes true only through Jaffrey's acts. By dispossessing Clifford and sending him to a living death he reenacts the sin of his forefather, and when he returns to drag Clifford's secret from him he repeats it once again. The pattern of generations, expressed in the linked portraits, determines the meaning of his action, but it is his action that revives the pattern and places him within it. He and Clifford must experience as an unfolding plot what the portraits express as a predetermined pattern.

This kind of interaction between symbolically expressed and progressively experienced meaning provides an important clue to the place of plot in *The House of the Seven Gables*. The first fourteen chapters amble along so slowly and undirectedly that the book almost seems to have no plot at all. Some of its chapters do arouse our curiosity and thus direct our interest forward in time, but Hawthorne never teases us for long. We are made to wonder what momentous action Hepzibah can be about to undertake, and then we find out: she is opening a cent-shop. We wonder who Phoebe hears breathing in the darkened parlor, and soon enough we learn that Hepzibah's mysterious guest is Clifford. The climaxes in these instances are nearly bathetic, but that bathos is intentional. Hawthorne makes us forgo the false excitement of manipulated plot and accept instead homely and unexceptional events as a reality more worthy of our interest. The appearance of plotlessness is reinforced by Hawthorne's technique of cutting away from the action of his foreground to analyze the essences of his characters and to place them in thematic and historical patterns. This technique enriches our perception at the cost of making the characters seem static. But in their low-key daily lives the characters are also dynamic, changing and evolving, and the relation between their fixed places and the action of their development resembles that between the portraits and the story.

We know, for instance, what Phoebe's essence is. In terms of the fixed contrasts in the book she is the Actual; freedom from and ignorance of the past; physical and mental health; the new plebeianism, in which the graces of a lady are combined with a practical talent for home economics; sunshine, blooming nature. Her place in the historical pattern of the book, its romance drama of expiation, is equally clear. Like the Perditas and Mirandas of Shakespearean romance, her vital purity embodies a redemptive potential. She is the exorciser; her homely witchcraft is what avails against the accumulated gloom and decay, sin and sorrow, of the house. She is presented in terms of these static structures of meaning so frequently that it comes as something of a surprise when we are told that she is also changing. But at several points Hawthorne does stop to comment on her growth, to note how, through her daily contact with the house and its inmates, she becomes less gay, less girlish, but more a woman. While she is exorcising the gloom she is also learning from it, learning of the past, of shadows and sorrow. Her education goes hand in hand with her sexual maturation—"the bud is a bloom!" (220)—and both of these processes of development are shown as functions of her evolving relationship with Holgrave. Her growth reaches its culmination in "The Flower of Eden," in which she both first encounters "awful death" (305) and then, moments later, first declares her love. Her fixed role in the drama of expiation is never in doubt, but it is only through her evolving experience that she can grow into and act out the full role that the historical pattern forecasts for her.

The best place to observe the relation between the historical and psychological pattern and the developing present action, the respective plots of romance and novel in *The House of the Seven Gables,* is in Holgrave's tale and its aftermath. Holgrave presents "Alice Pyncheon" as a conscious experiment in the use of romance. He includes even more gothicisms—a gesticulating portrait, a skeleton with a missing hand— than Hawthorne does in his initial historical sketch. Through his use of a supernatural mode Holgrave presents the book's clearest vision of the dynamics of the strife of Pyncheon and Maule; this occurs in the scene of mesmeric communication with the dead, in which the Colonel tries to tell where the deed is hidden, the Maules grasp him by the throat, and he once more coughs up blood. His tale also contains the book's clearest presentation of Pyncheon history as a psychic and psychosexual conflict. "Alice Pyncheon" is the story of Gervayse Pyncheon's reenactment in the third generation of his grandfather's act of greed and human sacrifice. In exchange for the deed to the land in Maine, Gervayse knowingly becomes a pander, offering Matthew Maule his daughter's virgin spirit. Alice's aristocratic pride, artistic training, and "womanly mixture" all combine in her haughty sexual appraisal of Maule:

> A glow of artistic approval brightened over Alice Pyncheon's face; she was struck with admiration—which she made no attempt to conceal—of the remarkable comeliness, strength, and energy of Maule's figure. But that admiring glance (which most other men, perhaps, would have cherished as a sweet recollection, all through life) the carpenter never forgave.
>
> (201)

In both of them sexuality is perverted into a struggle for domination; their meeting is a battle of sexual wills, pitting "woman's might against man's might" (203). Maule defeats and enslaves Alice's psyche—"Mine, by the right of the strongest spirit!" (206)—but the tale's conclusion, with its extraordinarily powerful vision of Alice's degradation and of Maule's final remorse, shows the double defeat that this kind of contest must produce.

As he tells his tale Holgrave brings about a repetition of its central moment. The spell an earlier Maule casts through mesmerism this later Maule casts through fiction; the strength of his tale's illusion gives him power over Phoebe, Matthew Maule's original power to achieve "empire over the human spirit" (212). But he has learned through his fiction. Recognizing the power of his rough magic, he rejects it; he refuses to violate Phoebe's "individuality" (212), the sanctity of her human heart. Respectful love wins out over the sort of heartless curiosity to which Holgrave has been prone, and his choice makes mutual sexual love possible. The chapter now modulates into a lyrical and moonlit love scene.

Holgrave's decision marks the turning point in his personal development, and it marks the turning point in the persisting historical conflict as well. As he completes his tale and re-creates its central situation the historical plot and the present plot merge completely. But the result of this is that the present characters, having returned to this crucial point in the cycle, can now reverse the earlier action and its outcome. The tale defines the importance of what is passing between Holgrave and Phoebe, and simultaneously it is the change in their own present lives that releases them from the pattern of domination and psychic revenge that the tale illustrates.

When we reconsider the sequence of action in *The House of the Seven Gables* in the light of this episode we can detect a curious degree of logic behind its apparent meanderings. Hepzibah is forced to abandon the Pyncheon position of aristocratic withdrawal and open a door to the world, and as soon as she does so Phoebe, the world's best ambassador, arrives to begin her work of comfort and renewal. When Holgrave and Phoebe first meet in the garden, when their love has its remote beginning, Clifford and Hepzibah are reunited. Holgrave's renunciation of the Maules' power seems by a ghostly causality to bring about the "fifth act" (218), as he calls it, the catastrophe in which Jaffrey's assertion of the Pyncheons' power destroys not others but simply himself. The plot too, it would seem, has its secret character. Because the characters exist within a large pattern of conflict, when any of them change the shape of their own lives they change the shape of the whole pattern. Holgrave's action in the garden, then, can free Clifford from Jaffrey in the parlor.

But the plot also has its merest surface—its simple and low-key daily life, with its ordinary and varied exigencies, its explicable present motives, its fortunate and unfortunate accidents, its opportunity for relationships slowly to develop. The secret plot, the romance plot of continuing psychic strife, explains the meaning and supplies the logic of what happens in this merest surface. But the simple daily life has its importance as well. This is where the characters can do and become, where they can choose to remain what they are, as Jaffrey does, and thus repeat the historical cycle, or else choose to change and develop, as the others do, and thus escape from the cycle. The homely foreground of *The House of the Seven Gables* supplies its characters with a crucial margin of indeterminacy. It is only here that they can achieve a measure of self-determination and freedom from their past. Time in *The House of the Seven Gables* is, as Blake says, the mercy of eternity.

The two possibilities the present plot offers to the characters reach their respective culminations in the climactic chapters of the book, "The Flight of the Two Owls" and "Governor Pyncheon." These chapters form a pair; essentially they are a diptych of life and death. Clifford and Hepzibah leave the house's retirement and are "drawn into the great current of human life" (256); with his wonderful paean to the ascending spiral curve of progress Clifford declares the independence of the present from the past as well as their own independence from the house's familial past. Involvement and presentness are values Hawthorne associates at the level of art with the novel, so that in his extended realistic descriptions here he creates in his fiction the sort of world his characters move into in their lives. In these descriptions the past is no longer seen as present in things; the details of the busy interior of the railway car are not grimly symbolic but simply actual and lively. Hawthorne concludes this description: "Sleep; sport; business; graver or lighter study;—and the common and inevitable movement onward! It was life itself!" (257). Clifford's speech finally comes to seem as much maniacal as Orphic, but this indicates the complexity of his newly real life, not its invalidity; the freedom he wins in it is a mixed state of exhilaration and anxiety.

While Hepzibah and Clifford leave the house to embrace real life, Jaffrey returns to the house and sits in the ancestral chair to embrace death. Hawthorne's rushing rhetoric of questions and taunts in "Governor Pyncheon" reviews the round of Jaffrey's busy day, but it does so to indicate how completely his life in the active world of men has ended. His focus on Jaffrey's watch and its record of passing time emphasizes, similarly, how completely the present has become inaccessible to him. By choosing to repeat the family pattern Jaffrey relinquishes the freedom to live in the actual and present world. Hawthorne's self-conscious use of the Maules' magic mirror at the end of this chapter shows Jaffrey as passing into a world of pure romance, into a ghostly gathering of ancestral spirits in which he can only take his place in line and go through once more the ritual motions of the Pyncheons who have come before him. Finally he becomes, as Clark Griffith notes, the corpse that his palace of selfhood has concealed all along.[8]

The House of the Seven Gables has a happy ending with a vengeance.

With the marriage of a Pyncheon and a Maule—romance's marriage of the children, which both concludes its conflict and provides for the continuance of human generations—the dark history of guilt and retribution is transcended. The ancestral portrait topples, the sluggish spring revives, the chickens begin to lay eggs by the dozens. Alice's posies bloom; these white flowers with a red spot, recalling the bloodstained ruffs of the Pyncheons, suggest that now the curse has passed out of the family and has been transformed into a principle of natural beauty and fruition. Holgrave recants his dangerous radical views, and the new community moves into a new house—Jaffrey's—to enjoy its inheritance.

This inheritance more than gratifies Phoebe's desire for "a house and a moderate garden-spot of one's own" (156). The recompense is huge; and further, the dark green barouche and the "couple of hundred thousand" (318) that the characters come into are not obviously appropriate rewards for those who have suffered so long the consequences of the Pyncheons' urge to acquire and hoard material wealth. This is what gives rise to ironic readings of the ending, for instance to Lawrence's sneering suggestion that the family spirit has simply found a more up-to-date incarnation: "the new generation . . . is setting up in the photography line, and is just going to make a sound financial thing out of it."[9]

In the book's terms the reward has more justice to it than Lawrence is willing to allow. After all, Hawthorne does not urge us to worry very much one way or the other about the new community's enhanced position in a competitive world. In the ending he is willing to forget about the forces and tensions his book has shown to be at work in the larger society and to envision a private resolution to those tensions, one in which aristocracy and plebeianism marry and cease to vie, and one in which the wealth that has been the exclusive property of public and grasping men is united to the softer virtues of sentiment and imagination. Further, the inheritance has a value over and above its cash assessment. Throughout the book the Pyncheon family's unrealizable fortune has stood for all the riches that the split and persisting strife within the personality has made unattainable to the characters. The marriage at the end marks the healing of this split as well, so that when the survivors inherit Jaffrey's house and wealth they are not just expropriating the expropriators but truly coming into their own, into the wealth of whole selfhood.

The new fortune also indicates a change in the family's relation to the past. In the ending all the story's missing links—Holgrave's identity, the hiding place of the deed, the truth about the uncle's death—come into the open. In *The House of the Seven Gables* only those who do not understand the past are condemned to relive it, so that as the characters uncover their family's potent secrets those secrets lose their power to determine their lives. And as soon as they understand the past they also become free to forget it: they can now receive an inheritance not as a curse but as a rich legacy for use in the present. At the end all the characters achieve the state of being Holgrave describes in the moonlit garden:

> "After all, what a good world we live in! How good, and beautiful! How young it is, too, with nothing really rotten or age-worn in it! This old house, for example, which sometimes has positively oppressed my breath with its smell of decaying timber! And this garden, where the black mould always clings to my spade, as if I were a sexton, delving in a graveyard! Could I keep the feeling that now possesses me, the garden would every day be virgin soil, with the earth's first freshness in the flavor of its beans and squashes; and the house!—it would be like a bower in Eden, blossoming with the earliest roses that God ever made."

>   (214)

Love purifies the mind, to which everything then becomes pure—and new. It rescues the lover from perceptions of a past persisting in things and ushers him into a world of redeemed and self-sufficient presentness.

Having reached this condition of understanding and perception the characters have no more need of romance. They ride off into a book more devoted to the substantial and the contemporary, a book in which there is, as Hawthorne says in the preface to *The Marble Faun,*

> no shadow, no antiquity, no mystery, no picturesque and gloomy wrong, nor anything but a common-place prosperity, in broad and simple daylight.

But he does not accompany them into this new book. In his last paragraph he returns to the house that they have in every sense left behind them.

> Maule's well, all this time, though left in solitude, was throwing up a succession of kaleidoscopic pictures, in which a gifted eye might have seen fore-shadowed the coming fortunes of Hepzibah and Clifford, and the descendant of the legendary wizard, and the village maiden, over whom he had thrown love's web of sorcery.

>   (319)

One last time he observes a connection with the long past; one last time he reminds us of what the characters are prepared to ignore—the old house, the cyclical history, the ancestral romance. The well, the elm, the ghost of Alice Pyncheon—these are the last clouds of the legendary mist which, in the preface to *The House of the Seven Gables,* Hawthorne says that "the Reader, according to his pleasure, may either disregard, or allow ... to float almost imperceptibly about the characters and the events, for the sake of a picturesque effect" (2).

By this point, however, we are not simply left with a choice among different possible ways of reading. As at the end of *The Scarlet Letter,* we know what the choices are, and we know what each of them implies. All through the book Hawthorne has led us back and forth between various kinds of fiction, and he has done so in such a way as to make us see what kind of an understanding of experience each of them is capable of and committed to achieving. To disregard the legendary mist—to choose the exterior views of character, the plot of our own day, and the passages of realistic description as the book's reality—is to see as, in different ways, Phoebe and Jaffrey do. They love no shadows; their concern is with the actual, the palpable, the present. To the extent that they reject shadows they also fail to understand their lives and their story. Jaffrey is finally victimized by the imagination he disregards,[10] and Phoebe must be schooled in the moonlight before she can begin to comprehend or to take an effective part in the tragedy of the Pyncheons. On the other hand, to see only the legendary mist—the ghostly inner characters, the symbolic places, and the compulsively repeated psychic plot of romance—is in effect to adopt Clifford's mode of vision as he looks into Maule's well. The present is obliterated by his fantasy, which can only see his past reenacting itself in the well's flickering lights. Clifford's repetitive fantasy vision is a symptom of his mental illness, and his development in the book must be toward increased contact with the substantial present.

To allow the mist to float before the story for the sake of a certain effect—to join in all the complex optical illusions that Hawthorne's modulation between different fictions engenders—is to adopt something like Holgrave's mode of vision. His tale draws upon a double source. It is compounded of history and tradition, documented fact and "wild, chimney-corner legend" (197). He trusts the imagination, both his own and that of popular rumor, as a vehicle of truth. Thus he is willing to make use of the supernatural—"not as a superstition, however—but as proved by unquestionable facts, and as exemplifying a theory" (185). He is willing to believe in the spooky magic of romance for the sake of discovering, through it, the logic that gives facts their coherence and importance. As such he is the reader's friend in *The House of the Seven Gables.* His attitude illuminates the value of the credulity the book's magic asks from us, and it clarifies the possibility of an imaginative acceptance of wonders that is not compulsive but freely chosen, for the sake of what they reveal at another level.

Hawthorne's own tale draws upon the same double source that Holgrave's does, and the division between them mirrors the larger division in his work between the fictions of realism and the fictions of romance. He makes a strong commitment to both but resists an ultimate commitment to either. He strives to record the humble texture of ordinary present life, but at the same time he distrusts appearances and finds this record unable to explain the historical and psychological dynamics that give the present its shape. His romance can supply that missing logic, but he finds its supernaturalism as well as its determinism unfaithful to the indeterminacy and freedom of nature and real life. He solves his dilemma by making use of and making us enter into the worlds yielded by both these modes of vision. And he keeps the odds between them from seeming simply absurd, not by seeking to efface their differences—magical portraits and hereditary curses are, if anything, the most blatant of romance mechanisms—but rather by passing his own consciousness of their discrepancy on to us and making us aware of the procedures and presuppositions that inform their versions of reality. As in *The Scarlet Letter*, he complicates our perception of his fictional world in such a way as to heighten our awareness of the imaginative activities that create it, and thus to engage us in a consideration of the kinds of truth that those activities can achieve. His double exposures all have the function of inviting us as readers to join him and his characters in a self-conscious attempt to make sense of their story. They make us see their experience as individual and historical, as substantial and as meaningful, as present and free and as determined by a prolonged past—and then they leave us with the task of forging for ourselves, on the basis of our clear understanding of the choices involved, the representation that we think most appropriate.

5 | "Who the Devel Aint a Dreamer?" The Blithedale Romance

Especially at this day, the volume is welcome, as an antidote to the mooniness of some dreamers—who are merely dreamers——Yet who the devel aint a dreamer?

Melville to Hawthorne, on *The Blithedale Romance*, 17 July 1852

When he completed *The Blithedale Romance* in April 1852, Hawthorne had written three novels in as many years, and this book provides a useful vantage point from which to review his work with the novel. The central drama of *Blithedale* once again turns on perversions of relationship and acts of willed violation. In subjecting others to his prying curiosity Miles Coverdale is a new incarnation of Roger Chillingworth and the unregenerate Holgrave; Zenobia's willingness to return Priscilla to an inhuman bondage to gain her own ends gives her a kind of kinship with Jaffrey Pyncheon. At every stage of the book's action we can hear Dimmesdale's assessment of Chillingworth in the background: "He has violated, in cold blood, the sanctity of a human heart" (*SL* 195).

At this level there is a striking degree of continuity in Hawthorne's work—indeed he seems to be telling the same story over and over. But when we look at the ways he tells his story and at the fictional worlds in which he sets it, what is equally striking is how remarkably little his books have in common. The genial domestic realism and the playful use of romance in *The House of the Seven Gables* are so much at odds with the intensely lurid and tragic grimness of *The Scarlet Letter* that it seems as if Hawthorne had purposely set out to make his second book's world as different from his first book's as he could. Hawthorne was well pleased with *The House*—the high mirth of its conclusion seems in part a reflection of his own satisfaction with his creation—and on the basis of this he might have been expected to continue working in this more congenial mode. But this is not the case: in vision and technique *Blithedale* is as different again from *The House* as *The House* is from *The Scarlet Letter*. Rather than allowing the success of one book to suggest the direction for the next, Hawthorne to a remarkable extent puts each achievement aside and starts all over. In this respect the only continuity that his novels possess is that of their experimentation.

Hawthorne had trouble choosing a title for *The Blithedale Romance*—

in addition to the one he finally selected he considered "Hollingsworth,"
"Blithedale," "Miles Coverdale's Three Friends," "The Veiled Lady,"
"Priscilla," "The Arcadian Summer," and "Zenobia"[1]—and it is not
hard to discover the origin of his quandary. *Blithedale* contains several
distinct centers of interest. The experiment in socialistic community, the
passionate intrigue involving the community's most interesting residents,
Coverdale's experience of their experience as an involved spectator, and a
more magical drama of clairvoyant maidens and evil wizards all compete
with one another as the book's central experience. As a choice of subjects
this is an embarrassment of riches, and Hawthorne accepts it as such;
rather than adopting any one of them at the expense of another he chooses
to choose them all.

This decision begins to suggest what makes *Blithedale* so different from
the works that precede it. *The Scarlet Letter* focuses unremittingly on the
experience flowing from the act and exposure of adultery, and for all its
apparent diversity of surface life *The House of the Seven Gables* is equally
single-minded in its attention to Pyncheon family history. By comparison
Blithedale is striking for its freedom of range. It makes room for all sorts
of characters and dramas, from the central ones already mentioned to a
host of minor ones: the broad humor of Silas Foster and the Blithedale
barnyard; wonderful satiric insets like its description of the hocus-pocus
of a lyceum-circuit sorcerer; social tragedies like that of Old Moodie, who
as he stands admiring his daughter's splendor in his tenement room takes
on something of the quality of Père Goriot.

This book is Hawthorne's open house, and the welcome he extends to
all sorts of subjects goes along with his willingness to try out all sorts of
tones and techniques in his narrative—*Blithedale* is, as Richard Chase
says, a "medley of genres and intentions."[2] Occasionally these get in
each other's way in the novel. For instance, at a theoretical level it is not
easy to reconcile Coverdale's authoritative irony as commentator on the
comedy of Blithedale with his unreliability as the hero of a Jamesian
tragedy of a prying narrator. But if it makes for a certain amount of chaos,
Hawthorne's eagerness to do too many things at once is what gives
Blithedale its special pleasure. By giving up the tautness of formal
organization of the earlier novels he gains for this book a kind of
freewheeling exuberance; and by refusing to confine himself to a strict
consistency Hawthorne allows himself to reveal abilities and interests
whose existence is only dimly suggested in his previous works.

This aspect of *Blithedale* suggests that criticism has less to gain by
considering it in its unity than by noticing the variety of new directions it
explores. One of these is evident in the book's urbanity. The use of

Coverdale as speaker here permits Hawthorne to show off a sort of sophisticated wit not manifest in his other books. We see this at its best in Coverdale's descriptions of the community's daily life—for instance, in his musings on how the participants' wearing of their old clothes makes them look like "a gang of beggars or banditti" (63), or like "the denizens of Grub-Street, intent on getting a comfortable livelihood by agricultural labor" (64). The playful fancies with which he surrounds his observations enable him to suggest ironic discrepancies between the community's sober theory and its frivolous practice and at the same time to avert harsh judgment, leaving room for recognition of the fun and benign folly that goes along with these contradictions.

The book's urbanity is evident in another form in its exchanges of badinage. In their conversations about throwing off such aspects of "the life of degenerate mortals" as housework to recover "the life of Paradise" (16), or about Coverdale's potential transformation into a tobacco-chewing farmer, Zenobia and Coverdale exhibit a lively freedom of mind that allows them to use Blithedale's official language of serious purpose as the basis for witty hyperbole. To Coverdale's mock-heroic musings on the Edenic life Zenobia replies that the snowstorm must postpone their adoption of "the Paradisaic system": " 'As for the garb of Eden,' added she, shivering playfully, 'I shall not assume it till after Mayday!' " (17). Such an element of flirtatious innuendo is almost always present in their duets, and it reveals another aspect of their witty freedom, the ease with which they allude to their own sexuality.

Finally the strain of urbane humor recedes into the background in *Blithedale*. But its presence does indicate a talent and interest not really evident in the author of *The Scarlet Letter* and *The House of the Seven Gables*, a flair for a sophisticated sort of social and sexual comedy. And the book's witty dialogues also point toward another innovation in *Blithedale*, its new method of dramatic presentation. *The House* scales down the dimensions of individuated consciousness in its characters for the sake of emphasizing overarching patterns. Hawthorne endows the characters of *Blithedale* with something closer to the full presence and power of selfhood that the characters of *The Scarlet Letter* possess. But the use of a dramatized narrator here, a narrator deprived of access to the inner workings of others' minds, means that Hawthorne cannot resort to *The Scarlet Letter*'s method of analytic interior observation. This self-erected obstacle leads to a breakthrough in Hawthorne's fiction: in *Blithedale* he learns to reveal the full psychological complexity of his characters through their external presentations of themselves.

Zenobia affords the best example of this. She shares with Hester

Prynne what Coverdale calls "a certain warm and rich characteristic" (17), a fullness of sexual presence. But much more than Hester, Zenobia seems to have a body—over and over Coverdale refers to her exposed shoulder, her full bust, her large hands—and as a result this heroine's sexual presence is not asserted but vividly seen. We know more about the details of Zenobia's clothing; we see, for instance, her simple dress of American print and her silk kerchief. And, again, her appearance subtly reveals her character; the presence of both something obtrusively simple and something obtrusively luxurious in her dress gives us our first hint of the element of play-acting involved in her commitment to the community's rustic life. Zenobia's body, her clothing, her gestures, and her looks express her. What is even rarer in Hawthorne, so does her speech. Thus during the first afternoon at Blithedale Coverdale asks her if she knows Hollingsworth personally:

> "No; only as an auditor—auditress, I mean—of some of his lectures," said she. "What a voice he has! And what a man he is! Yet not so much an intellectual man, I should say, as a great heart; at least, he moved me more deeply than I think myself capable of being moved, except by the stroke of a true, strong heart against my own. It is a sad pity that he should have devoted his glorious powers to such a grimy, unbeautiful, and positively hopeless object as this reformation of criminals, about which he makes himself and his wretchedly small audiences so very miserable. To tell you a secret, I never could tolerate a philanthropist, before. Could you?"
>
> (21–22)

No speech in Hawthorne's previous books sounds so much like actual conversation, and no speech is so revealing of its speaker's nature. All of Zenobia is present here: her sexual self-consciousness and flirtatiousness; her tendency to subject questions of social belief to personal and sexual response; her modish urbanity, hinting at a lurking triviality in her social concern; her self-confidence and vivacity, present in the cadences of her speech.

The dramatization of Zenobia is indicative of a whole new method in Hawthorne's fiction. He reverses, here, the assumption of *The House of the Seven Gables* that the "merest surface" and the "secret character" are antithetical. Here he understands the apparent and external details of character as parts of an intricate system of self-presentation, so that they can be allowed to reveal, not conceal, the features of the true self. As a result, instead of authoritatively explicating their secret lives he shows us the characters in their masks, allowing us to make what sense we can of them through their own dramatizations of themselves.

The kind of vitality and significance with which surface character is endowed in *Blithedale* makes it possible for Hawthorne to be more fully dramatic in his scenic art. By contrast with his other works it is remarkable how much conversation there is in this book, and at the same time how masterfully Hawthorne records what Nathalie Sarraute calls the *sous-conversation,* the advances and recoils, attractions and repulsions that go on within the characters while they are talking.[3] Thus in the great debate scene in "Eliot's Pulpit" the theoretical argument about the position of women moves in one direction while the buried action moves in precisely the opposite. Zenobia emotionally submits to Hollingsworth's masculine strength of vision even while her side, now defended by Coverdale, seems to be winning the argument. In the fifteenth chapter, "A Crisis," the debate between Coverdale and Hollingsworth over the respective rights of the community and Hollingsworth's plan to use Blithedale as the base for his project of reforming criminals is again a cover under which another curious love scene is taking place. Hollingsworth breaks off his moral exhortations and, as he pauses, his eyes fill with tears.

> "Coverdale," he murmured, "there is not the man in this wide world, whom I could love as I could you. Do not forsake me!"
>
> (133)

This emotional plea pulls at Coverdale's heart with "an almost irresistible force" (134). He replies with two questions that seem to him to ask themselves involuntarily. Their subterranean logic is not that of moral concern but of suspicious jealousy—Coverdale, we remember, finds it "an insufferable bore" (126) to occupy a secondary place in the affections of others: "Is Zenobia to take part in your enterprise? ... What is to become of Priscilla?" (134). Hollingsworth is stunned and makes an evasive reply. This in turn angers Coverdale, who is also glad for the strength his new anger gives him to resist Hollingsworth's final demand.

Such scenic renderings of emotional dialectics and battles of will both through and beneath the dialogue are common in *The Blithedale Romance.* The most superb instance comes in "Zenobia's Drawing-Room," in which both characters are fully conscious that their polite conversation is really a surface beneath which Coverdale is attempting to expose and Zenobia to conceal her secret feelings. In all these scenes there is a complexity and dynamism of interaction that is new in Hawthorne's fiction. But what truly distinguishes them from scenes of comparable intensity in his earlier works has as much to do with what they leave out as with their sophistication of staging. These scenes never make us switch back and forth between the characters and symbolic features of setting—fourfold scarlet letters or allegorical roosters and hens. Instead of distancing us and allowing us to understand their experience in more abstract terms these scenes work to give us an immediacy of involvement with the characters' motives and modes of passion as they unfold themselves in their encounters. And this change in technique is itself part of a more general shift in Hawthorne's work with the novel. In the silvery veil *Blithedale* contains an object potentially as rich in symbolic overtones as the scarlet letter,[4] but Hawthorne does not organize his book's presented world so cohesively around this symbol, nor does he ever force us to encounter it directly *as* a symbol. Similarly, like *The House of the Seven Gables* this book articulates dichotomies of crucial terms, but it does not line its characters up as figures in the pattern of an overt thematic structure. In *Blithedale* Hawthorne commits himself more unequivocally to his characters and the plot that their evolving relationships enact, refusing to make sense of their experience in terms of any order of meaning other than the dramatic one. He gives up the suggestiveness of a symbolic mode for the sake of achieving a new realism of dramatic presentation.

The subtlety of the presentation of character and scene in *Blithedale* is one feature that made this book a particular favorite of a later generation of realistic novelists, particularly Henry James and William Dean Howells. Their esteem is also at least partly based on the book's concomitant suppression of the methods of romance. Thus Howells, who inherits the generic definitions of Hawthorne's preface to *The House of the Seven Gables,* makes his highest tribute by calling *Blithedale* ''nearer a novel than any other fiction of the author.''[5] Howells sees in this book instances of what he calls ''palpitant naturalism,'' and James is similarly impressed by its ''vulgar, many-coloured world of actuality.''[6] These phrases reveal their own preoccupations as novelists but they do also point to real features of Hawthorne's work. In particular they draw our attention to the care he takes here to fill in the varied life of a larger world in which the characters' drama takes place.

The Blithedale Romance does not aim at a panoramic presentation of society. When Coverdale decides that he ought to return to the city and ''hold a little talk with the conservatives, the writers of the North American Review, the merchants, the politicians, the Cambridge men, and all those respectable old blockheads'' (141) he indicates the existence of social classes and institutions that we see almost nothing else of in the book. Hawthorne's focus on the Blithedale community is in this respect like his focus on the group gathered around the Pyncheon house. Rather than seeking to present a whole society frontally he chooses to concentrate on those who are estranged from society and thus to evoke a larger social world indirectly by studying the lives of its antagonists. But it is nevertheless remarkable how much we get around in *Blithedale*. In addition to the community we visit urban drawing rooms and barrooms, working-class tenements and suburban villages. Certainly the spatial range of the work is one of the major manifestations of its open inclusiveness; by comparison with *Blithedale* the worlds of Hawthorne's earlier novels seem not only small but even claustrophobic.

And Hawthorne's effort in *The House* to embrace what he calls the opaque substance of today, the varieties of contemporary life, seems almost timid compared with that in *Blithedale*. The reason seems to be not only that *Blithedale* contains a wider range of representation but also that the version of an actual world that it presents is so completely different from that of *The House*. The kind of minute description lavished on the pleasant pastimes in the Pyncheon garden is here devoted to the portrayal of the haunts and habits of urban alcoholics. Whereas Phoebe comes out of the bloomingly healthy life of the New England village, Priscilla comes out of a darker milieu. According to Zenobia, as a poor seamstress Priscilla has been "stifled with the heat of a salamander-stove, in a small, close room, and has drunk coffee, and fed upon dough-nuts, raisins, candy, and all such trash, till she is scarcely half-alive" (34). In *Blithedale* Hawthorne does not feel so compelled to be faithful to the tender and familiar influences that brighten nature and real life. As a result his realistic mode can now be put in the service of a more ironic vision, one that can be faithful to the squalor and poverty of urban life. It can be faithful, as well, simply to the strange new creations of that life; thus in "The Hotel" Hawthorne provides what may well be fiction's first documentary description of the backyard of a city apartment house.

Blithedale includes an unobtrusive richness of social representation, and an interesting feature of this representation is that it does not hurry to tie together its fragments of a world into a coherent social vision. Phrases such as "it was an age" or "in a republican country" are significantly missing here. A result of Hawthorne's willingness not to give a premature coherence to the world he presents is that it frees him simply to observe the local curiosities of that world. He can note the decor of the drawing room of a stylish boardinghouse, with its "pictures, marbles, vases," its "various methods of costly self-indulgence and splendid ease" (164); then he can put this aside and go on to note with fine ironic precision the decor of the barroom, with its idealized paintings of tempting entrées, its bartender with his magnificent mental endowments, and its gaudy fountain full of goldfish. Finally through these realizations of individual places a kind of coherent image does begin to emerge. The absence of connection between Zenobia's and Old Moodie's milieus repeats the absence of connection among the lives Coverdale observes going on behind the various windows of the boardinghouse; the very lack of meaningful relation among the parts of the world it shows is one of the novel's most salient points. And different as they are from one another in one sense, the drawing room and the barroom are alike in their insistent artifice. In this they belong to a larger pattern of artificial paradises, a pattern that includes the Blithedale community itself. All of these testify to the need the characters of this world feel for a more ideal life, and they ironically suggest as well the limits of their ability to imagine creatively such an alternative life.[7]

A chapter such as "The Village-Hall" clearly demonstrates the new fictional direction implicit in Hawthorne's detailed descriptions of milieu. It contains a crucial moment in the plot—Hollingsworth's freeing of Priscilla from Westervelt's exploitation. But this is quickly handled in one page, and the great bulk of the chapter is made up of an extended account of the activities of a New England lyceum. The scene is rendered with a fullness completely out of proportion to the requirements of the plot, and it suggests that in *Blithedale* Hawthorne is less interested in his plot itself than in the chance it gives him to hold a mirror up to the activities of contemporary social life. The vignette here also shows with special clarity how the New England of this day differs from the earlier one of *The Scarlet Letter*. Once more we see a community gathered together before a platform to observe a ceremony. But the ceremonies that take place in the lyceum are of a different order from those of the Puritan scaffold; "here is to be heard the choir of Ethiopian melodists, and to be seen, the diorama of Moscow or Bunker Hill, or the moving panorama of the Chinese wall" (196). The list suggests the quality of randomness or disconnection that we have seen elsewhere in *Blithedale*, and it suggests as well that the only continuity of the audience's interest is its demand for exotic escapist entertainment. On the day in question the entertainment consists of an appearance of the Veiled Lady, who is presented with an elaborate rigmarole of veils and wizard robes and magic exhortations—"She beholds the Absolute!" (201). The high moral seriousness of the Puritans' punishment of Hester gives way, here, to a carnival atmosphere. Whereas the Puritans' rituals are their way of acting out and reinvigorating their genuine spiritual beliefs, in the village hall the spiritual is placed in the service of spectacle and leisure pastime. When Hawthorne holds his mirror up this is what it shows: a world vacant of transcendent value, a world in which the trappings of ideality are present only in inverted forms.

In founding their community the characters of *The Blithedale Romance* work to create a new system of shared values and a new mode of serious purpose. But they belong to the world they oppose, so that the society they create ends by repeating and intensifying the features of the one they resist. For all its talk of selflessness and mutual aid, the real life of the community is one of tableaux vivants, charades, and costume parties, of artifice and frivolous play. And the spirit of the age infects the quality of their private as well as their group experience. Like Hester's gorgeously embroidered letter, Zenobia's personal emblem—her tropical flower—expresses a luxuriance of passionate vitality. But whereas Hester's letter is a seriously chosen sign of her own felt guilt and integrity, Zenobia's hothouse flower suggests a pleasure in rich adornment and a love of stylish self-display. The difference of their symbols carries over into their characters and careers. Zenobia too suffers the fate of loving a man incapable of returning her powerful generosity, but even in her most intense anguish there is always a quality of self-consciousness and theatricality; she seems to be watching herself play the part of Zenobia. In the middle of her passion in "Zenobia and Coverdale" she turns to Coverdale and says with a sharp laugh, "It is genuine tragedy, is it not?" (223). Coverdale notes as well that she is "not quite simple in her death. She had seen pictures, I suppose, of drowned persons, in lithe and graceful attitudes" (236). Her inability to escape from her own worldliness and artfulness makes her not, like Hester, a genuine tragic heroine, but rather a "tragedy-queen" (142). In her ironic tragedy, as in the ironic comedy of Blithedale, Hawthorne explores with extraordinary subtlety the condition of a world that has lost access to all sorts of significant forms of experience—of spiritual affirmation, of social relation, of self-expression, and even of suffering.

The character who best embodies the quality of life of Hawthorne's presented society is Miles Coverdale. In the comfortable retirement of his hermitage Coverdale broods on the projects he might accomplish in his leisure: he might write a poem; or, inspired by the sweet breeze, he might "meditate an essay for the Dial" (99); or he might put the ventilation to another good use and smoke a cigar.[8] In its bathos this progression is worthy of Pope. It shows Coverdale as incapable of entertaining a conception of art as anything more than an elegant pastime. Writing poetry for him accompanies the drinking of particularly fine sherries and the playing of billiards as part of the round of pleasures available to a wealthy man of sensibility. In fact Coverdale is no more satisfied by his urban existence than any of the others are; but he has incurred a worldliness of outlook that keeps him from committing himself to a larger vision and that makes him treat his own enthusiasms with constant self-deprecation. He can neither believe nor be quite comfortable in his unbelief; and as a result his voice in the novel traces an intricate ironic pattern of inflation and deflation:

> Whatever else I may repent of, therefore, let it be reckoned neither among my sins nor follies, that I once had faith and force enough to form generous hopes of the world's destiny— yes!—and to do what in me lay for their accomplishment; even to the extent of quitting a warm fireside, flinging away a freshly lighted cigar, and travelling far beyond the strike of the city-clocks, through a drifting snow-storm.
>
> (11)

It is this habit of mind, with its sophisticated freedom, its longing for and refusal of commitment, and its tendency to turn the serious into mockery or self-mockery that qualifies Coverdale as the spokesman for the world of *Blithedale*; he is, in effect, the man of the hour.

The figure of Coverdale embodies the most radical new fictional direction in *The Blithedale Romance*. Nothing in Hawthorne's previous novels prepares for his relinquishing his authoritative stance and his adoption here of a dramatized narrator; nor is there outside evidence to shed light on the intentions behind this innovation. To understand Hawthorne's purposes it is necessary to consider the use he makes of his narrator within the book.

Hawthorne's distance from Coverdale is not a consistent one. In his evaluations of Blithedale Coverdale's judgments often have a sane balance suggesting that they have his author's approval, whereas at other points he exhibits a moral obtuseness that makes him seem to be the object of Hawthorne's scorn. The relation of author and narrator varies from page to page, and sometimes even from sentence to sentence; but Hawthorne is careful to establish a degree of ironic distance from the outset. In the brief first chapter Old Moodie asks a favor of Coverdale, and Coverdale's reply—first he brushes aside the troublesome request, then he asks what the favor is, and when Moodie refuses to tell him he becomes full of eagerness to help—establishes a permanent trait of his character. He is slow to respond to appeals to his generosity but quick to respond to appeals to his curiosity.

As narrator Coverdale is the central figure in a drama of curiosity, and this fact helps to account for the variations of his credibility in the book. He is not generally unreliable either in his information or even in his surmises—the guesses he makes about the other characters' secrets are usually remarkably accurate—but he is unreliable in explaining his own motives. As his curiosity becomes increasingly obsessive this unreliability turns into a frenzy of rationalization. As he sets out to extract Moodie's secrets by getting him drunk he says:

> What else could possibly be done for him? How else could he be imbued with energy enough to hope for a happier state, hereafter? How else be inspirited to say his prayers?
>
> (180)

Coverdale has a remarkably libidinous imagination. He dreams of Hollingsworth and Zenobia exchanging passionate kisses, and when he is awake his fantasies take a similar turn. Zenobia's comment about donning the garb of Eden leads him to imagine her naked; he spends a considerable amount of time while convalescing from his cold speculating on Zenobia's sexual past, asking himself if she is "a woman to whom wedlock had thrown wide the gates of mystery" (47). He is also wonderfully responsive to Hollingsworth's care, which, as he repeats, exhibits an almost feminine tenderness. And Coverdale's prying curiosity seems to be a displacement of his suppressed erotic desire. He first tries to make Priscilla betray her feelings about her past life after he first senses that Zenobia and Hollingsworth have supplanted him in each other's affections. He again attempts to "come within her maidenly mystery . . . to take just one peep beneath her folded petals" (125) just after he sees Zenobia passionately press Hollingsworth's hand to her bosom. Feeling excluded, he taunts Priscilla with the fact of her exclusion; then he adds:

> There may have been some petty malice in what I said. Generosity is a very fine thing, at a proper time and within due limits. But it is an insufferable bore, to see one man engrossing every thought of all the women, and leaving his friend to shiver in outer seclusion, without even the alternative of solacing himself with what the more fortunate individual has rejected.
>
> (126)

His ungenerous curiosity is energized by his frustrated desire, and indeed prying inquisitiveness is the form his love takes. In this sense he is right to acquit himself of the charge of being cold and detached: "if I erred at all, in regard to Hollingsworth, Zenobia, and Priscilla, it was through too much sympathy, rather than too little" (154)—although "sympathy" is not the word that most precisely describes Coverdale's feelings.

Coverdale's unreliability is a function of the way that he admits this drama of attraction into his consciousness. The more emotionally involved he becomes, the more elaborately self-deceptive are the reasons he invents for his behavior. When he first sets out to pry into Priscilla's past he does so on the grounds that he has a "duty" (71) to protect her from the strong wills of others, though his actions seem anything but protective. When Zenobia pulls the curtain of her drawing room, closing off the "theatre" of his observation from his hotel window, he is at first furiously resentful at being shut out of the other characters' lives, then he becomes yet more curious, and finally he decides that it is his "duty" (162) as an old acquaintance to call on her. This is the typical pattern of his thought: a feeling of emotional exclusion fuels his desire to know, and then he finds a moral imperative to second—and excuse—his wish.

Coverdale's finest and most fully developed conception of his duty is found in his slowly evolving idea that he has been singled out to take the part of Chorus to the tragedy of his three friends' lives, to observe faithfully, to judge rigorously, and yet to sympathize to the full. This is the only position open to him after Hollingsworth has engrossed the affections of all the women, and the more shut out he feels the more it seems to him his duty to occupy this role. When Zenobia draws her curtain he feels "a revengeful sense of insult," and his personal pain makes him exclaim:

> was mine a mere vulgar curiosity? Zenobia should have known me better than to suppose it. She should have been able to appreciate that quality of the intellect and the heart, which impelled me (often against my own will, and to the detriment of my own comfort) to live in other lives, and to endeavor—by generous sympathies, by delicate intuitions, by taking note of things too slight for record, and by bringing my human spirit into manifold accordance with the companions whom God assigned me—to learn the secret which was hidden even from themselves.
>
> (160)

Here his exclusion from their affections is converted into a sign of an equally intimate relationship. As spectator he becomes a necessity to his friends; and his perceptual faculty becomes evidence of a noble vocation, an agency of divine justice and truth. In a passage like this, self-deception reaches truly heroic proportions and even commands a kind of admiration.

In his portrayal of Coverdale's passionate purposes and delusions Hawthorne creates a drama of perverse curiosity that places *The Blithedale Romance* in a line extending backward to William Godwin's *Caleb*

Williams and forward to James's *The Sacred Fount*. And here we see most clearly what the strategy of the dramatized narrator permits the author to accomplish. Rather than analyzing Coverdale's mental life he re-creates the whole texture of his narrator's consciousness, thus allowing us both to listen to Coverdale's own understanding of his project and to observe, behind that, the operations of his more hidden mind out of which his actions and his self-deceptions emerge.

This method of double revelation also helps to explain the appropriateness of Hawthorne's narrative technique to the other dramas of *The Blithedale Romance*. In every part of his story Hawthorne is concerned with the relationship between the private and internal and the public and external. During the debate scene in Eliot's pulpit Coverdale says, "I could measure Zenobia's inward trouble, by the animosity with which she now took up the general quarrel of woman against man" (121), and the rule of thumb that he establishes here holds throughout the book. The publicly presented self and its language of public abstraction are, to the observant eye, an index to the psychological and emotional state of the buried self. In *Blithedale* public creeds of all sorts are seen as expressions of private needs.[9] The credo of the Blithedale community is familiar love in place of pride, mutual aid in place of selfish competition, but, as Coverdale notes, the bond of the Blithedalers is actually negative, not affirmative. Their "little army of saints and martyrs" is predominantly composed of "individuals who had gone through such an experience as to disgust them with ordinary pursuits" (62). They are united less by their beliefs and affirmations than by their feelings of estrangement and frustration. Zenobia's feminism is, like their communitarianism, the expression in public and social terms of her passionate nature's misery. Coverdale surmises that she has wrecked herself on a man whose shallow nature contains no depths of feeling to respond to her "real womanhood," and her frustrated love now finds an outlet in her militant crusade and her "character of eccentricity and defiance" (103).

Zenobia's feminist stridency waxes and wanes, following the involuted course of her emotional life. Hollingsworth is more consistent in his ideological affirmations, but this is because his ideology expresses his needs more completely than Zenobia's does. A persistent feature of Hawthorne's battle of the sexes is that, at the same impasse, his women are able to achieve a temporary dislocation of personality that enables them to maintain their capacity to love, while his men become self-absorbed and monomaniacal. Thus just as Chillingworth's whole energy of love and creativity is channeled into his mission of vengeance and Dimmesdale's into his obsession with his guilt, so Hollingsworth's entire life-force is channeled into his crusade for the reformation of criminals. The love that might have gone outward to others is turned inward toward his self-generated ideal. As Coverdale notes, Hollingsworth draws a plan of his edifice of reform as lovingly as another man might draw the house he intended to occupy with his wife and children. If Hollingsworth is a more consistent ideologue than Zenobia it is because he has completely sublimated into his social purpose the energy that she only temporarily transfers into hers.

Coverdale's relation through curiosity to the other characters is similar to Hollingsworth's to his cause. As the book progresses he gets a sickened sense that "these three had absorbed my life into themselves" (194). Obsessed by his own single purpose, he becomes increasingly willing to sacrifice the rights of others to the demands of his own curiosity and increasingly blind to his own true motives. If the characters of *The Blithedale Romance* have one trait in common, it is the massive dislocation of their desires; by making Coverdale his narrator Hawthorne builds into his book's form an enactment of its central subject, an illustration of the process by which a capacity for loving relationship becomes perverted. He also provides an acting out of another crucial subject, the relation between perverted love and perverted belief. In their final encounter at Eliot's pulpit Zenobia rages at Hollingsworth: "Self! self! self! You have embodied yourself in a project. You are a better masquerader than the witches and gypsies yonder; for your disguise is a self-deception" (218). But her words might apply just as well to all the book's characters. All their ideologies are disguises, subterfuges through which the self couches its private desires and needs in public terms. In this respect the process by which Coverdale converts his wishes into a conception of duty is akin to that by which Zenobia converts her misery into a belief in women's rights, or that by which Hollingsworth converts his love into his crusade. Simply put, a self-deceiver tells a story about self-deception; in the twists and turns of his unreliable narrative we can watch the process by which a hidden emotional stratum generates the conceptions and beliefs entertained by the conscious mind. In Coverdale's mental experience and in the interactions of the other main characters Hawthorne shows as private drama what he sees elsewhere as a more widespread social condition, a life devoid of valid forms of relation and affirmation; but here he sees this condition as proceeding from an inner state of psychological disturbance.

On a warm summer evening described early in *The Blithedale Romance* Coverdale sees Priscilla sitting at Hollingsworth's feet and Zenobia, at a distance, looking on with a strange gaze. As he observes the three of them he is held fast: "I could not turn away my own eyes" (77). His words forcefully recall Hawthorne's own words in "The Custom-House": "My eyes fastened themselves upon the old scarlet letter, and would not be turned aside" (*SL* 31). Like the letter, the configuration of the three characters affects its observer as a "vortex" (70), drawing his whole mind to it with a centripetal force. And just as Hawthorne felt obliged to work out an interpretation of his symbol, so too Coverdale finds in the three "the indices of a problem which it was my business to solve" (69). Hawthorne's effort in the moonlit room to get to know his illusive guests, by calling up imagined scenes and then analyzing their characters' motives and modes of passion, also has its equivalent in Coverdale's experience. He converts his friends into the "characters . . . of my private theatre" (70); as he watches them acting out actual scenes he is always trying to guess what they are thinking and feeling and to guess the secret connections among them. "What are you seeking to discover in me?" Zenobia asks him; he replies, "The mystery of your life" (47). All of this suggests another reason for Hawthorne's adoption of a dramatized narrator: in the figure of Coverdale he presents his own process of imaginative creation as a dramatic action.[10]

In the narrative role Hawthorne adopts in *The Scarlet Letter* and *The House of the Seven Gables* his judgment is authoritative and has its sanction in his total knowledge of his characters' hidden lives and of the pasts that have shaped those lives. What the narrator of the earlier novels always knows is exactly what Miles Coverdale wants to find out. His is a quest for privileged information; he searches for the "casual opening" in others which, like the path in the forest, will admit him "into the long-sought intimacy of a mysterious heart" (90). The secrets of their pasts are the subject of his heated speculation, and, as he comes to prey upon Moodie, Zenobia, and Priscilla, of his active pursuit.

As we have seen, one of the major ways in which Hawthorne gains access to a hidden stratum of psychological and psychohistorical truth in his earlier works is through the calculated use of a fictional mode of primitive romance. In his attempt to solve the problem his friends present him with, Coverdale has access to a similar imaginative mode in his own mind. Left to himself he is always composing mental dramas peopled with strange spirits whose spheres attract or repel one another in a magical way. This is the sort of story he invents when his actual information fails him, as when Zenobia and Westervelt hold inaudible conversations beneath his hermitage and behind the window of the drawing room. When Priscilla first arrives at Blithedale he sees her as a Lucy Gray figure, "some desolate kind of creature, doomed to wander

about in snowstorms'' (27); then as he watches her behavior toward
Zenobia he abruptly revises his fantasy, seeing her as a spirit who seeks to
enslave herself to a master spirit.

To Zenobia, of course, Priscilla has another mode of being entirely; it
is at this point that she delivers her devastating comments about
seamstresses who drink too much coffee and eat too many doughnuts.
But Coverdale will have nothing to do with such social realism. He prefers
to make a character ''out of the texture of a dream'' (32). This
interchange is one of several moments in the book suggesting that
Coverdale's pronounced streak of romance imagination may be part of
the equipment ensuring his status as a minor author. He himself is
sometimes inclined to see the intricate machinery of sorcery and telepathy
he erects around Priscilla not as corresponding to her ''realities'' but as
''fancy-work with which I have idly decked her out'' (100).

But at other points his romance imagination seems less idle and
precious and more a mode of valid insight. During his illness he enters a
state of feverish fantasy in which he experiences moments of almost
preternatural intuition: ''Zenobia is an enchantress! . . . She is the sister
of the Veiled Lady! That flower in her hair is a talisman'' (45). Even after
he recovers, his daydreams about the others lead him to anticipate major
discoveries. He describes his mental experience of Hollingsworth:

> in solitude, I often shuddered at my friend. In my recollection of
> his dark and impressive countenance, the features grew more
> sternly prominent than the reality, duskier in their depth and
> shadow, more lurid in their light; the frown, that had merely
> flitted across his brow, seemed to have contorted it with an
> adamantine wrinkle. On meeting him again, I was often filled
> with remorse, when his deep eyes beamed kindly upon me, as
> with the glow of a household fire that was burning in a cave.
> —''He is a man, after all!'' thought I—''his Maker's own truest
> image, a philanthropic man!—not that steel engine of the
> Devil's contrivance, a philanthropist!''—But, in my wood-
> walks, and in my silent chamber, the dark face frowned at me
> again.
>
> (71)

The dusky face with its lurid light recalls that of Roger Chillingworth; the
dark face frowns at Coverdale just as Jaffrey's does at Clifford as he looks
into Maule's well. The passage illustrates the process of imagining a
villain of Hawthornesque romance. Coverdale's imaginative distortion
works as Hawthorne's romance always does, to bring into focus the secret

character beneath the "reality," to discover within the complexity of his presented self Hollingworth's essential and demonic intensity of will. In discussing his observations of Hollingsworth Coverdale becomes extremely self-conscious about the nature of his perception. "Of course, I am perfectly aware," he says, "that the above statement is exaggerated." It "may remain, however, both for its truth and its exaggeration, as strongly expressive of the tendencies which were really operative in Hollingsworth, and as exemplifying the kind of error into which my mode of observation was calculated to lead me" (71). He wonders how much trust to place in his imagination as a vehicle of truth; but he is also aware that he does not have much choice about this. Asking himself whether it was not a "great wrong" to believe in his own intuited discoveries, he answers: "I could not help it. Had I loved him less, I might have used him better" (69).

This supplies a crucial clue to the sources of Coverdale's romance. He imagines a dark and demonic Hollingsworth after he feels excluded from his affection, and then when Hollingsworth once more beams at him kindly he feels not just erroneous but remorseful. The dialectic of his perception is less one of abstract truth and error than of jealous resentment and guilty love. Meeting Westervelt in the forest, Coverdale sees him too not in his actual appearance but in his "spectral character" (95): his coal-black hair, his gleaming eyes and teeth, his serpent-like walking stick, and his stickpin that "glimmered . . . like a living tip of fire" (92) converge to make him look like the devil in "Young Goodman Brown." And again Coverdale's spectral perception is fueled by his emotional response, his furious resentment of Westervelt's excessive intimacy of address and his apparent closeness to the characters from whose lives he feels shut out. The narrative of *Blithedale* thus enables us to see both Coverdale's fantasies and the emotional origins of those fantasies. In this way the novel provides Hawthorne's most thorough exploration of the energies of romance.

The presentation of Coverdale's fantasy life points to another interesting difference between this book and *The Scarlet Letter* and *The House of the Seven Gables*. Here again two somewhat separate impulses inform the construction of the novel's fictional world, one of which moves to give that world the reality of a complex and indeterminate actuality, the other to give it the more spectral and magical reality of an imaginative projection. But instead of allowing these two impulses to create their own fictional structures, here Hawthorne grounds them in the consciousness and the perceptual processes of his narrator. Thus in

Blithedale as in *The Scarlet Letter* the characters seem to possess different sorts of ontological status; if Zenobia is the triumph of Hawthorne's dramatic realism, Westervelt shares with the Model in *The Marble Faun* the distinction of being his most completely ghostly and demonic character. Here, however, the difference is a function not of their actual modes of being but of the ways in which Coverdale sees others.

In his earlier works Hawthorne's alternate fictional structures complicate our perception of his world in such a way as to make us consider the procedures of our own imagination and the sorts of truth that different ways of imagining reality can achieve. In *Blithedale* the role of the reader is a less self-conscious and tricky one; because its oscillations of mode take place within Coverdale's mind we do not have to keep shifting the angle of our imaginative involvement. But in another sense *Blithedale* is the most self-conscious of all Hawthorne's fictional exercises. Because all of Coverdale's recognitions demonstrate both "tendencies ... really operative" in the book's world and the processes of "my mode of observation," the question of the nature and validity of imagination is being explored continually throughout the book's narrative. Because Coverdale has to struggle to put his story together at every point, the activity of fictional creation, the activity of making sense of experience, becomes the major action of *Blithedale*. In this light Hawthorne's use of a dramatized narrator may be seen not as a radical departure but actually as the culmination of a strain of development in his previous works.

Having said this much, we must now add that Hawthorne does not entirely give up the tactics of a mixed medium in *The Blithedale Romance*, nor is the magical mystery tour of its romance always so consistently grounded in a drama of mind. The association of Priscilla and Westervelt with a magical drama of good and evil spirits cannot be entirely understood as a fancy-work emanating from Coverdale's imagination; and in particular the novel's two interpolated tales invite us to see a more ghostly stratum in the book directly, not as a function of the narrator's surmise.

Zenobia's "The Silvery Veil" is, like Holgrave's "Alice Pyncheon," a "wild, spectral legend" (107), a conscious experiment in romance narrative. And her tale performs a function parallel to his in clarifying the central design of the book's conflict. In response to wild rumors that the Veiled Lady is either a beautiful maiden or a Medusa-like hag and that the magician who exhibits her has "bartered his own soul for seven years' possession of a familiar fiend" (110), Theodore, the tale's hero, sets out to learn the mystery of her nature. The Veiled Lady, gifted with a preternatural ability to detect his intention, offers him two choices. He may kiss the veil and release her as the fulfillment of all his desires, or he may lift the veil without kissing her and thus release her as his "evil fate" (113). He must choose between "holy faith" and "scornful scepticism and idle curiosity"; and his choice mirrors the larger one offered to all the characters in the book between a generous and loving commitment that frees others and a selfish intention that enslaves others to their own purposes. (In his desire to know without giving of himself Theodore is particularly close to the curious Coverdale.) At its close the tale's action comes to coincide with the present situation of the characters exactly as they did in "Alice Pyncheon." And nothing is more indicative of the difference of moral atmosphere in these two books than the fact that, where Holgrave chooses to learn from his story and respect Phoebe's sanctity, Zenobia spreads the gauzy veil on Priscilla, knowingly violating her by returning her to the hateful bondage of Westervelt.

In the second tale interpolated in *Blithedale,* "Fauntleroy," Coverdale retells what he has learned from Old Moodie, again making use of a "romantic and legendary license" (181). This mode of procedure enables him to suggest a secret system of relationships: by pairing Moodie's daughters as "the reflection of their [parents'] state" (185) he links Zenobia and Priscilla as manifestations of the extreme conditions of a materialistic society. Coverdale has recourse here to Hawthorne's and Holgrave's favorite source of supernatural suggestion, the "wilder babble" (188) of popular rumor. The whispers of the neighbors portray Priscilla as a ghost child to whom silence is audible and hidden things are visible; Westervelt becomes a wizard whose body is a "necromantic contrivance" and whose remarkable dental work is the token of his pact with the devil. The rumors here connect with the suggestions of "The Silvery Veil" and of Coverdale's surmises to hint at a magical drama underlying the book's apparent action, a battle of good and evil waged between a pure spiritual maiden and various dark powers intent on violating or imprisoning her virgin soul.

After we have warmed up on *The Scarlet Letter* and *The House of the Seven Gables,* the raw-romance presentation of the drama in *Blithedale* can scarcely faze us as readers. We are used to leaving more realistic narratives to enter into a more enchanted vision that reveals a secret pattern to the action of the novels. The medical mystery by which Priscilla's anemia and "tremulous nerves endow her with Sybilline attributes" (2) is not so different from that by which hereditary apoplexy comes to signify a family curse, or that by which an A-shaped discoloration of skin comes to embody a deeper mystery of guilt and punishment; we are willing to entertain a physical implausibility for what it reveals at another level. But although it takes the same form, the magic of *Blithedale* has a somewhat different quality from that of the earlier works. For one thing, while "Alice Pyncheon" is one of the strongest chapters in *The House*, "The Silvery Veil" and "Fauntleroy" are among the weakest in *Blithedale*. Their narratives are chaotic and even their styles seem loose and vague. A reason for their disorganization is that the tales are called on to tie together the loose ends of the plot. *Blithedale* is like *The Marble Faun* in its possession of a plot that arouses all sorts of interests extraneous to Hawthorne's purposes. Zenobia's real relation to Westervelt and the features of that relation that make her willing to turn Priscilla back to him, Old Moodie's transference of his brother's legacy from Zenobia to Priscilla—such details are crucial to the unfolding action of *Blithedale*, but Hawthorne is either unwilling or unable to work them out at the level of action. Instead he relegates them to his interpolated tales, and as a result the magic in these tales at least partly serves to conceal a larger incoherence; as Marius Bewley says, in *Blithedale* "Hawthorne uses shadows for refuge rather than for definition."[11]

But the real problem with the romance in *Blithedale* lies in its relation to the book's other elements. In Hawthorne's earlier books a supernatural mode suggests meanings of another order from a realistic or dramatic one, but these orders of meaning can be synthesized, and by being included in such a synthesis the supernatural enriches the book's sense. In *Blithedale* the orders of meaning that he invokes tend to be competitive, not complementary. Well might the other characters look at Coverdale with incredulous scorn when he theatrically whispers, " 'Zenobia is an enchantress! . . . She is the sister of the Veiled Lady!' " (45). In the book itself Zenobia is something more complicated and finally more interesting than an enchantress, and the book explores much more interesting webs of relationship than her quasi-allegorical sisterhood with Priscilla. If Priscilla is a legitimate clairvoyant she cannot also be a sham, though if she is not a sham the novel's satire of degenerate spiritualism and its study of her as an insulted and injured figure in a drama of social poverty makes no sense. The features of the book that might have led Hawthorne to entitle it *The Veiled Lady* are a distraction. Whereas the realistic present action of *The House* is in a crucial way incomplete without the supplementary romance history of an inherited curse, the dramatic and social plot of *Blithedale* actually make better sense without the encumbering mechanisms of enchantment.

But their function *as* a distraction helps, I think, to account for the place Hawthorne gives to these features of his book. The whole impetus of the Veiled Lady plot is to resuscitate in the figure of Priscilla a locus of absolute spiritual value and thus to erect an objective standard against which the charity or villainy of the other characters can be measured. Elsewhere in the book Hawthorne shows a society based on inversions of spiritual value, and he suggests as well a permanent discrepancy between the terms in which the conscious mind forms its affirmations and the psychic processes that produce such affirmations. But someone—I do not think it makes much difference whether we call him Coverdale or Hawthorne—is intensely uncomfortable with this strongly ironic vision. The second half of the novel is full of evidence of this. When, in ''The Village-Hall,'' Hollingsworth releases Priscilla from Westervelt's sorcery, his seems to be the strength of a rival magician; we might even see him here as making Matthew Maule's proud boast, ''Mine, by the right of the stronger spirit!'' But Coverdale insists on interpreting the scene not as a new enslavement but as a genuine release:

> the true heart-throb of a woman's affection was too powerful for the jugglery that had hitherto environed her. She uttered a shriek and fled to Hollingsworth, like one escaping from her deadliest enemy, and was safe forever!
>
> (203)

And the book never exposes his apparent error. Similarly when Hollingsworth chooses Priscilla over Zenobia, the apparent motive for his choice— he has just learned that she, not Zenobia, is to inherit Moodie's brother's legacy—is covered over. In ''The Three Together'' he is in effect converted to generous love, even though such a change of heart is utterly implausible and unprepared for. The dead Zenobia's hands seem to be clenched in immitigable defiance, but Coverdale says, ''Away with the hideous thought!'' (235) and concludes that she is actually kneeling in prayer. *The Blithedale Romance* is the darkest of Hawthorne's novels. Although it shares with his earlier works as its one central value the refusal to violate and victimize others, in it no one is sufficiently free from his own compulsions to be able to respect the sanctity of the human heart. But its author is reluctant to embrace this dark vision. Even at the cost of being unconvincing or deliberately falsifying, he makes a determined effort to salvage the possibility of holy faith and generous love. And the romance plot centered on the Veiled Lady is the book's main attempt to make another kind of sense of itself, to avert the deepest implications of its drama of experience.

Finally Hawthorne solves the problems of *Blithedale* not by making order of its chaos but by cutting his losses. After ''Fauntleroy'' and ''The Village-Hall'' he throws over his spectral plot and returns to the dramatic interactions of his characters, producing, by doing so, a succession of narrative chapters as strong as anything else in his work. Coverdale returns to Blithedale as if by gravitational force to find his three friends engaged in a passionate crisis. From this point on Zenobia usurps the book's center stage. In the agony of her rejection by Hollingsworth she reaches her fullest development. Her harangue against his egotism and her expressions of sexual contempt for the "blind, instinctive love" and "little, puny weakness" (224) of Priscilla that he has preferred to "that proud, intellectual sympathy which he might have had from me" have a dignity that is matched by the dignity of her humble recognition of herself as a "miserable, bruised, and battered heart, spoilt long before he met me!" (225). The majesty of her suffering is not diminished but magnified by the element of self-conscious theatricality in her behavior. Perhaps the finest stroke of all is that, in the middle of her passion, Zenobia is seen as taking pleasure in Coverdale's admiration of her beauty. In her stature and her complexity of response Zenobia is here reminiscent of Shakespeare's Cleopatra. Nothing is allowed to interfere with her final grandeur. The romance fable of maidens and wizards, the realistic portrayal of society, and the drama of Coverdale's prying curiosity all give way to a taut and grave narration of her agony and death. Finally Hawthorne does find a way to rescue his book from irony and to affirm a value in human experience—through tragedy.

But the strong concluding movement of *The Blithedale Romance* does not entirely save the novel from its confusions of form and vision. There is evidence that Hawthorne was acutely sensitive to the book's problems. The fact that he sent the manuscript to the critic Edwin P. Whipple "to have it looked over by a keen, yet not unfriendly eye" suggests his awareness of faults in it. At the same time he seems to despair of mending those faults, so that in the same letter in which he invites Whipple's criticisms he also makes what sounds like a secret plea for him to go easy on the book: "After all, should you spy ever so many defects, I cannot promise to amend them; the metal hardens very soon after I pour it out of my melting-pot into the mould."[12] And the preface to *Blithedale* is full of hints of dissatisfaction or anxiety. To ward off comparisons of Blithedale with Brook Farm he stresses that his treatment of the community is "altogether incidental to the main purpose of the Romance" (1); he has used the community, he says, "merely to establish a theatre," as "an available foothold between fiction and reality" (2). But by his own testimony he has found that foothold slippery indeed. He has made use of his actual recollections "in the hope of giving a more lifelike tint to the fancy-sketch" (1), and the method has worked only too well: the sort of actuality with which he endows his characters inadvertently establishes a set of realistic expectations such that "the beings of [his] imagination are compelled to show themselves in the same category as actually living mortals" (2). And, thus exposed to criteria of verisimilitude, he fears that "the paint and pasteboard of their composition" will be "but too readily discernible." In a kind of subdued grumble he deplores his deprivation of "a certain conventional privilege" that readers of the Old World allow to their authors, the privilege to create "an atmosphere of strange enchantment" in which the imagined and the real will seem to blend.

If the tone here is somewhat new, the problems Hawthorne addresses are not. The gap between his "fancy-sketch" and his lifelike tints is similar to that in *The House of the Seven Gables* between what Hawthorne calls the romance and the humble investiture; it corresponds to the tension in all his work between a fiction that creates the imagined world of the romance and a fiction that creates a semblance of actuality. The difference between *Blithedale* and the earlier novels is not that they have a thicker atmosphere of enchantment in which to conceal this tension but that they place the parties to it in more coherent and significant relationships. Similarly the sense of "paint and pasteboard" is not absent in *The Scarlet Letter* and *The House*. Hawthorne is, for instance, fully conscious of his red-eyed devils, his family curses, and his magic portraits as creaky machines, and he works in his fiction not to make us forget this but exactly to heighten our awareness of it. By doing so he frees us from the necessity of taking these devices literally and allows us to accept them for the sake of the sense they make at another level; we are allowed to believe in them, as Holgrave says, as illustrating a theory. The problem with *Blithedale* then is not that its means of representation are less elegant but rather that its own internal confusions make it difficult for its readers to accept its wizards and veiled ladies in this more detached and sophisticated sense.

The phrase "paint and pasteboard" harks back to the sketch "Main Street," and this short work illuminates the nature of Hawthorne's difficulty here. In "Main Street" a showman makes use of a series of cardboard images attached to a moving wire to present the history of Salem. He is repeatedly interrupted by a carping critic in his audience, a man of sense, as he calls himself, who refuses to be taken in: instead of vivid scenes of the past he sees only a "pasteboard figure, such as a child would cut out of a card, with a pair of very dull scissors" (*SI* 56). The speaker encourages him to see the cardboard as "an airy and changeable reflex of what it purports to represent" (*SI* 63); he asks the man of sense to take another seat, or another point of view, from which "the proper light and shadow will transform the spectacle into quite another thing" (*SI* 57). But finally, during the Great Snow of 1717, the machine itself destroys its own illusion: the wire breaks.

"Main Street" was written shortly before Hawthorne started *The Scarlet Letter,* and it illustrates the sort of self-consciousness about his art of illusion that persists throughout his experimentation with the novel. In employing the devices of primitive romance he works with fictive means that he knows at one level are shopworn and absurd. But he attempts to use them as the "reflex" of a layer of psychological truth not otherwise accessible to representation; and he passes on to us his own awareness of his artifice as a way of forestalling our objections and engaging us, instead, in a consideration of the possible validity of the imagination that informs such means. The failure of the romance techniques in *Blithedale* to mesh with the rest of its presented experience makes him fear that his audience will see his devices not as a means to truth but simply as a cheap trick. Thus at the end of the book, having solved its problems in one way by turning his narrative over to Zenobia's tragedy, he solves them in another way by announcing his fiction's absurdity from within. In a line apparently added on the same day that he wrote the preface,[13] he in effect breaks his own machine's wire: "I—I myself—was in love—with— PRISCILLA!" (247).

The shift in Hawthorne's attitude toward his fictional methods from a sense of them as artifices in the service of a larger truth to a sense of them simply as hollow artifices parallels a larger shift in his attitude toward the imaginative construction of experience. As we have seen, in all his books he qualifies the sense that he makes of life by noting the sort of imaginative outlook that his presentation issues from. But in *The Scarlet Letter* and *The House of the Seven Gables* he draws attention to this not to undermine his vision's worth but to establish its tentative and relativistic validity. By contrast with his other books *Blithedale* is saturated with a sense of illusion. The village society that gathers to watch the Veiled Lady comes to see not a spiritual spectacle but an exercise in "ingenious contrivances of stage-effect" (199). Blithedale's communitarians flee from society's "artificial life" (16) to create a new life of artifice and masquerade. And the characters' beliefs are considered not in their social value but as parts of another masquerade, one in which the mind dresses up and disguises its own psychic needs in the language of duty and cause. Coverdale's infamous confession is the culmination of these elements in the book. It seems to be a big lie. From what we have seen, we know that he was also in love with Zenobia, and perhaps most of all with Hollingsworth. If Coverdale's confession is true, then nothing else in the novel is. His last line must make us wonder whether we should have trusted him to make sense of anything in the book, or whether the whole of it has not been the most elaborate deception of all, or even whether anything in the story has actually taken place except in his own mind. We are left stranded as in a series of surrealistic perspectives; we seem to have become, along with Coverdale, prisoners of a set of shifting mental illusions none of which lead outward toward reality. Melville's comments are the most astute criticism of the novel that we have: however much it may set out to make an ironic study of self-deception, it ends up suggesting that self-deception is a universal and inevitable condition—"who the devel aint a dreamer?" Fiction as a form of truth gives way to fiction as a form of delusion.

When he arrives at this point Hawthorne has reached an impasse both in his formal practice and in his sense of life. It is no wonder that he did not publish another novel for seven years. The preface of *Blithedale* indicates the way in which he finally got around this impasse. In *The Marble Faun* and his late fragmentary romances the atmosphere of strange enchantment sets in with almost impenetrable thickness. He turns to old country settings, with the hope that they will provide a haven of pure romance in which "the creatures of his brain may play their phantasmagorical antics" (1) with no scandal to anyone's sense of reality. And whatever might be said in favor of *The Marble Faun*, the sacrifices involved in this shift are enormous. All Hawthorne's achievements in dramatic realism and in recording and making sense of social and historical reality are pushed aside to give his phantasms more elbow room. No longer braced against his fictions of reality, his romance comes to be often merely extravagant; because the tension between these elements is suppressed, the later works no longer conduct the exploration of the activity of imaginative sense-making so central to his major works. Hawthorne never again attempts the creative experiments in form that his three great novels represent because he never again comes to terms with the double impulse that has informed his art and vision.

III|

Melville

Some burn damp faggots, others
    may consume
The entire combustible world in
    one small room
As though dried straw, and if we
    turn about
The bare chimney is gone black out
Because the work has finished in
    that flare.

        Yeats, "In Memory
      of Major Robert Gregory"

6 | The Art of the Diver

Le roman ... n'est pas conçu en vue d'un travail défini à l'avance. Il ne sert pas à exposer, à traduire, des choses existant avant lui, en dehors de lui. Il n'exprime pas, il recherche.

Robbe-Grillet, "Du réalisme à la réalité"

Exuberance is Beauty.

Blake, "The Marriage of Heaven and Hell"

Of the many critical works on Melville the one whose angle of appreciation seems to me most nearly to coincide with the genuine interest of Melville's work is Warner Berthoff's *The Example of Melville*. Berthoff locates the final value of Melville's work not in its specific accomplishments but in the quality of mind that informs it: "The particulars of the work itself—themes, ideas, procedures, forms—come to seem to a degree incidental. We grow aware of something further, of a continuous imaginative presence and energy sustaining these particulars and positively generating them."[1] This is the sort of appreciation that Melville himself desired. In his reply to Hawthorne's "joy-giving and exultation-breeding letter" on *Moby-Dick* he tries to second-guess the motives for Hawthorne's praise:

> You did not care a penny for the book. But, now and then as you read, you understood the pervading thought that impelled the book—and that you praised. Was it not so? You were arch-angel enough to despise the imperfect body, and embrace the soul.[2]

And in any case it is the sort of appreciation that Melville's peculiar production requires. He loves to philosophize, but in the end his philosophical statements are less interesting for their intellectual content than for the animated activity of thinking they manifest. He sees himself as a committed artist, but in the end his works are less remarkable for their achieved artistic perfection than for the spiritedness with which he goes about creating his art. This is why Berthoff stresses not Melville's achievement but his example—an example of a prodigal and forceful imagination throwing its whole energy into an earnest attempt to articulate its own insights.

The special nature of Melville's imagination is evident in all his works, but it can be seen with particular clarity in his letters. His first exposure to Emerson came when he heard him lecture in Boston in 1849. He describes his response in this way:

Now, there is a something about every man elevated above
mediocrity, which is, for the most part, instinctuly perceptible.
This I see in Mr Emerson. And, frankly, for the sake of the
argument, let us call him a fool;—then had I rather be a fool
than a wise man.—I love all men who *dive*. Any fish can swim
near the surface, but it takes a great whale to go down stairs five
miles or more; & if he dont attain the bottom, why, all the lead
in Galena can't fashion the plumet that will. I'm not talking of
Mr Emerson now—but of the whole corps of thought-divers,
that have been diving & coming up again with bloodshot eyes
since the world began.[3]

What is striking here is Melville's extraordinary magnanimity. His sense
of his own power leads him not to denigrate other artists but to embrace
them gregariously; he shares with Keats a genius-loving heart. It is also
worth noting that his appreciation is based not on the content of
Emerson's lecture but on the spirit of his enterprise. Characteristically,
Melville does not try to discuss this analytically. He adopts a tentative
hypothesis—Emerson is a fool—and then reverses its judgment. To
explain this reversal he throws out a metaphor, and then he works out the
implications of his figure by elaborating it in a series of inventive bursts.
By allowing his imagination to unfold in this way he moves from a
statement of personal enthusiasm to an increasingly precise formulation
of the object of his enthusiasm; he reaches his thought by giving himself
to the process of his thinking. "I'm not talking of Mr Emerson now"; by
bringing his own resources of mind to bear on Emerson he transforms a
particular man and a particular occasion into a vision of a whole mode of
being, an activity of intrepid thought that includes both Emerson and
Melville within itself.

A similar operation of mind can be seen in Melville's tribute to *The
House of the Seven Gables*. The opening of this letter, cited above as the
epigraph to Part Two, again shows Melville's remarkably disinterested
generosity. It also shows his habit of metaphorical exposition. He likens
the book to a fine old chamber, then pursues the likeness by inventing a
string of furniture images; as it expands and develops, his figure comes to
describe the texture of the book's world more and more fully. At this
point Melville drops his image and praises Hawthorne's craft more
directly, listing his favorite scenes and commenting on the skillful
characterization of Clifford. Then he takes off.

There is a certain tragic phase of humanity which, in our
opinion, was never more powerfully embodied than by Hawthorne. We mean the tragicalness of human thought in its own

unbiassed, native, and profounder workings. We think that in
no recorded mind has the intense feeling of the visable truth
ever entered more deeply than into this man's. By visable truth,
we mean the apprehension of the absolute condition of present
things as they strike the eye of the man who fears them not,
though they do their worst to him,—the man who, like Russia or
the British Empire, declares himself a sovereign nature (in
himself) amid the powers of heaven, hell, and earth. He may per-
ish; but so long as he exists he insists upon treating with all Powers
upon an equal basis. If any of those other Powers choose to
withhold certain secrets, let them; that does not impair my
sovereignty in myself; that does not make me tributary. And
perhaps, after all, there is *no* secret. We incline to think that the
Problem of the Universe is like the Freemason's mighty secret, so
terrible to all children. It turns out, at last, to consist in a
triangle, a mallet, and an apron,—nothing more! . . . There is
the grand truth about Nathaniel Hawthorne. He says NO! in
thunder; but the Devil himself cannot make him say *yes*. For all
men who say *yes,* lie; and all men who say *no,*—why, they are in
the happy condition of judicious, unincumbered travellers in
Europe; they cross the frontiers into Eternity with nothing but a
carpet-bag,—that is to say, the Ego. Whereas those *yes*-gentry,
they travel with heaps of baggage, and, damn them! they will
never get through the Custom House. What's the reason, Mr.
Hawthorne, that in the last stages of metaphysics a fellow always
falls to *swearing* so? I could rip an hour.[4]

Here again he might as well add, "I'm not talking about *The House of
the Seven Gables* now." He lunges past a specific occasion to discuss the
whole nature of Hawthorne's genius, and then he imaginatively transforms this particular author into an exemplification of a version of the
human condition. He seizes Hawthorne and uses him to define the
position of man keeping the open independence of his seas in a
mysterious universe. He formulates this in a statement, then in a
metaphor, then he twists and turns his image, expanding it, revising it,
pressing it on into new contexts, then revising it again. At each moment
he states his conclusions with the utmost definiteness, but the whole force
of the letter is in its forward motion; exactly by pouring the entire energy
of his intellect and imagination into each statement he acquires a new
energy and a further vision that lead him to a new formulation. "I could
rip an hour"; his thought moves not to a conclusion but to renewed self-
generation. It is no wonder that his letters overflow with triple post-
scripts, or that in a more humorous mood he asks Evert Duyckinck, "Can

you send me about fifty fast-writing youths, with an easy style & not averse to polishing their labors?"⁵

In *The Confidence-Man* Melville defines the original character as being "like a revolving Drummond light, raying away from itself all round it—everything is lit by it, everything starts up to it (mark how it is with Hamlet)" (*CM* 271). Like so many of his descriptions of men of vision, this sounds like a self-portrait. The analogy with Hamlet is an apt one; the quality of mind by which, for instance, Hamlet sees in Fortinbras an exemplum of true greatness is extremely close to Melville's own. Both go out to what they see with an extraordinary responsiveness, seize it, and, out of the urgency of their personal concerns, transfigure it into a larger image of human potential. And like his own diver with bloodshot eyes, Melville values this outreaching activity of perception for itself as much as for what it enables him to attain.

Melville's generous and forcefully mobile imagination must appeal to the genius-lover in us, but at the same time it might be noted that the same features of mind that make his letters such exhilarating reading also make somewhat peculiar equipment for a novelist. In this respect what Melville passes over in his letters is as revealing as what he is excited by. In his discussion of *The House* his comments on the book's running interest, its presentation of Clifford, and the fine stroke by which Holgrave turns out to be a Maule sound sincere enough but also somewhat perfunctory; in any case when he goes on to consider the tragic phase of humanity and thunderous nay-sayings he leaves such details far behind him. This way of thinking deserves comment for what it suggests about Melville's approach to fictional composition. The careful dramatization of character and the careful plotting of action are of only subsidiary interest to him. Unlike that of most novelists the natural bent of his imagination is not toward submerging its own identity and evoking images of the experience of others, envisioning an action unfold through their interactions. In his novels he presents relationships fitfully, sometimes even haphazardly— the relations of Ishmael and Queequeg or of Pierre and Lucy are obvious examples of this. The dramatic rendering of complex character and interaction is always one sort of organization among others in Hawthorne's novels, but, compared with Melville, Hawthorne embraces the means of the dramatic novelist almost forthrightly.

No other nineteenth-century novelist has so little commitment to the basic storytelling procedures of the novel as Melville has; on the other hand, none has so large a commitment elsewhere. What makes him slight the craft of *The House* is his impetuous eagerness to get on to larger topics, to explore man's position before the powers of heaven, hell, and earth. He is not content to swim near the surface; he wants to dive. His abrupt movement from the specific data before him to speculations about the ultimate coordinates of existence is characteristic of both his interests and his temper. Intellectually, Melville affects the metaphysics; he relishes his own "ontological heroics,"[6] his meditations on the nature of man, God, and Truth; he can use a phrase like "the Problem of the Universe" almost unblushingly. Further, he possesses the sort of imagination that E. M. Forster terms prophetic—his perception instinctively extends specific experience in the direction of infinity.[7] His letter comes out of the same habit of mind that sees a shark as a symptom of the sharkishness of nature, or that sees a revelation of the chance operation of the universe in a giant squid.

It is the metaphysical and cosmological thrust of his imagination that makes Melville a bull in the novel's china shop. In the chapter "Moby Dick" he dissects the psychic processes that compose Ahab's motive as minutely as Hawthorne does Hester's or Dimmesdale's, but finally to complete his account of this particular character he feels the need to refer to a lower depth of shared experience that defies analysis—a place where the "proud, sad king," the deposed demigod who is our common sire, sits in ruined state, keeping "the old State-secret" (*MD* 183) of human fallenness. He shows the restrictive social codes and the personal emotional urges in face of which Pierre defines a new ethical system for himself as skillfully as Hawthorne does in "Another View of Hester," but again he insists on going further; he presses on to inquire how this system corresponds to "Heaven's own Truth" (*P* 211). His impatience with the ordinary procedures of the novel is a function of his refusal to remain within the orders of reality with which those procedures deal. His vision impels him to be less interested in the actual processes of human experience, understood in its social, psychological, moral, or historical aspects, than in the meaning of experience seen in its largest conceivable dimensions. As a result he feels the "plain, straightforward . . . narrative of personal experience" in a novel like *Redburn* to be an inhibition; his ambition is to create an art that can take "probings at the very axis of reality."[8]

Melville's letters reveal another reason for this impatience as well. He is no more willing carefully to elaborate a coherent image of reality in its cosmological aspect than in any other; his thought is in surging motion, always moving beyond its own attainments toward a further reach. The idea of discovery as an ongoing process rather than as a completed act is essential to an understanding of Melville. He feels this himself. With urgent candor he writes to Hawthorne:

I am like one of those seeds taken out of the Egyptian Pyramids, which, after being three thousand years a seed and nothing but a seed, being planted in English soil it developed itself, grew to greenness, and then fell to mould. So I. Until I was twenty-five, I had no development at all. From my twenty-fifth year I date my life. Three weeks have scarcely passed, at any time between then and now, that I have not unfolded within myself.[9]

"Lord, when shall we be done growing?"[10] To his own amazement, and sometimes to his pain, he feels himself in process, perceptibly unfolding. Something of this awesome growth can be observed taking place in his letters. He leaps from a specific subject to a large hypothesis, then proposes another and another, until finally he has touched on everything and at each point revolutionized his thinking about everything. And Melville understands that his own articulation of his insight is the means by which he enables himself to grow. In *Pierre* he says that when the novelist is at work "two books are being writ" (*P* 304): he unfolds his vision through the act of composing his book. In *Mardi* Babbalanja explains that in creating his epic the poet Lombardo "did not build himself in with plans; he wrote right on; and so doing, got deeper and deeper into himself." Finally, by giving expression to all that stirs in him, he gains access to an inner source of pure power; he can now discard his creations because, by means of them, he has "created the creative" (*M* 595).

Melville accordingly courts expression as a means to deepened insight and to self-generating creativity, and this too puts a distinctive mark on his work with the novel. It is noteworthy how little his works have in common in subject or technique. It is difficult to think of another artist who produced in such quick succession works so fundamentally unlike one another as *Typee, Mardi, Moby-Dick, Pierre, Benito Cereno,* and *The Confidence-Man.* In devising techniques for his fiction he combines the conscious care of a dedicated craftsman with a remarkable tentativeness, a remarkable lack of commitment to his own achievements; he discards as readily as he invents. What we have just seen of his attitude toward creativity explains why this is so. Because each formulation seems to him to open up further vistas that require new formulations, he is always sailing on. His fictional techniques, like the hypotheses in his letters, are both brilliantly adequate and instantly obsolete.

Even within individual books Melville's methods change radically from beginning to end, and sometimes even from chapter to chapter. Like Lombardo, his wish to unleash his creative self urges him to write without plan. Having begun one sort of book he is often willing to throw that over in the middle and pursue an entirely new direction. In describing *Mardi* to its prospective publisher he tells how he became bored with "my narrative of *facts*" and so set to work composing another sort of novel. As a result *Mardi* "opens like a true narrative—like Omoo for example, on ship board—& the romance & poetry of the thing thence grow continually, till it becomes a story wild enough I assure you & with a meaning too."[11] None of his other works is quite so freely improvised as *Mardi* is, but both *Moby-Dick* and *Pierre* share with it this sense of explosion. They start out operating according to the established procedures of nautical adventure narrative and sentimental romance, but then Melville bursts out of the fetters of genre, introducing all sorts of new subjects and trying out all sorts of new techniques. Walter Bezanson defines a characteristic shared by all of these books when he writes that *Moby-Dick* has a "peculiar quality of making and unmaking itself as it goes."[12]

It is Melville's commitment to the unfolding of his vision as much as the cosmological dimension of his interests that makes his works such special cases within the general context of the novel. In particular it makes his works significantly different from Hawthorne's. Next to Melville's books, with their uncouth designs and their vigorous processes of self-shaping, Hawthorne's novels seem like models of deliberate and finished formal production. Further, Hawthorne's fictional worlds seem relatively stable next to Melville's, which are always being created, dissolved, and created anew. The features I have emphasized in Hawthorne's fiction are even more central in Melville's: instead of adhering to a uniform conception of reality and seeking to represent it in his fiction he tries out various modes of representation and explores different versions of the real; instead of attempting to give what he shows the status of an independent actuality his active presence makes us conscious of it as a function of the imagination that creates it.

Mardi is the most eccentric of Melville's novels, and for this reason it illustrates better than any other what happens when the impulses I have been discussing are acted out without restraint. Plot and character are of the most minimal interest in this book. The nominal action, Taji's quest for Yillah, seems to exist for the sake of being side-tracked, and the character of Melville's quester changes abruptly from page to page. Instead of dealing with the processes of individual experience Melville reaches out to embrace all the varieties of experience. His book leaps from sexual idyll to religious inquisition to social satire, from meditations on the psychological mystery of a stranger in the self to discourses on the beauty and inhumanity of nature to discussions of the nature of truth. In an equally disjointed manner the novel tests out the visions and versions of truth accessible to history, poetry, and philosophy. "Oh, reader, list! I've chartless voyaged" (*M* 556). The unity of *Mardi* is that of its author's spiritedly wayward imagination, seizing a subject and pressing as far as it can toward its final implications, then dropping it to seize another. And in a deeper sense the true plot of *Mardi* is Melville's self-creation. This novel is an almost unique experiment in which an author attempts to give birth to his own creative self by giving form to whatever surfaces in his mind. It is comparable to Keats's effort to make himself a poet by writing *Endymion*.[13]

In the letter in which he explains the course of the composition of *Mardi* Melville cavalierly brushes aside objections to its strangeness. "My *instinct* is to out with the Romance, & let me say that instincts are prophetic, & better than acquired wisdom."[14] This statement should be juxtaposed with his explanation near the end of *Pierre* that in order for the artist to fashion his intuitions into a significant creation he must quit the quarry of his own mind and "go and thoroughly study architecture" (*P* 257). These two passages can be seen as the end points of a period of gigantic ambition and brilliant accomplishment in Melville's career as a novelist. They suggest as well the distinctive features of that accomplishment. Melville never wrote another novel so completely innocent of imposed form as *Mardi*, but at least until the writing of *Pierre* he continued to believe in the value of instinctive composition and to use his fiction to further his personal unfolding. At the same time, during this period he came to discover his own artistic need for a more rigid formal discipline. Out of the tension between these antithetical needs he composed the idiosyncratic works that are his contribution to the novel, each of them striking its own balance between representation and exploration, narrated action and speculative diving, closed coherence and open inclusiveness.

It should be stressed at this point that if the sort of form Melville creates is a function of his peculiar imagination, it is also the product of a particular philosophical outlook. Melville does not have a well-defined philosophy—or rather he has a hundred of them. But what all his formulations have in common is a sense of reality as something finally mysterious and unknowable. In *Mardi* when the historian Mohi asks, "What is truth?" the philosopher Babbalanja replies, "That question is more final than any answer" (*M* 284). Melville's thought-diver cannot attain the bottom; man in his tragic phase of humanity confronts Powers that keep their secrets from him. In *Moby-Dick* Melville's internal descent into his hero finally stops short before "the old State-secret"; and in this book the external world is correspondingly enigmatic. Try as he may to submit the whale to his consciousness Ishmael must conclude at last, "I know him not, and never will" (*MD* 376). Pierre encounters a mysterious face outside himself, and his powerful response to it opens up a previously unsuspected region of mystery within him, inhabited by troops of hooded phantoms. His situation is the characteristic one of human consciousness in Melville's world; he feels a "confounding feeling" before an intuition of "one infinite, dumb, beseeching countenance of mystery, underlying all the surfaces of visible time and space" (*P* 52).

The sense of reality implicit in these examples plays a crucial role in shaping Melville's understanding of the nature of fiction. In the Fieldingesque fourteenth chapter of *The Confidence-Man*, "Worth the consideration of those to whom it may prove worth considering," he addresses readers' demands that authors present their characters consistently. He insists that "in real life, a consistent character is a *rara avis*" (*CM* 76); and in light of this he suggests that the desire for consistency is not, as such readers think, a demand that fiction be true to life, but really a demand that it offer a comfortably comprehensible replacement for reality. He recognizes that readers are willing to be mystified by "certain psychological novelists" who present characters seemingly full of baffling complexity, until, by the magic of their art, they reveal a deeper consistency—"in this way throwing open, sometimes to the understanding even of school misses, the last complication of that spirit which is affirmed by its Creator to be fearfully and wonderfully made" (*CM* 78). Here the process by which fiction seems to be faithful to the mystery of reality is only a subtler cheat, a cheat enabling the reader, with only a pleasant shudder of anxiety, to discover that life is even more comprehensible than he had thought. Melville concludes:

> Upon the whole, it might rather be thought, that he, who, in view of its inconsistencies, says of human nature the same that, in view of its contrasts, is said of the divine nature, that it is past finding out, thereby evinces a better appreciation of it than he who, by always representing it in a clear light, leaves it to be inferred that he clearly knows all about it.
>
> (*CM* 77)

He makes a related point in *Pierre*. As Pierre ponders the first installment of Isabel's weird autobiography he instinctively realizes that its mysteries admit of no elucidation. As Melville describes his hero's discovery his novel grows self-conscious.

> Like all youths, Pierre had conned his novel-lessons; had read more novels than most persons of his years; but their false, inverted attempts at systematizing eternally unsystemizable

elements; their audacious, intermeddling impotency, in trying
to unravel, and spread out, and classify, the more thin than
gossamer threads which make up the complex web of life; these
things over Pierre had no power now.... He saw that human
life doth truly come from that, which all men are agreed to call
by the name of *God;* and that it partakes of the unravelable
inscrutableness of God. By infallible presentiment he saw, that
not always doth life's beginning gloom conclude in gladness;
that wedding-bells peal not ever in the last scene of life's fifth
act; that while the countless tribes of common novels laboriously
spin veils of mystery, only to complacently clear them up at last;
and while the countless tribe of common dramas do but repeat
the same; yet the profounder emanations of the human mind,
intended to illustrate all that can be humanly known of human
life; these never unravel their own intricacies, and have no
proper endings; but in imperfect, unanticipated, and disappointing sequels (as mutilated stumps), hurry to abrupt intermergings with the eternal tides of time and fate.

(*P* 141)

The countless tribe of common novelists attacked here are the heirs of
Ann Radcliffe, the romancers whose invented mysteries and terrors turn
out to have some perfectly sensible explanation in the last chapter. Leslie
Fiedler acutely summarizes the final implication of their work: "it
embodies in the very technique of fiction a view of the world which
insists that though fear is real, its causes are delusive."[15] It denies that
there is anything permanently incomprehensible or terrible either in the
self or in the world, and accordingly it is a fiction that ends with wedding
bells as inevitably as life itself ends with a death.

But clearly what Melville is attacking in this paragraph is not so much
one genre of romance as something about novels in general. He is calling
into question the validity of any work in which the novelist assumes an
authoritative power to describe reality, to show all the interlocking
attributes and exigencies that make character, or to know all the strands
of causation that shape the course of events. To catch the full force of his
point it helps to remember what James says in his preface to *Roderick
Hudson:* "Really, universally, relations stop nowhere, and the exquisite
problem of the artist is eternally but to draw, by a geometry of his own,
the circle in which they shall happily *appear* to do so."[16] James's point is
elementary: fiction is not life, but a reduced and clarified image of life;
the novelist cannot help being selective, and the art of his selectivity
consists in providing a representation sufficiently full that we will not
miss what he has left out. But the exquisite art of making relations

happily appear to end somewhere is precisely what Melville is objecting to. It involves, for him, a systematizing of the eternally unsystemizable. It builds into fiction the implication that the complex web of life can be finally understood by author and reader.

The qualities of imagination that make Melville an explorer rather than the re-creator of a stable vision of reality receive a powerful second from the views he expresses in passages like these; in effect he is challenging the credentials of any representational art. These passages also suggest the nature of the procedures that a more valid fiction will have to adopt. What Melville stresses is that human life partakes of the inscrutable mysteriousness of God. His philosophical commitment as a novelist is faithfully to represent *this* reality, or reality under *this* aspect. But immediately there is a problem. The inscrutable cannot, by its very nature, be represented directly; and the novel cannot, by its very nature, *not* organize its presented experience in some way or other. As an artist Melville is thus engaged in the paradoxical task of seeking to make sense of something that he insists from the outset defies comprehension. His effort as a novelist is to construct a fiction sufficiently organized to evoke as a real presence a mystery that lies beyond its own powers of explanation.

Melville's titanic heroes reflect his own keen desire to find out what lies beyond; they also embody a practical solution to this problem of artistic strategy. With their obsessive awareness of Powers concealed behind the masks of the visible world and their total commitment to an assault on the mysteries within and without—"henceforth I will see the hidden things; and live right out in my own hidden life!" (*P* 66)—these heroes make a force of cosmic secrecy a powerfully felt presence in their books. They attempt to find out more than can be humanly known of human life, and their quests have no proper endings. The white whale is as unknown at the end of *Moby-Dick* as it was at the beginning. The scene in the picture gallery at the end of *Pierre* makes the secret of Isabel's true paternity, and thus of the value of Pierre's ethical sacrifices, more ambiguous, not less so. Instead of unraveling the mysteries that task and heap them, Ahab and Pierre achieve a final moment of tragic self-recognition, and then "hurry to abrupt intermergings with the eternal tides of time and fate."

Melville's narrators—Ishmael and the Magian narrator of *Pierre*—also feel the burden of the mystery. In its presence they alternate between an urgent desire to assault the bastions of the secret-keeping world and a consciousness of the futility of such an assault. We see this in their alternation between metaphysical diving and straight narration, and between a sympathetic identification with their heroes and an ironic distancing of themselves from them. Their final response to the condition of their world is to tell a story. And within the books, the activity of making and unmaking that I discussed earlier becomes a function of their efforts, as narrators, to find an appropriate way to tell their story. They try out fictional techniques, then drop them and adopt new ones, changing the method and direction of their books again and again in search of an adequate means of representation. The very way that this search goes on within the novels serves to reinforce our sense of the ultimate elusiveness of the experience that they make momentarily comprehensible. In the construction of their fictions they act out a drama akin to that of their heroes, an attempt, always defeated and always renewed, to systematize unsystemizable elements.

One of the most conspicuous features of Melville's novels is their peculiar system of decorum. Toward the end of *Moby-Dick* such chapters as "The Grand Armada," "The Castaway," "A Squeeze of the Hand," "The Try-Works," and "The Doubloon" follow closely upon one another, and although they share certain affinities of method, what is striking is how fully Melville realizes the visions implicit in each of their separate incidents without regard to how these visions might fit together. At least these chapters have in common their impulse to forge a major statement of the novel's issues. Such an aim does not seem to govern Melville's presentation of a British lawsuit, or of the bill of lading of a Dutch whaler, or of how Pip's father found a wedding ring around a pine tree, but he includes these as well, and again, without undue concern for their relation to the rest of the book. In the second half of *Pierre* he produces in quick succession and without transition a philosophical pamphlet, a lurid vision of the city as nightmare, a satire of the business of arts and letters in America, and a dream vision of the Titan Enceladus. This proliferation of independent parts illustrates what W. J. Harvey, in a discussion of Dickens, calls "episodic intensification": "the impulse to exploit to the full possibilities of any particular scene, situation or action without too much regard for the relevance of such local intensities to the total work of art."[17]

Certainly Melville's procedure of energetically creating parts rather than carefully orchestrating wholes is a product of his preference for writing without plan, for seizing passing opportunities as a means to unfold his own understanding. But in his intensification of episode his personal preference also coincides with the requirements of his theory of fiction. Here is another way in which he contrives to introduce a highly visible amount of inconsistency and disorderliness into his work's organization of experience. It is above all his way of keeping his books open—open both to new information and to new ways of understanding information. Finally Melville cannot disagree with James that the novelist must draw the circle. But by freely including such heterodox material and dilating on it for its independent interest he succeeds in drawing a circle with a difference—with "nimble center, circumference elastic" (*P* 54), as he puts it. The effect of this kind of circle is exactly the opposite of James's. Rather than making relations happily appear to end somewhere it alludes to the arbitrariness of its own exclusions, reminding us of the existence and potential significance of everything it has left out.

The peculiar air of open-endedness that Melville's novels possess is itself a skillful creation, and his art of elastic circumference helps to show how he produces it. His novels seem so open not because he takes the varied world for his subject and then tries to tie it up into a bulging bundle, although this is the illusion he creates; rather it is because he adopts coherently selective fictional forms and then breaks down their boundaries, reaching out to incorporate what they have excluded. Thus at the end of *Billy Budd* he writes:

> The symmetry of form attainable in pure fiction cannot so readily be achieved in a narration essentially having less to do with fable than with fact. Truth uncompromisingly told will always have its ragged edges; hence the conclusion of such a narration is apt to be less finished than an architectural finial.[18]

But the first twenty-seven chapters of *Billy Budd* are themselves the perfection of polished architectural form. What Melville does—and it is characteristic—is to include as an aftermath three disconnected chapters which suggest alternate versions of the story he has just told. By incorporating these chapters he purposely mars his work's formal perfection and unsettles the settled sense it has made; and these "ragged edges," by roughening his form and making its meaning tentative, give his work the appearance of "truth uncompromisingly told." As a novelist Melville must systematize, but he avoids the presumption of having made a final sense of experience by undoing his own systematization in such a way as to emphasize its incompleteness.

The paragraph from *Billy Budd* is Melville's last and most artful statement on a subject that has preoccupied him at least since the time of *Mardi.* At one point in that book the poet Yoomy offers to relate a legend, and the historian Mohi grumbles "something invidious about frippery young poetasters being too full of silly imaginings to tell a plain tale." Yoomy replies:

"Old Mohi, let us not clash. I honor your calling; but, with
submission, your chronicles are more wild than my cantos. I deal
in pure conceits of my own; which have a shapeliness and a
unity, however insubstantial; but you, Braid-Beard, deal in
mangled realities."

(*M* 280)

Their debate is actually between two kinds of fictional form. Yoomy
defends the form the poet creates when, turning his back on the actual,
he evolves an imaginative vision that renders experience with a height-
ened coherence and significance. The historian would have his form
correspond as nearly as possible to the structure of facts and actual events.
That his narrative seems mangled is a sign of his fidelity to the
inconsistency of real life.

Melville reformulates and extends this debate in the thirty-third
chapter of *The Confidence-Man,* where he distinguishes between a
fiction aiming at a "severe fidelity to real life" and "another class" that
frankly declares its imaginative independence from the actual but gains
thereby the ability to present "more reality, than real life itself can
show"—"nature unfettered, exhilarated, in effect transformed" (*CM*
206–7). This formulation shows how closely the distinction Melville is
drawing parallels Hawthorne's distinction between the novel's "very
minute fidelity ... to the probable and ordinary course of man's
experience" and romance's non-verisimilar exhibition of "the truth of the
human heart" (*HSG* 1).[19] Like Hawthorne, Melville sees these modes as
differing not just as artistic methods but as ways of envisioning and
imaginatively re-creating reality; as theoreticians of fiction they are
preoccupied with these methods' rival modes of and claims for truth.
And like Hawthorne, rather than joining in this dispute as a partisan
Melville finds it more natural to entertain both sides by turns. This is true
of his practice as well. In his novels he enacts a strong imagined design
but always eventually gives in to the impulse to look over his shoulder to
see how it squares with the texture of actual life; he creates shapely and
self-enclosed forms, and then makes room within them for the ragged
edges of mangled realities. In *Mardi*'s terms Melville as a novelist wants to
be both poet and historian. He constructs his engagingly unstable novels
by making use of both these modes of vision, presenting his work to us
not as a consistent imitation of any reality but as a consistent exploration
of ways of imaging a reality that must finally remain unknown.

All of Melville's varied impulses and concerns come together in the
creation of *Moby-Dick* and *Pierre. Mardi* is as ambitiously experimental
and as fully representative of the range of his interests, but it pays a price

for its chosen incoherence, and it suffers as does no other work by Melville from what Wallace Stevens calls "the greatest poverty," "not to live / In a physical world." After *Pierre* Melville continued to invent new forms for the novel, but in his later work he is closer to adopting Yoomy's position; he is more willing to turn his back on the variety of the actual world for the sake of evolving self-contained fables. By confining himself within the discipline of the fable he produces some of his richest work, but he suppresses, in doing so, the exuberance of personal inventiveness and discovery that informs his earlier novels. In their including all the dimensions of his creative project *Moby-Dick* and *Pierre* are Melville's most authentic books. They are his most significant experiments in creating the sort of fiction to which his imagination and his sense of reality commit him.

7 | The Uncommon Long Cable: *Moby-Dick*

All that we saw was owing to your metaphysics.

Blake, ''The Marriage of Heaven and Hell''

In the novel the theory of description is the theory of life. What sets the novelist's work apart from the philosopher's is that he articulates a vision of existence not in the internally coherent terms of logical abstraction but through his particularized representation of experience as it is lived. Whatever view of human nature he may subscribe to, it is his specific presentation of the contents and dynamics of his characters' personalities that creates his work's distinctive version of human nature. Whatever belief he may hold about the forces that determine or shape human destinies, it is through his presentation of particular agencies of causation in particular situations that his book implies a sense of how things happen. Lawrence says, "Never trust the artist. Trust the tale."[1] The author may be bristling with opinions or majestically indifferent to them, but in either case the vision of life he communicates is to be caught from his detailed specification of the texture of life within his narrative itself.

In his direct addresses to us Melville insists again and again that life is mysterious, inscrutable, past finding out. Such assertions are, in Lawrence's terms, of the artist. What makes them seem important and valid to us as we read his fiction is not his bald statement of belief but rather his ability to evoke a sense of life from within the particular reality that he images forth in his tale. In *Moby-Dick* he does this by presenting a world whose most persistent quality is its strangeness; and from the first he conducts his description in such a way as to emphasize the strangeness of what he shows.

The scenes that Ishmael passes through before the *Pequod* sails are studded with objects seen detached from their recognizable names or functions—objects like the one Ishmael finds in his room in the Spouter Inn:

> But what is this on the chest? I took it up, and held it close to the light, and felt it, and smelt it, and tried every way possible to arrive at some satisfactory conclusion concerning it. I can

compare it to nothing but a large door mat, ornamented at the edges with little tinkling tags something like the stained porcupine quills round an Indian moccasin.

(19)

Even the things and places that seem more recognizable are oddly unlike their counterparts in our familiar experience. A bar is framed with the arch of a whale's jawbone; a chapel has a prow for a pulpit; a ship's bow is so inlaid with ivory teeth as to look like a whale's mouth. The people of this world are as unaccountable as its physical environment. Captain Bildad's derivation of Ishmael's salary—the seven hundred and seventy-seventh lay—from a biblical text, an act seen separate from an explicable motive, seems vaguely maniacal. In the person of Queequeg the familiar human body becomes something grotesquely foreign—"his very legs were marked, as if a parcel of dark green frogs were running up the trunks of young palms" (22). The "everlasting itch for things remote" that makes Ishmael resolve to go a-whaling need not take him so far afield: from the beginning he inhabits a "wonder-world" (6).

This wonder-world is also a world of terrors. Going through the first invitingly open door that he encounters in New Bedford Ishmael stumbles on what looks like "the great Black Parliament sitting in Tophet" (8); and when he succeeds in bringing the actual nature of this place into focus it does not lose its portentous gloom. The black preacher's sermon on "the blackness of darkness, and the weeping and wailing and teeth-gnashing there" strengthens his sense of having entered the real presence of a living hell. Similarly the darkly indefinite painting that he encounters in the Spouter Inn calls up horrific visions of primal powers; and his final surmise that this painting obscurely represents a sperm whale impaling itself on the masts of a ship during a hurricane deepens, not alleviates, its sublime terror. This world is not just unfamiliar. Demonic forces seem near at hand in it, palpably present in its surface actuality.

Ishmael says that the indefiniteness of the painting "fairly froze you to it, till you involuntarily took an oath with yourself to find out what that marvellous painting meant" (11). This is his characteristic response to the forest of enigmas he passes through. Its mysteries arrest him and seize him with a sense of what he calls "significant darkness" (461). To release himself from their halting power he instinctively attempts to decipher their meaning, and thus to incorporate them within the familiar categories of his experience. He has several ways of doing this. The queer nautical appointments of Father Mapple's chapel seem, as the painting does, "full of meaning" (39). Asserting that the world is a ship on its

passage out, and that the pulpit is its prow, he deprives the scene of its
strangeness by giving its furnishings the fixed significance of allegorical
symbols.

The mystery of Queequeg cannot be handled in this way. Each new
detail that Ishmael learns about his savage bedfellow increases his fright.
He keeps forging explanatory hypotheses to make this stranger seem less
scary. Seeing his purplish-yellow face, he surmises that he is a sailor who
has been in a fight; then, seeing that the black squares on his skin are not
sticking-plasters but stains, he decides that this is a white man who has
been tattooed by savages. But these comforting explanations are shattered
one after another, until finally he must recognize that he is seeing the
abominable cannibal himself. This discovery gives him a final moment of
pure terror, until, in a last turn of thought, he says:

> For all his tattooings he was on the whole a clean, comely
> looking cannibal. What's all this fuss I have been making about,
> thought I to myself—the man's a human being just as I am. . . .
> Better sleep with a sober cannibal than a drunken Christian.
>
> (24)

Ishmael's tactic for releasing himself from the terrors of strangeness here
is a comic one. By positing a lowest common denominator of human
identity he makes the stranger just like himself; by reversing his
preconceived definitions of civilized and savage he makes the cannibal
not only acceptable but actually desirable as a companion.

But in a third type of experience neither symbolism nor sociable
accommodation can help Ishmael. He is "riveted" (92) by Elijah's dark
hints about Captain Ahab. Peleg's similar hints inspire in him "a certain
wild vagueness of painfulness" (80) that he cannot explain away. The
only relief he can find from this enigma lies in temporary forgetfulness:
"for the present dark Ahab slipped my mind" (80).

For all their variations of outcome these episodes share a common
pattern. Ishmael encounters something that is unfamiliar and that, in its
unfamiliarity, fills him with dread. The drama in these scenes is that of
his mind's attempt to make sense of what he sees, and thus to make
himself at home and at ease with it.[2] After the *Pequod* sets sail in the
chapter "Merry Christmas" the scope of the book's world and the
procedures of its narrative change abruptly, but the pattern of confrontation that Melville so carefully establishes in the opening chapters
continues throughout *Moby-Dick*. The occasional strangeness of the
shore gives way to the perpetual strangeness of the sea. As Ishmael's
meditations on sharks and dogs and on the whale's mode of vision make
clear, the sea is the locus of a life that simply bears no relation to the

forms and structures of ordinary experience. In the face of this life the sense of mysterious powers momentarily evoked in the black church and the painting becomes a permanent presence. The appallingly pathetic death of the old and maimed whale in "The Pequod Meets the Virgin"; the discovery of a stone lancehead, presumably of prehistoric origin, within this whale; the strangely beautiful vision of mother whales nursing their cubs in "The Grand Armada"—in scenes like these we seem to see into the mystery of primordial nature. The *Pequod* sails through a world of continuous sublimity, inhabited, in Wordsworth's words, by "huge and mighty forms, that do not live / Like living men."

During the voyage Ishmael's individual attempts to make sense of local marvels similarly give way to a perpetual endeavor of questioning and surmise. At some points this effort is applied to specific mysteries, as in Ishmael's struggles to discover the real nature of the whale's spout or of its skin. But at other points the characters are moved to address a larger enigma. In "The Candles" Ahab demands of his fierce father the fire god: "my sweet mother, I know not. Oh, cruel! what hast thou done with her?" (500-501). Ishmael repeats and modifies his question in "The Gilder": "Where lies the final harbor, whence we unmoor no more? In what rapt ether sails the world, of which the weariest will never weary? Where is the foundling's father hidden?" (486-87). Even the otherwise stolid Stubb has fits of ontological insecurity: "I wonder, Flask, whether the world is anchored anywhere" (504). Like *King Lear,* *Moby-Dick* puts its characters through an experience so alien and extreme that they seem to reinvent spontaneously every philosophy of existence. And as in *King Lear,* what is finally most remarkable is not the answers they achieve but the questions they are impelled to ask. Frozen before the appalling strangeness of nature, they involuntarily seek to discover what it means: what is the nature of the world? what god or gods govern it? what origin are we moving from, and to what end?

At the center of *Moby-Dick* is Ahab's crucial act of interpretation. When he reveals his fierce purpose of vengeance in "The Quarter-Deck" Starbuck resists:

> "Vengeance on a dumb brute!" cried Starbuck, "that simply smote thee from blindest instinct! Madness! To be enraged with a dumb thing, Captain Ahab, seems blasphemous."
>
> (161)

Ahab replies:

> "Hark ye yet again,—the little lower layer. All visible objects, man, are but as pasteboard masks. But in each event—in the

living act, the undoubted deed—there, some unknown but still
reasoning thing puts forth the mouldings of its features from
behind the unreasoning mask. If man will strike, strike through
the mask! How can the prisoner reach outside except by
thrusting through the wall? To me, the white whale is that wall,
shoved near to me. Sometimes I think there's naught beyond.
But 'tis enough. He tasks me; he heaps me; I see in him
outrageous strength, with an inscrutable malice sinewing it.
That inscrutable thing is what I chiefly hate; and be the white
whale agent, or be the white whale principal, I will wreak that
hate upon him."

(161-62)

"All that most maddens and torments; all that stirs up the lees of things;
all truth with malice in it; all that cracks the sinews and cakes the brain;
all the subtle demonisms of life and thought"—all that makes this world
seem alien to us or hostile to our human existence—"to crazy Ahab, were
visibly personified, and made practically assailable in Moby Dick" (181).

Through Ahab's symbolic act the elements of the world of *Moby-Dick*
are given the specific shape and the forward motion of a dramatic action.
The whole force of dreadful mystery in the novel is given a local
habitation in the white whale; and the whole urge to subject the
inscrutable to human understanding and control becomes particularized
in Ahab's mission of vengeance. All the impulses that make the
characters ask questions of their world come to energize this quest. And at
the same time, the quest raises in concrete form the questions they must
otherwise ask at a more abstract level. Whether nature is maliciously evil
or merely dumb; whether it operates by intention or accident; whether it
is governed by an intelligent power beyond itself or by physical and
biological processes—these questions become directly visible and potentially answerable in the more specific question whether Moby Dick inflicts
destruction by brute instinct or by design.

Ahab's interpretation of the whale as an intelligent force of evil has a
peculiar status in *Moby-Dick*. The book cannot validate his theory. If it
did, it would settle the problem of the nature of the world too
definitively. But on the other hand it cannot allow his theory to seem
merely mad or merely personal. If it did so, the voyage of the *Pequod*
would lose its point; the narrative action of hunting Moby Dick would no
longer raise and explore real cosmological questions. The novel must use
Ahab's interpretation as a scientist uses a working hypothesis—as a
tentatively accepted conclusion formulated in advance to give significant
direction to an experiment.

Accordingly Melville makes a major effort in *Moby-Dick* to give Ahab's sense of the whale a qualified plausibility. Thus in the chapter "Moby Dick" Ishmael engages in a piece of brilliant exploratory argument. With firm pacing and fine precision he brings forward one by one the possible reasons for the legendary stature the white whale possesses in the minds of the whalers: their daily contact with "whatever is appallingly astonishing in the sea" (177); their frequent experience of the disastrous consequences of the whale's ferocity and cunning; the special terror that has always attached to the sperm whale; the sailor's natural susceptibility to superstition. Every time he invokes the whalers' rumors he then goes on to present evidence that might have provided the initial reasonable foundation for their wild surmises. They think that Moby Dick is ubiquitous; and this is not so strange, Ishmael continues, since whales travel at such speeds that they can be encountered in widely separate parts of the globe within a short span of time. The result of this procedure is that, although Ishmael's apparent purpose is to show how it can be that some men believe strange things, the actual effect of his discussion is gradually to break down our sense of incredulity and to move us closer and closer to entertaining their beliefs ourselves. Like Hawthorne, he evokes "outblown rumors" and "wild, strange tales" (177) in such a way as to encourage us to enter into a superstitious frame of mind. And when we make even a partial imaginative acceptance of "half-formed foetal suggestions of supernatural agencies" (177) associated with Moby Dick we are on our way to joining Ahab in his vision of an "unknown but still reasoning thing."

The sense of the whale that this chapter produces is reinforced by the news of Moby Dick's actions presented in the *Pequod's* gams. Captain Boomer of the *Samuel Enderby*, having lost his arm to Moby Dick, joins Doctor Bunger in arguing against Ahab that the evil it causes stems not from malice but only from its awkwardness. But as we see Boomer's whalebone arm next to Ahab's whalebone leg we receive, at the least, strong evidence of this whale's power, and specifically its power to inflict pain. Other encounters hint more unequivocally that Moby Dick destroys by purposeful design. In "The Town-Ho's Story" the white whale spills the ship's boat in such a way that only Radney is killed. This by itself suggests a cunning selectivity of destruction; but occurring as it does after Radney's willful humiliation of Steelkilt and at the time when Steelkilt plans to execute his vengeance, it also inevitably suggests more than this. Its act seems like a "visitation of one of those so called judgments of God" (241): Moby Dick becomes the agent of a divine power that takes the justice of human retribution into its own hands.

Certainly its acts wear a similar aspect in "The Jeroboam's Story," in which the chief mate, Macey, assaulting Moby Dick in defiance of Gabriel's prophetic assertion that this whale is "the Shaker God incarnated" (314), is smitten into the air and killed without his boat's being otherwise harmed. Again Moby Dick seems like the purposeful agent of a divine visitation; and again we are moved closer to an imaginative acceptance of Ahab's vision of the whale.

Episodes like these have an effect on our view not just of Moby Dick but also of the operation of the world. They imply the existence of powers beyond the natural world that act in and watch over that world. In them what happens in human experience is the product not of chance or will but of a providential necessity. Ishmael can thus call Radney "the predestinated mate" (247), and he can see in the chain of events in "The Town-Ho's Story" "a strange fatality . . . as if verily mapped out before the world itself was charted" (257). He calls this felt design "the secret part of the tragedy," and he carefully distinguishes it from the "publicly narrated" (241) version of the tale. His terms recall Holgrave's discrimination of the "secret character" from the "merest surface," and his procedure recalls Hawthorne's as well. In presenting these episodes his fiction takes us beyond the apparent order of ordinary causality and lets us see the dark consistency of a more ghostly design. Within this design the separate events of human experience are seen enacting and reenacting fixed patterns, patterns that recur independent of individual characters' knowledge or will. Just as in *The House of the Seven Gables* each distinct incident of Pyncheon history exemplifies the same rhythm of self-assertion and self-defeat, so too from within "The Town-Ho's Story" and "The Jeroboam's Story" the world seems to contain no actions other than willful assaults by domineering men and destructive retributions performed by the white whale. We have reentered the enchanted and cyclical world of romance.

Set off as a tale within a tale told in a special style, "The Town-Ho's Story" bears a special resemblance to "Alice Pyncheon" in *The House* and "The Silvery Veil" in *Blithedale*. It serves to distance us from the novel's ongoing action for the sake of clarifying a pattern underlying that action. Ahab is as "overbearing" (242) as Radney and as willing as Macey to assault the whale in spite of denunciations of blasphemy; and since his character and purpose resemble theirs, their fates seem to prophesy his own. But in *Moby-Dick* this sense of romance design is evoked not just at second hand through its tales but also directly as a presence in its actual world. In discussing the sort of reality presented by what he calls prophetic novelists Forster says, "It is the ordinary world of fiction, but it reaches back."³ A chapter like "The Spirit-Spout" shows what this means in the context of *Moby-Dick*. This chapter describes a scene which, without ever ceasing to seem starkly natural, is simultaneously haunted. The storm-tossed sea is perceived as heaving and heaving like a guilty conscience. The strange birds and fish that surround the *Pequod* seem like "guilty beings" transformed into lower orders of life and "condemned to swim on everlastingly without any haven" (233). Nature is, here, fully animistic; and the silvery jet that appears before the *Pequod* night after night "seemed some plumed and glittering god uprising from the sea" (230). A supernatural force reveals itself in nature, seeming to guide the *Pequod* on to its appointed end as the Polar Spirits of "The Ancient Mariner" do. Though their nature remains mysterious, we feel ourselves in touch with the world of spirits, in a reality inhabited by ghostly powers.

At times, too, the actual world of *Moby-Dick* seems to obey the sort of magical causality that operates in its tales. The first time Ahab asks another ship for news of the white whale, its captain's speaking-trumpet falls into the ocean. When the captain of the *Jeroboam* tries to tell Ahab other tidings than Gabriel's prophecy of the blasphemer's doom, the waves repeatedly wash his boat out of earshot. The letter Ahab would deliver turns out to be addressed to Macey, and, as he fails to pass it to the captain, it falls at his own feet. A phrase Angus Fletcher cites from Aristotle describes the feeling these events convey: "incidents like that we think to be not without a meaning."⁴ Actual occurrences seem charged with symbolic significance, with dark portent. Apparent accidents seem the products not of chance but of a preternatural necessity. Reality itself here solicits our superstition.

Extending our perception as he does in these chapters is crucial to Melville's purposes. By giving us our own experience of intuitive recognition of purposeful powers in nature he makes Ahab's vision of the world seem not only intellectually plausible but urgently real to our imagination. We too see the physical world and its succession of ordinary events as a pasteboard mask, a surface beneath which we discern the operation of a dark intelligence. And whether or not Ahab's quenchless feud seems ours, it is by making us feel this preternatural force as present and real that Melville is able to sustain his action on the scale that he intends, to make Ahab's mission palpably a quest for "audacious, immitigable, and supernatural revenge" (184).

Melville's ability to raise his story to the height of this great argument is one of the wonders of *Moby-Dick*. He transcends the ordinary dimensions of the novel, giving to his tale the scale and scope of full-blown myth. But another wonder is that *Moby-Dick* also contains within it what amounts to a completely different book. Thus after passing on to us the haunted and ominous vision of "The Jeroboam's Story," Ishmael's narrative pauses for a moment and then begins again:

> In the tumultuous business of cutting-in and attending to a whale, there is much running backwards and forwards among the crew. Now hands are wanted here, and then again hands are wanted there. There is no staying in any one place; for at one and the same time everything has to be done everywhere.
>
> (317)

What other novel changes its gears so abruptly between chapters as *Moby-Dick* does? With a plunk Ishmael returns to the practical present business of whaling, then passes on to describe a specific scene in which Queequeg, in his shirt and socks, flounders about on the whale that is being stripped, Tashtego and Daggoo flourish their spades to protect him from sharks, and Ishmael, tied to Queequeg by the "elongated Siamese ligature" (318) of the monkey-rope, looks on from the deck. This scene too moves outward toward a vision of cosmological forces; "so strongly and metaphysically" does Ishmael "conceive of my situation" (318) that it blossoms into a full-fledged allegory of Life. But the way that "The Monkey-Rope" reaches back, in Forster's phrase, could not be more different from that of "The Jeroboam's Story." Instead of the fanatically insistent rhythms of Gabriel's earnest speech Ishmael pronounces his vision with metaphorical exuberance and colloquial humor. Where the world itself seemed to call for and support Gabriel's dark interpretation, Ishmael's allegory is a moment's conceit playfully superimposed on his situation. Thus whereas "The Jeroboam's Story" leaves us in gloomy meditation over the "many strange things" that "were hinted in reference to this wild affair" (317), in "The Monkey-Rope" Ishmael's vision collapses as Queequeg comes back on deck and the scene returns us from the mysteries of life to the comic security of hard ground, tepid ginger-jub and strong spirits.

"The Monkey-Rope" exemplifies the other side of *Moby-Dick*, the side concerned not with preternatural powers and supernatural revenges but with the works and days of ordinary life on board a whaleship. This side of the novel takes many forms, and it makes many sorts of contributions to its total strength. We see one of its forms in such chapters as "The First Lowering" or "Stubb Kills a Whale." D. H. Lawrence says that "Melville is a master of violent, chaotic, physical motion,"[5] and these chapters prove his point. They manage to convey in "one welded commotion" (223) of simultaneous action the mates' lively exhortations and their crews' responses, the complex motions of men, harpoons, and lines, and the whale's divings and mountings through churning, bloody water. These chapters magnificently communicate the thrill and violence of the hunt without ever ceasing to be descriptively precise; in them Melville achieves for the action-narrative a kind of realistic sublimity. Less exhilarating but no less fully circumstantial are the chapters in which Ishmael describes the tools of the whaler and the procedures of his work—cutting in, baling the case, trying out blubber, and so on. In these Melville reveals a feeling for and a skill at evoking the processes of human labor matched, I think, only by Zola's. An offshoot of this strain in *Moby-Dick* are the chapters that present the more relaxed leisure activities of the crew—"Stubb's Supper" is the finest example of these in the novel.

These chapters show off interests and abilities of Melville's other than those we encounter in the portentous scenes discussed earlier, but what should be emphasized here is that they also engage us, as we read them, in a completely different vision of reality. This reality is solid, tactile, and mobile. In it the characters make use of man-made physical objects—boats, lines, harpoons, knives—to cope with an equally physical natural adversary. It is not inhabited by supernatural agencies or charged with symbolic significance; its spouts are spouts, and signs to the hunters of the timing of their prey—not spirits. When the conception of an order beyond the natural occurs at all in these chapters it is usually invoked in order to be laughed at. Thus when Stubb makes Fleece bring the glad tidings of available grace to the sharks in "Stubb's Supper"—"You is sharks, sartin; but if you gobern de shark in you, why den you be an angel; for all angel is not'ing more dan de shark well gobberned" (294)—his Christian gospel is ludicrously at odds with the actual situation, and theology itself comes to seem comically irrelevant to the real nature of things. Seeing that his sermon falls on deaf ears, Fleece curses the sharks, and they and Stubb go on eating.

Differing in their sense of the nature and dimensions of reality, these chapters have a correspondingly different vision of the world's causal order. In hunting and stripping the whale the members of the crew use their brawn and skill to manipulate their environment. There are no strange fatalities here: man makes things happen. And again, when these chapters hint at a larger order of causality they do so mockingly. When Tashtego falls into the whale's tun while baling the case in "Cisterns and Buckets" Ishmael, in a burst of humorous Hawthornism, offers us our choice of explanations:

> Whether it was that Tashtego, that wild Indian, was so heedless
> and reckless as to let go for a moment his one-handed hold on
> the great cabled tackles suspending the head; or whether the
> place where he stood was so treacherous and oozy; or whether
> the Evil One himself would have it to fall out so, without stating
> his particular reasons; how it was exactly, there is no telling
> now . . .
>
> (340)

But, secure in the confines of a solid if slippery world, we must find this
theory of demonic agency and special providence ludicrously overcon-
ceived. We laugh at its very possibility and go back to watching the
action.

As "Cisterns and Buckets" shows, this world has its own mode of evil,
its own potentials for doom and destruction. Death is a constant presence
in *Moby-Dick;* Ishmael shows each tool and each procedure of the
whaleman's work as presenting its own peculiar perils and as affording its
own unique way to die. But death here seems like a bad accident, not an
appointed fate, and more often than not its possibility is simply
overlooked. Like Stubb, the whalers contrive to convert "the jaws of
death into an easy chair" (115). In their constant exercise of their own
skill and ingenuity they lose sight of the limits an inhuman world places
on their powers; and in his descriptions of the processes of their daily
activities Melville does so as well. As a result these descriptions have the
quality of low-key celebrations of ordinary human freedom. Their realism
is comic in Susanne Langer's sense of the term: they exhibit and revel in
"a brainy opportunism in face of an essentially dreadful universe."[6]

The uniqueness of *Moby-Dick* as a novel lies in its ability to include
both the intense and eerie supernaturalism of "The Spirit-Spout" and
the pure comedy of ingenuity of "The Pequod Meets the Rosebud,"
both Ahab's lofty address to nature's dark, Hindoo half and Ishmael's
casually chatty aside: "Porpoise meat is good eating, you know" (141). It
embraces the epic and the everyday, the cosmic and the trivial, the world
of spiritual presences and the world of physical acts and facts. But it does
not just mix these helter-skelter: its narrative divides them up and plays
them off against each other. This procedure is what gives *Moby-Dick* its
characteristic rhythm. To choose a characteristic sequence, the book leads
us from the broad humor of Stubb's diddling of the French captain in
"The Rosebud" to the high tragedy of Pip's isolation and divine vision in
"The Castaway" to the work of squeezing sperm in "A Squeeze of the
Hand." This scene of ordinary labor suddenly turns into an ecstatically
loving vision of angels; then we plunge equally abruptly back down into

the factual world of plum-pudding, gurry, and nippers. Then comes the inverted religiosity and phallic wit of "The Cassock" and the night work of trying out blubber in "The Try-Works." Here again the novel opens out, this time onto a vision of the ship as inferno; and then we touch down once more to learn how whalemen light their ships in "The Lamp." At one moment the surface of the opaque world opens up to reveal a spirit, angelic or demonic; then, inevitably, we return to business as usual in a world whose hard surface seems to be all that there is.

Melville's fiction bounces us back and forth between two visions of reality that are radically incommensurate and arranged in such a way that from within one of them we simply cannot see the other. Where is the unknown but still reasoning thing within the mask of the whale Stubb captures? The actual whale is so completely present that it never occurs to us to look for a lower layer. To call Radney "the predestinated mate" means something serious in "The Town-Ho's Story." But when, later on, Ishmael says, "The predestinated day arrived, and we duly met the ship Jungfrau" (348), and when the object of this predestination is a chauvinistic race against the foolish Germans, the very idea that the world has a secret part becomes a good joke. Fleece's sermon is a piece of fun, but when Ahab stands on the same deck and addresses his fiery father in "The Candles," we cannot be so sure that no one out there is listening. The propriety of worship, even if by defiance, becomes a matter of deadly earnest.

Ishmael tells us that since the whale's eyes are on different sides of its head he "must see one distinct picture on this side, and another distinct picture on that side" (328). The alternation of portentous romance and comic realism in his narration makes us see in a similar way. It makes us enter into both of its visions and see each, by turns, as yielding a true image of reality, but we cannot, if we would, put the two of them together. This is what accounts for some of the strangest features of the experience *Moby-Dick* gives its readers—the fact that as we read the novel the whale seems now genuinely godlike, now simply so much blubber or, in the ultimate reduction of "The Whale as a Dish," "a meat-pie nearly one hundred feet long" (297); the fact that its natural world is at one moment a place of strangeness and terror, only to become, a chapter later, downright cozy; and finally the fact that its action engages us in a quest of genuinely mythic proportions to slay the leviathan that keeps man shut out from a redeemed world—but then for long stretches it lets us forget all about Ahab, the white whale, and the whole larger purpose and significance of the *Pequod*'s voyage.

The divided narrative of *Moby-Dick* also works to make us see man under radically different aspects. In its most intense scenes we observe "high abstracted man alone; and he seems a wonder, a grandeur, and a woe" (462). But in its more everyday chapters the characters seem, if not quite "a mob of unnecessary duplicates," at least not so unlike such busy ordinary mortals as ourselves. Ahab's soliloquies reveal a complex interiority in which an intense self-consciousness combines with an equally intense energy of overreaching will. By fitting him out with a "bold and nervous lofty language" (73) drawn from Shakespearean tragedy and *Paradise Lost* Melville removes him from the circle of our familiar experience and endows him with a grandeur commensurate with the heroic scale of his mission. He is equally careful to give Stubb a language of his own, and in its way the racy vernacular in which Stubb addresses his crew is as much a triumph of linguistic invention as the Ahab music is; but instead of working to distance and elevate Stubb, this characterization gives him the accessible reality of a vital *homme moyen practical*. Stubb's character possesses a completely different set of contents from Ahab's. He has nothing to correspond to Ahab's deep psyche, analyzed by Ishmael in "Moby Dick" and "The Chart"; he has almost no self-consciousness, and little will beyond what allows him to make the most of passing opportunities. Instead he possesses all the knack for ordinary business and ordinary pleasure that Ahab so singularly lacks. Thus while Ahab is a "mighty pageant creature, formed for noble tragedies" (73), we see Stubb at his best pulling after whales, diddling fools, and enjoying a dinner and a pipe.

It is almost impossible to visualize Ahab and Stubb standing alongside each other; like Hester Prynne and Roger Chillingworth, they differ not just in the individual attributes of their characters but in their very modes of being. And in *Moby-Dick* as in *The Scarlet Letter* the sorts of reality that these characters are given in the book's fiction are intimately associated with the ways in which they themselves envision and understand reality. As the ordered sequences of soliloquies in "The Doubloon" and the chapters following "The Quarter-Deck" show, Melville insistently presents his characters as representatives of distinct modes of consciousness, each of which conceives of and responds to the world in its own characteristic way. Ahab is obsessively conscious of inhuman supernatural powers. Ordinary actuality simply evaporates before his boiling mind as he projects himself out of it to engage in cosmic contests. "I laugh and hoot at ye, ye cricket-players, ye pugilists, ye deaf Burkes and blinded Bendigoes!" (166). These are what is real to Ahab, and when he does occupy himself with the solid objects of present situations he does so as a way of making contact with the forces beyond. Thus he has the carpenter squeeze his hand in the vise so that he can feel the localized pressure of an adversary force; he grabs the ship's lightning-rods so that he can feel the might of the fire-god and defyingly resist it; and finally he assaults one natural creature, Moby Dick, so that he can eradicate once and for all the inscrutable source of human suffering.

As Ahab's consciousness always moves to expand the world outward, Stubb's moves to scale it down to more comfortably manageable proportions. Stubb approaches the whale chase "as if the most deadly encounter were but a dinner" (115). He dismisses ominous mysteries by labeling them "queer," and since for him "a laugh's the wisest, easiest answer to all that's queer" (168) he can accommodate strange fatalities to his cheery outlook by treating them as practical jokes. He responds to Ahab's terrible revelation of his dark purpose by telling himself, "'one comfort's always left—that unfailing comfort is, it's all predestinated'" (168), and though at first glance this would seem to indicate his sensitivity to a larger cosmological order, in fact it illustrates how he eludes such a sensitivity. By asserting a providential philosophy he denies his own need to consider his situation further. For Stubb metaphysics is a tactic of self-preservation by which he overcomes uneasiness and returns himself to the comforts of a song and a smoke.

Within *Moby-Dick* the schematized contrast between Ahab and Stubb is only one version of a larger opposition. We encounter it in another form in the mixture of representational modes in the novel's narrative, which presents by turns the sort of reality inhabited by terrifying invisible agencies that Ahab sees and the sort of comfortably demystified workaday world that Stubb sees. We meet it again in a division of Ishmael's mind and voice—for example, in the alternation of his dread before the deadly cosmic voids that are so forcefully present to him in the tombstones of Father Mapple's chapel and his comic reductions of apparent cosmic mysteries to the lower mysteries of the body: "In one word, Queequeg, . . . hell is an idea first born on an undigested apple dumpling" (85); or in the alternation between his riveted response to Elijah's portentous prophecies and his cagy dismissal of "Mr. Elijah" as a bamboozler, "a humbug, trying to be a bugbear" (93). In the first chapter Ishmael says:

> I am quick to perceive a horror, and could still be social with it—
> would they let me—since it is but well to be on friendly terms
> with all the inmates of the place one lodges in.
>
> (6)

Ahab inherits his quick perception of and itch to make contact with the horrible, Stubb his urge to fraternize and make the world a cozy haven.

At the center of *Moby-Dick*'s concern, and organizing its fictional presentation, is a conflict between two attitudes toward and two visions of the nature of the world. At the level of characterization, representation, and narrative voice *Moby-Dick* insists on an opposition between a sense of reality as something inhuman that lies beyond the actual and apparent and a sense of it as something visible, tangible, and finally supportive of human security. This is the opposition Ishmael formulates most clearly in "The Whiteness of the Whale": "Though in many of its aspects this visible world seems formed in love, the invisible spheres were formed in fright" (193).

The mixed narrative mode of *Moby-Dick* and its assimilation of its characters to the terms of this dichotomy are symptoms of the book's preoccupation with these two senses and their rival claims to yield a true picture of the world. And whenever Ishmael becomes seriously thoughtful, this becomes the subject of his meditation. "The Lee Shore" provides his first full-scale attempt to mediate between them. To evaluate the fate of the intrepid quester Bulkington, Ishmael compares him to a storm-tossed ship seeking to fend off from the land. "The port would fain give succor; the port is pitiful; in the port is safety, comfort, hearth-stone, supper, warm blankets, friends, all that's kind to our mortalities" (105). But in the storm this image of a world that is familiar and kind to our basic human needs becomes "that ship's direst jeopardy"; the ship can find security only in its solitary self-assertion against the inhuman forces that would destroy it. By a brilliant reversal of value the shore becomes "treacherous, slavish," the return to its comforts a cowardly evasion of the true condition of the world. The resolute encounter with the "howling infinite" emerges as an act of necessary heroism, leading to sure destruction but finally to an apotheosis.

"For worm-like, then, oh! who would craven crawl to land!" (105). In "The Lee Shore" Ishmael throws his personal allegiance and his rhetorical weight behind the Ahabian sense of reality and human mission. Elsewhere his meditaitons are less resolved. In "Brit" he turns from the sea, so calm and loving on its surface and so murderously active in its depths, to consider the mind, which likewise has its "one insular Tahiti, full of peace and joy, but encompassed by all the horrors of the half known life" (274). Similarly in "The Grand Armada" the calm center of generative joy surrounded by the destructive fury of the wounded whales makes him think of himself:

> even so, amid the tornadoed Atlantic of my being, do I myself still for ever centrally disport in mute calm; and while ponderous

planets of unwaning woe revolve round me, deep down and deep inland there I still bathe me in eternal mildness of joy.

(387)

As in "The Lee Shore," Ishmael's metaphorical models here relate something loving and something frightful, but here he refuses to choose between them. Instead he simply accepts the dual aspect of nature and uses its duality to forge a model of the mind.

In "The Try-Works" he tries to press this sense of observed coexistence toward a philosophical conclusion about the nature of the world. After his terrifying experience of inversion he tries to extract a lesson from what has happened, and at first he states it thus: "Look not too long in the face of the fire, O man!" (422). He rejects the "artificial fire" as a liar and its ghastly vision as an illusion, choosing as the true image of the world the gentler version produced by the "golden, glad sun." But here Ishmael stops to consider what this gospel of good cheer excludes: the "dark side of this earth" (422), the woeful wisdom of Solomon, the reality of graveyards in addition to operas, Young and Pascal in addition to Rabelais. In face of the reality of the woeful both in the world and in the mind he overturns his first conclusion, but he finds his second formulation equally partial. To give oneself up wholly to woe, he sees, is a kind of suicide: "There is a wisdom that is woe; but there is a woe that is madness" (423). To do justice to the realities of both glad sun and ghastly fire, joy and woe, he abandons his static maxims and evolves the dynamic image of the Catskill eagle, the noble bird who can both "dive down into the blackest gorges, and soar out of them again and become invisible in the sunny spaces." Now instead of the either/or of "The Lee Shore" his metaphor makes possible an embrace of a both/and; and instead of the intrepid defier he finds an example of a mind adequately responsive to the condition of its world in a flexible figure capable of entering into both the howling infinite and the peacefully secure without being imprisoned in either of them.

But the serenity of achieved insight that Ishmael attains at the end of "The Try-Works" is only momentary; the problem so decisively solved here is reopened in "The Gilder." On a day of dreamy quietude he forgets once more the tiger's heart concealed in the sea's beauty and feels instead "a certain filial, confident, land-like" (486) sensation, an intimation of a world formed in love. But an intervening consciousness of the temporariness of this ecstasy breaks his mood's illusion and unleashes a statement of the full frustration of the mind that so desperately longs for a stable and supportive world.

Would to God these blessed calms would last. But the mingled,
mingling threads of life are woven by warp and woof: calms
crossed by storms, a storm for every calm. There is no steady
unretracing progress in this life; we do not advance through
fixed gradations, and at the last one pause:—through infancy's
unconscious spell, boyhood's thoughtless faith, adolescence'
doubt (the common doom), then scepticism, then disbelief,
resting at last in manhood's pondering repose of If. But once
gone through, we trace the round again; and are infants, boys,
and men, and Ifs eternally. Where lies the final harbor, whence
we unmoor no more? In what rapt ether sails the world, of which
the weariest will never weary? Where is the foundling's father
hidden? Our souls are like those orphans whose unwedded
mothers die in bearing them: the secret of our paternity lies in
their grave, and we must there to learn it.

(486-87)

Mood gives way to mood, one vision of reality gives way to another.
Instead of acting out some cumulative progression or moving closer to an
essential truth the motion is simply a random rhythm, a cycle without a
dialectic. The Catskill eagle may dive or soar, may see grounds for
disbelief, doubt, or faith, but it can never alight. We will never achieve a
fast repose of final knowledge either of ourselves or of our world; we can
only have a self and a world in mutable motion, the experience,
sometimes satisfying, sometimes desperately wearying, of the weaving of
the warp and woof of existence.

The search for a true image of and an appropriate mental stance toward
experience in these chapters is also a search for the principles on which a
valid fiction could be constructed, and Ishmael's efforts to sort out his
discordant experience invite us to become self-conscious about our own
experience of seeing as readers of his book. Subscribing to the golden,
glad sun is equivalent to swearing by "Rabelais as passing wise, and
therefore jolly" (422); to choose the condition of darkness and woe as the
world's truth is to endorse Solomon and the poets of melancholy as
authors of the supreme fiction. Within *Moby-Dick* the first yields Stubb,
the comic Ishmael, and their comfortably solid world; the second, Ahab
and the world of ghastly mystery.

The way of truth Ishmael embodies in the figure of the Catskill eagle is
similar to the book's own way. In its alternation of portentous romance
and comic realism it commits itself by turns to each of these visions, but it
refuses to become trapped in either of them. Ishmael sees and re-creates
in his fiction a vision of dark intelligences operating in nature's visible
spheres, and ominous patterns of fate recurring in human actions; then

he soars out of this blackness and presents an equally compelling representation of exhilarating shared activity in a completely this-worldly setting. He shows a world so fully inhuman that Ahab's rite of cosmic defiance seems like a noble and necessary response; then he returns us to an everyday world in which canny skill and cheerful sociability seem like sufficient images of ultimate value. Is the world governed by a reasoning thing, or by a configuration of human will and natural chance? Is it a place of horrors, or is it more like a home? *Moby-Dick* keeps these questions open by answering them now one way, now another. In its mixed narrative we enter into each chapter's representation as if it yielded the only possible image of reality and thus the only possible basis for an answer. But if, like Ishmael in "The Gilder," we want to hold on to one of these, we do so at the cost of being unprepared for the next metamorphosis of the novel's world. And if we try to reconcile its discordant visions we are defeated by their sheer heterogeneity.

Having once gone through its cycle, we must get ready to go through it again; the novel too has no steady unretracing progress. It has, instead, the progressive motion of an open series of generated perspectives; and Ishmael's meditations explain why his book must proceed in this way. Since the world is a process of ceaseless change, no representation of reality can pretend to a final validity. It can have only the tentative and temporary validity of a moment's perspective. And an unsettled oscillation of view akin to the Catskill eagle's is the only mode of vision that can hope to be faithfully responsive to the nature of a world that is itself strangely compounded of opposites.

The peculiar willingness of *Moby-Dick* to be in uncertainty, to embrace contradictions without resolving their antinomies, is in large part a function of the character of its narrator. Ishmael's most persistent traits are his energy and his flexibility. Alfred Kazin stresses that we know Ishmael primarily as a voice, and that the "I" of Melville's narrative "sees the world through language."[7] At the level of voice Ishmael has a remarkable habit of catching a style from a situation. Entering the bar in "The Spouter-Inn" he starts talking in the melodramatic alliterations of a temperance tract; discoursing on the whale's magnitude in "The Fossil Whale" his language itself becomes full of "portly terms": "Fain am I to stagger to this emprise under the weightiest words of the dictionary" (452). He dons these styles of speaking and parades around in them with considerable flair, but he also drops them with perfect equanimity, going on to adopt another. Ishmael throws himself into his thinking with a similar verve. Whether he is arguing with comic eagerness that the spine reveals the man or pursuing with grave earnestness the relations of wisdom, woe, and madness, the pattern is the same: in face of a specific situation he catches at a large hypothesis, then presses and presses his insight, revising and extending it in line after line. As with his language, having vigorously pursued his conclusions he then effortlessly drops them. He inherits the part of Melville's mind that is more concerned with the act of diving than with attaining bottom; he refuses to be hemmed in even by his most profound discoveries.

Within *Moby-Dick* Ishmael's habit of mind can be seen most clearly in his essays of leviathanic revelation. As Leo Marx notes, he resolves to know the whale in much the same spirit that Thoreau in *Walden* resolves to know beans: he is determined to subject one piece of organic reality to consciousness.[8] His pursuit of this endeavor provides one line of narrative continuity in *Moby-Dick,* a plot of curious inquiry that embodies his personal alternative to Ahab's plot and to Ahab's more obsessive conception of how the whale is to be comprehended and subdued.

In the chapters that compose this subplot Ishmael marks off a particular aspect of the whale for scrutiny, and he also carefully specifies his own approach; he is by turns art historian, geologist, phrenologist, physiological lecturer, or expert witness for the defense. But for all the care that he takes in presenting his queer credentials and defining his angle of inquiry, his scientific procedures are almost without exception extravagant failures. Sometimes they break down because he gives in to an urge to indulge in his personal fantasies—he is, we know, both scientist and poet; in King Tranquo's whale-temple he has to record the whale's measurements crowdedly on his right arm, since he is saving "the other parts of my body" as "a blank page for a poem I was then composing" (449). But even when he adheres to his adopted approaches more rigidly, more often than not they collapse from within. In his pioneering physiognomical analysis of the whale in "The Prairie" he keeps trying to coerce his object into the categories of his science, only to run up against the final fact of the whale's utter lack of facial features. Finally he concludes:

> Physiognomy, like every other human science, is but a passing fable. If then, Sir William Jones, who read in thirty languages, could not read the simplest peasant's face in its profounder and more subtle meanings, how may unlettered Ishmael hope to read the awful Chaldee of the Sperm Whale's brow? I but put that brow before you. Read it if you can.
>
> (345)

In "The Tail" he is able to record with great objective precision the five modalities of motion of the whale's tail, but when he finishes his work and reviews his accomplishment he senses its permanent inadequacy: "Dissect him how I may, then, I but go skin deep; I know him not, and never will" (376). Over and over again Ishmael's efforts at systematic knowledge lead him to the Emersonian insight that thoughts never reach their object. The mind that moved out to incorporate the world turns back on itself and becomes self-conscious about its own procedures, discovering that the sense it had made of its objects is not that of objective fact but of a self-contained mental construct.[9] And at the same moment that Ishmael understands the fictiveness of thought he comes to see the world as "full of strangeness" (376), with a renewed sense of its final impenetrable mystery.

But this double discovery only seems to doom his inquiry to failure. By releasing him from the strictures of objectivity it actually frees him to expand his range. Instead of using them as a means to truth he can now play with closed systems of thought *as* constructs. He handles the special terminologies of law, of bibliographical pedantry, of science, and in "Jonah Historically Regarded" even of the higher criticism of biblical scholarship with the sort of feeling for their final absurdity and local delightfulness that we find in authors such as Rabelais, Swift, and Sterne, his predecessors in the tradition of learned wit.[10] He can also turn his attention from the unknowable whale to the variety of the human mind's responses to the whale. In this aspect he produces his *catalogue raisonné* of whale paintings, monstrous and otherwise, and his encyclopedic "Extracts," which he asks us to consider not as "veritable gospel cetology" but as "affording a glancing bird's eye view of what has been promiscuously said, thought, fancied, and sung of Leviathan" (xxxix). Similarly in his own encounters he is freed to present not just the whale in itself but the whole range of personal imaginings and feelings that are his responses to what he sees. If the whale cannot be finally known, no theory is entirely improbable; so Ishmael rises from the ashes of his scientific failures to proclaim his own hunches. The nature of the whale's spout can be discovered only through empirical observation, but if you get close enough to observe it "it will blind you." But "still, we can hypothesize," and "my hypothesis is this: that the spout is nothing but mist." It must be mist: after all, the whale is a genius, and from the heads of

> all ponderous, profound beings, such as Plato, Pyrrho, the Devil, Jupiter, Dante, and so on, there always goes up a certain semi-visible steam, while in the act of thinking deep thoughts.

> While composing a little treatise on Eternity, I had the curiosity
> to place a mirror before me; and ere long saw reflected there, a
> curious involved worming and undulation in the atmosphere
> over my head. The invariable moisture of my hair, while
> plunged in deep thought, after six cups of hot tea in my thin
> shingled attic, of an August noon; this seems an additional
> argument for the above supposition.
>
> (371)

If the whale's brow is not susceptible to phrenological analysis, it can at
least touch off a lively metaphorical meditation:

> Few are the foreheads which like Shakespeare's or Melancthon's
> rise so high, and descend so low, that the eyes themselves seem
> clear, eternal, tideless mountain lakes; and all above them in the
> forehead's wrinkles, you seem to track the antlered thoughts
> descending there to drink, as the Highland hunters track the
> snow prints of the deer.
>
> (344)

This mazy dance of mind is what Ishmael is left with. If the world is an
unreadable riddle, he can freely recognize the imaginativeness of his
thought and thus let each moment's experience release his own resources
of vital inventive exuberance.

Victor Brombert writes, "Reading Stendhal is an exercise in agility."[11]
Certainly this is also true of Melville. Ishmael is a master of the maze of
styles, tones, and roles, and his personal flexibility as a narrator creates a
plural and shifting role for us as readers. As the scientist of the brow he
requires us to take the position of attentive students; but when he passes
into his vision of mountain pools and antlered thoughts, yoking the most
heterogeneous things together with a gentle violence of mind that makes
the metaphysical poets seem tame and mechanical, we must become pure
poets, following with him the course of an image evolving through the
dynamic process of its own suggestiveness. The vapor hypothesis of the
spout at first seems well worth recording in our cetological notebooks, but
by the time Ishmael finishes supporting his contention we must wonder
whether he is mocking himself, or us, or some author we have not read,
or whether he has simply lost his mind. Here, as frequently in *Moby-
Dick,* he makes a communication that seems reasonable enough in a
language that seems calculated to arouse our suspicion, but that gives no
indication of what a proper response might be.[12] If we found this passage
in *The Tale of a Tub* we would know what was being parodied, and we
would recognize it as a piece of proud self-display that is also, unknown

to its speaker, an act of self-exposure. But here, finally, potential satire or self-satire seems less important than a gaudy gaiety, the gaiety of liberated thought.

Ishmael's narrative insists on and revels in its own imaginativeness. We must keep redefining our relation to this narrative, keep trying to catch the train of his thought and the nature of his tone as they change from phrase to phrase. His unfolding voice offers us as readers an experience comparable to his own in its variety, its mobility, and its alternations of faith and skepticism. He asks at one point, "And what are you, reader, but a Loose-Fish and a Fast-Fish, too?" (396), and this is what we are in his hands; both coerced by his expressions and freed to establish our own distance from them, both guided by his activity of mind and encouraged to enjoy that of our own imagination, the only condition being that we remain, as he is, in perpetual motion.

If Ishmael's efforts to know the whale can be called a plot in *Moby-Dick,* the most striking feature of this plot is its disorderliness. When he settles down to explore the whale's features in a roughly sequential manner the ship's business usually interrupts his progress. And when he is not hindered by outside interruptions he interrupts himself, taking off into a realm of wild surmise or reaching out to bring in odds and ends of whale lore that have slipped his mind. The Shandean system of progressive digression that he creates is the product of both a personal distaste for and an almost philosophical distrust of method. Like the systematization of knowledge, the organization of narrative seems to him an arbitrary imposition. He keeps his book open for the same reason that he leaves his bibliographical classification uncompleted in "Cetology"; because the world is huge, and full of unknown things, any attempt to impose a final order on its constituents must always be premature. "God keep me from ever completing anything. This whole book is but a draught—nay, but the draught of a draught. Oh, Time, Strength, Cash, and Patience!" (142). This, finally, is the spirit in which he constructs his persistently open form. The only book that can faithfully represent a world that is various and mysterious is one that is susceptible to endless extension and modification. It must leave room for each new aspect of things and each new motion of mind in a process of discovery that is, in the nature of things, still going on.

Like Stubb's, Ishmael's character and outlook are given definition in the novel by being contrasted with Ahab's. Ahab is a Hawthornesque figure of obsession and compulsion. Like Chillingworth or Hollingsworth, his thoughts have "created a creature" (200) in him; his entire energy of selfhood is channeled into a narrow intensity of purpose that domineers over him as he domineers over others. In these terms Ishmael is more like Hester. He has retained access to a whole range of emotional, intellectual, and imaginative potentials within himself, and the tendency of his fate and fortunes is to free him to engage in the new experiences that these open up for him.

In *Moby-Dick* as in *The Scarlet Letter* the opposition of these two sorts of temperaments signals the author's interest in a larger conflict between two ways of making sense of experience. Ishmael's flexible and open outlook, weaving a fabric of metaphorical meaning that it is endlessly willing to reverse or revise, plays against Ahab's sense of rigidly fixed significance. Ishmael says, "to any monomaniac man, the veriest trifles capriciously carry meanings" (235). Thus for Ahab when a school of fish deserts his boat to follow the *Goney* this natural event is a dark omen. He cannot see accident or neutral fact; everything he sees takes on a determinate meaning in terms of his own quest and fate. Nor can Ahab make room for symbolic suggestions that do not fit into his obsessed frame of mind. When a coffin-lifebuoy hints that death may lead to resurrection, he rejects its message rather than revise his vision of an inhuman world.

What most distinguishes Ahab from Ishmael is not his habit of symbolic perception but his inability to understand the meanings he sees as products of his own imagination. Personifying all that is evil and inscrutable in Moby Dick, he unwaveringly accepts his own figure as truth, as grounded in the actual nature of the world.[13] Like the Puritans of *The Scarlet Letter* he takes the meanings he perceives to be sanctioned by a cosmological order. Melville's contrast of fixity and flexibility of selfhood and interpretation, like Hawthorne's, is finally a conflict between a force that assigns determinate meanings to experience felt as derived from a higher order and a force that generates meaning from within the processes of its actual experience, entertaining these not as final truth but for the sense they make of that experience, and recognizing them as the products of its own angle of perception.

In composing *Moby-Dick* Melville strikes a balance between his own artistic urge toward undirected exploration and his desire for a more rigid formal coherence by playing off Ishmael's digressively open-ended searchings against the strict narrative unity of Ahab's quest. In doing so he also re-creates the crucial conflict I have been discussing within the novel's narrative itself. The free variety of the novel's great middle reproduces Ishmael's imaginative way; but for all its mad inclusiveness, mixture of media, and discontinuous rhythm, *Moby-Dick* returns to a continuous sequential narration conducted in a uniform style as it nears its end. After "The Grand Armada" the intervals between its major chapters of ominous tragedy grow shorter and shorter; after Ahab inaugurates the final stage of his quest by forging and demonically baptizing his enchanted weapon in "The Forge" the moments of comic realism and digressive inquiry cease entirely. Like the unsetting polar star

> Ahab's purpose now fixedly gleamed down upon the constant midnight of the gloomy crew. It domineered above them so, that all their bodings, doubts, misgivings, fears, were fain to hide beneath their souls, and not sprout forth a single spear or leaf.
> In this foreshadowing interval too, all humor, forced or natural, vanished. Stubb no more strove to raise a smile; Starbuck no more strove to check one. Alike, joy and sorrow, hope and fear, seemed ground to finest dust, and powdered, for the time, in the clamped mortar of Ahab's iron soul.
>
> (527)

The book's shift in narrative mode reproduces this change in the crew's life. As Ahab emerges to assert the full force of his bigotry or purpose the book's alternations of joyful activity and woeful insight cease, and the narrative takes on an intense single-mindedness akin to Ahab's absorption in his one dark idea. The book, like the crew, returns from "more common, daily appetites" (211) to "the full terror" (210).

In this part of the novel the current of changeful style and tone that elsewhere draws our attention to Ishmael's animated process of imagining gives way to an almost unbearably tense high style that points beyond itself to Ahab's tragic mission. Ishmael says of Ahab:

> The clothes that the night had wet, the next day's sunshine dried upon him; and so, day after day, and night after night; he went no more beneath the planks; whatever he wanted from the cabin that thing he sent for.
>
> (528)

And he says of the crewman who falls overboard:

> And thus the first man of the Pequod that mounted the mast to look out for the White Whale, on the White Whale's own peculiar ground; that man was swallowed up in the deep.
>
> (516-17)

This portentous style corresponds to the vision of the world that this part of the narrative creates. No incident is neutral now. The *Pequod*'s meetings with other ships are not occasions for the "abounding good

cheer'' (442) of sociable gams but moments of symbolic encounter. The
Bachelor is not simply a ship that has had good luck but an antithesis
revealing the *Pequod*'s joyless devotion to its end; the splash of the coffin
from the *Delight*'s funeral at sea gives Ahab's ship a baptism in death.
Nature itself yields up ominous prophecies. The gale in ''The Candles''
comes from exactly the direction in which Ahab plans to meet Moby
Dick; it destroys his boat alone. The electrical energy of the corposants
reverses the ship's needle as if nature were warning the *Pequod* away from
its appointed destination. Strange moans, heard in the ocean at night,
suggest to superstitious minds the voices of drowned men or prophecies
of impending deaths by drowning. A hawk snatches Ahab's hat as he
mounts the mast to look out for Moby Dick. We have reentered the
haunted and fatalistic world of ''The Spirit-Spout'' and ''The Jeroboam's Story,'' and in this world ''the least heedful eye seemed to see
some sort of cunning meaning in almost every sight'' (530). The
insistence of omens makes us enter into a frame of perception like Ahab's
own. The visible spheres become totally and claustrophobically meaningful, each incident charged with a fixed significance that seems to derive
not from the human imagination but from the intentional order of the
world itself.

The altered sense of significance here is also a function of an altered
sense of the shape of time. Ishmael's disjointed narrative works to
dissipate suspense. He confines our attention to the activities of present
scenes without letting these suggest what will happen next; when he
invokes the expectation of motion toward a goal he does so in order to
thwart it. Time in Ishmael's narrative takes the form Frank Kermode calls
chronos: instead of seeming to possess a larger order it unfolds as ''one
damn thing after another.''[14] We move through the perpetual present of
Ishmael's perception and inventively responsive imagination. But in the
narrative associated with Ahab time takes the form Kermode calls *kairos*:
its moments are felt as ''significant seasons,'' as ''charged with a
meaning derived from its relation to the end.''[15] We see a cunning
meaning in its incidents because they lead us forward to contemplate
Ahab's final encounter with Moby Dick. Because it is charged with the
sense of an ending in this way this narrative is genuinely and deliberately
suspenseful. It makes us pay attention to its individual episodes not for
their local interest but only as they move us nearer to a climax or enable
us to envision the form that climax will take. In its evocation of impatient
anticipation, too, the book makes us see as Ahab sees: ''looking straight
out beyond'' (121), an unremitting and direct thrust forward in space
and time, is Ahab's constant physical posture and imaginative condition.

As it approaches its end *Moby-Dick* reengages all its major thematic conflicts. Ahab's vision of the dying whale's natural reverence to the sun, his pitiful and charitable response to the mad Pip, and the demand of the captain of the *Rachel* that Ahab abandon his hunt and aid in the search for his lost son, like Ahab's son the child of his old age, all raise for Ahab the question whether the world is essentially beneficent or essentially inhuman, and the related question whether the highest value in human action lies in offices of reverence and human love or in a grim and fierce assault. Ahab enters into this debate most fully in the exquisite chapter "The Symphony." During the pause of a blazoned day "the step-mother world, so long cruel—forbidding—now threw affectionate arms round his stubborn neck" (533). In response to the loving beauty of the natural world he becomes, like Satan before Eve,

> abstracted . . .
> From his own evil, and for the time remain'd
> Stupidly good, of enmity disarm'd,
> Of guile, of hate, of envy, of revenge.

The moment opens up for him and allows him to review and understand lucidly the whole course of his life:

"Oh, Starbuck! it is a mild, mild wind, and a mild looking sky. On such a day—very much such a sweetness as this—I struck my first whale—a boy-harpooner of eighteen! Forty—forty—forty years ago!—ago! Forty years of continual whaling! forty years of privation, and peril, and storm-time! forty years of the pitiless sea! for forty years has Ahab forsaken the peaceful land, for forty years to make war on the horrors of the deep! Aye, and yes, Starbuck, out of those forty years I have not spent three ashore. When I think of this life I have led; the desolation of solitude it has been; the masoned, walled-town of a Captain's exclusive-ness, which admits but small entrance to any sympathy from the green country without—oh, weariness! heaviness! Guinea-coast slavery of solitary command!—when I think of all this; only half-suspected, not so keenly known to me before—and how for forty years I have fed upon dry salted fare—fit emblem of the dry nourishment of my soul—when the poorest landsman has had fresh fruit to his daily hand, and broken the world's fresh bread to my mouldy crusts—away, whole oceans away, from that young girl-wife I wedded past fifty, and sailed for Cape Horn the next day, leaving but one dent in my marriage pillow—wife? wife?—rather a widow with her husband alive! Aye, I widowed that poor girl when I married her, Starbuck; and then, the madness, the frenzy, the boiling blood and the smoking brow, with which, for a thousand lowerings old Ahab has furiously, foamingly chased his prey—more a demon than a man!—aye, aye! what a forty years' fool—fool—old fool, has old Ahab been!''

(534)

All the human comforts he has so single-mindedly excluded from his life—companionship, green country, marital and sexual love, even fresh food—now come back before his consciousness with an appeal that makes him half-willing to call his whole life a mistake, and half-willing to believe that to look on the beauty of a human eye is "better than to gaze upon God" (535).

Ahab's magnificent self-recognition is remarkably similar to Roger Chillingworth's in the seaside scene of *The Scarlet Letter;* and as Hester does there, so too here Starbuck steps forward to speak as a voice for the monomaniacal self's other urges, a voice proclaiming the reality of alternatives and insisting on the possibility of the free choice of a fully human self: "Away with me! let us fly these deadly waters!... See! see! the boy's face from the window! the boy's hand on the hill!'' (535-36). But even before he finishes his exhortation Ahab has retreated from the expanded moment's freedom back into his fixity of self and purpose. His self-recognition now yields him not release but a deepened awareness of the mystery of his being:

> "What is it, what nameless, inscrutable, unearthly thing is it; what cozzening, hidden lord and master, and cruel, remorseless emperor commands me; that against all natural lovings and longings, I so keep pushing, and crowding, and jamming myself on all the time; recklessly making me ready to do what in my own proper, natural heart, I durst not so much as dare? Is Ahab, Ahab? Is it I, God, or who, that lifts this arm?''
>
> (536)

He is moving toward his own embrace of Chillingworth's dark necessity. He is entering the fatalism of his last phase—"Ahab is for ever Ahab, man. This whole act's immutably decreed" (554)—a strange state of consciousness in which, as from an infinite distance, he watches himself act out the role of Ahab, the man whose special fate it is to become inhuman in his assertion of humanity, to enact an assertion of individual will that is itself part of a plot "rehearsed by thee and me a billion years before this ocean rolled" (554).

Having chosen not to choose in "The Symphony," Ahab is now ready finally to meet the white whale. And just as "The Symphony" presents one last time the novel's debate between the world of love and the world of fright, so too the superb chapters narrating the three-day chase raise in one last form the questions whether nature is intelligently malicious, whether it supports a cosmological interpretation and a determinate symbolism like Ahab's. On the first day the white whale, "as if perceiving" his assailants' strategy, dives and shoots himself beneath Ahab's boat; then he "slowly and feelingly" takes the boat's bows "full within his mouth," shaking it "as a mildly cruel cat her mouse" (541). Two days later, enraged by the hunt and "seemingly seeing" in the *Pequod* "the source of all his persecutions" (563), Moby Dick bears down on the ship. What are we to think? Does he act with intention, does he cause disaster with cunning cruelty and purposive design? Is there a reasoning thing behind the mask? In these chapters the white whale makes his long-awaited first appearance, a creature of appalling beauty and power. He almost toyingly breaks up the boats, then he tangles their lines, then he devastatingly destroys Ahab's boat and the *Pequod* itself; then he dives—and if we would know what he was and what he meant, we must go down after him. We are left where we began: confronting a sublime enigma that demands interpretation, that suggests and poten-tially supports several readings, but that finally refuses to yield up its mystery to human comprehension.

Like *The Scarlet Letter*, *Moby-Dick* is magnificently resolved at the level of action and magnificently unresolved at the level of meaning. Ahab's last stand is like Dimmesdale's confession: in his final moment of self-evaluation—"Oh, now I feel my topmost greatness lies in my topmost grief" (565)—and in his final fatal act of assault his book achieves the dramatic culmination it has moved toward so unswervingly. But *Moby-Dick* has its own equivalent to the resistance to its hero's finalities of *The Scarlet Letter*, its own equivalent to Hester's reply to Dimmesdale: "I know not! I know not!" Ahab's is a closed ending; but his story is included within Ishmael's, and his closed ending is followed by Ishmael's open one. Ishmael survives the wreck, living on to tell the story that is his personal account, the story that cannot achieve a completion or significance beyond what he himself has discovered in his experience. Ahab's quenchless feud has been his. Ahab's quest tests to the utmost the possibility of finding a fixed and final essence beyond the warp and woof of existence, and thus of escaping from the condition of uncertainty. But he survives it and resumes his ongoing orphan's life with his questions unanswered. In writing Ahab's book he similarly tests to the utmost the possibility of creating a final fiction, of committing himself to one narrative mode and its determinate version of reality, but in the end he must return to write a book that includes this as one fiction among many, a book that is more faithful to the uncertainty and variety of "this strangely mixed affair we call life" (225). At the end of this book he himself is still in the middle; and like Hawthorne's, his work ends with a conclusion that refuses to conclude. Having shown us what he can of this strangely mixed affair, having engaged us, in his narrative, in different visions of the world and clarified for us the nature and implications of the modes of perception that inform these visions, he finally releases us even from his own heterodox and relativistic outlook, freeing us to make what sense we can of an abiding mystery. He ceases to guide us so that we can share in his own central experience, the experience of active, self-conscious seeking in the face of a world that challenges us to read it if we can.

8 | The Fate of Candor: *Pierre; or, The Ambiguities*

> We ... have dreamed the world. We have dreamed it strong, mysterious, visible, ubiquitous in space and secure in time; but we have allowed tenuous, eternal interstices of injustice in its structure so we may know that it is false.
>
> Borges, "Avatars of the Tortoise"

It is only a slight exaggeration to say that since its publication *Pierre* has been a book that there were none to praise and very few to love. The reason for this is not hard to discover. It has a plot that is at best confused and at worst simply absurd. At times it insists that we take its characters and their drama seriously, but at other points it treats them with extravagant silliness. And these two moods are not always easy to distinguish: how is one to respond to, let alone love or praise, a novel whose hero and heroine exchange lines like these?

> "Conjure tears for me, Pierre; that my heart may not break with the present feeling,—more death-like to me than all my grief gone by!"
> "Ye thirst-slaking evening skies, ye hilly dews and mists, distil your moisture here! The bolt hath passed; why comes not the following shower?—Make her to weep!"
> Then her head sought his support; and big drops fell on him ...
>
> (113)

Is this meant to be poignant or ludicrous? Are we to accept it as an attempt at serious if non-naturalistic representation, or as serious parody, or as sheer flummery? Like the ambiguities of tone in *Moby-Dick,* those in *Pierre* keep our position as readers unsettled; but here the experience of unsettledness is seldom enjoyable. Next to the continuous beauty and verve of the verbal texture in *Moby-Dick* this book's overlush and melodramatic style often sounds hollow. The quantity of language in excess of its occasion here does what Ishmael's exuberant voice never does—it makes the novel's world seem perpetually out of focus. This effect is reinforced by the structure of feeling. The sympathies and hatreds the narrator expresses are so unbalanced and excessive that we can wonder about his emotional stability; we might even be tempted to conclude, as Raymond Nelson does, that the author of *Pierre* is suspiciously similar to Pierre himself.[1] In its mode of representation, its style, and its attitude *Pierre* is marked by a persistent quality of distortion. Moving through its world is like moving from mirror to mirror in a funhouse, except that we can never be quite sure whether we are in a funhouse or a real house of horrors.

After he completed *Pierre* Melville wrote to his English publisher Richard Bentley that his new book possessed

> unquestionable novelty, as regards my former ones,—treating of utterly new scenes & characters;—and, as I beleive, very much more calculated for popularity than anything you have yet published of mine—being a regular romance, with a mysterious plot to it, & stirring passions at work . . .[2]

Regular *Pierre* is not, but in some ways this description is accurate enough; the book unquestionably represents a major change of direction in Melville's fiction. The author who so masterfully narrated whale chases now describes breakfast scenes, rural picnics, and love duets; the author who created Captain Ahab and surrounded him with figures like Stubb and Ishmael now takes as his hero a genteel, milk-loving youth and places him between a light and a dark lady, Lucy Tartan and the mysterious Isabel. In composing *Pierre* Melville puts aside his achievements in adventure narrative and tries his hand at a sentimental romance. This in itself accounts for much of the book's strangeness. This genre is almost completely unsuited to Melville's own gifts and talents; and in a way, he scarcely seems to want to succeed in this new role. The odd combination of straightforwardness and secret mockery inherent in his handling of the style, characters, and characteristic situations of sentimental romance is evidence of his ambivalence, his desire both to make use of this genre and to assert his independence from it. The distortedness and chaos of *Pierre* are products of a tension, present from the first and explosive at the end, between the author and the literary form he has chosen to work in.

Melville suggests a reason for his attempt to work with this alien form when, in his letter, he links "regular romance" with "calculated for popularity." "Dollars damn me," he writes in a famous letter to Hawthorne:

> What I feel most moved to write, that is banned,—it will not pay. Yet, altogether, write the *other* way I cannot. So the product is a final hash, and all my books are botches.[3]

Melville was continually faced with the pressure of financial need, and thus also continually constrained to produce fiction that would meet the approval of a large paying audience. And from around 1848, when he began to conceive of himself as an ambitious genius, he increasingly felt this pressure as a cruel attempt to bastardize his talents. This feeling reaches the strength of paranoia in the second half of *Pierre*, with its obsessive concern with how "the bill of the baker" (258) forces the sincere artist to "hurl his deep book out of the window, and fall to on some shallow nothing of a novel" (305). Faced with this insoluble problem, Melville became fascinated with the possibility of duplicitous communication. This is what he discovers in Hawthorne's tales, which are, he exultantly announces, "calculated to deceive—egregiously deceive—the superficial skimmer of pages."[4] In this light "the *other* way" becomes not a hateful adversary but a strategic asset; the author can use the forms and conventions of popular fiction in such a way as to gain the approval of a popular audience, while at the same time smuggling a darker communication past their eyes. Clearly a wish to deceive in this way is present in Melville's letter to Bentley, and this suggests that the whole apparatus of sentimental romance in *Pierre* may embody a rather cold-blooded attempt to please and hoodwink the superficial skimmers among the reading public.

But if something of this sort is at work in *Pierre*, it provides an explanation of Melville's intentions and achievement that is finally inadequate. A strategy of cunning duplicity implies a cool detachment of the artist from his own creation; but in fact Melville is never more personally involved, or, indeed, more in earnest in his novels than he is in *Pierre*. Further, the theory of duplicity implies that Melville regards sentimental romance as a shallow nothing to be manipulated at will, an implication that belies the serious use he makes of this form and the complexity of vision he expresses through it. If we look past the surface novelty of *Pierre* we can recognize its fundamental continuity with the rest of Melville's work. He explores new aspects of his major preoccupations; and different as it obviously is from *Moby-Dick*, the form he creates for it is, like that of *Moby-Dick*, the product of a striking experiment at evolving a fictional shape in which to incarnate and study the implications of his ongoing discoveries. In terms of what it attempts, *Pierre* is a legitimate companion piece and genuine sequel to *Moby-Dick*. And considered in this way its failures can be understood not as the result of external pressures or of a collapse of inspiration but as the ultimate product of paradoxes and problems implicit in Melville's imaginative project all along. Seen in these terms *Pierre* emerges as one of the most interesting of Melville's novels, and also as the one that reveals most instructively the peculiar nature of his whole endeavor as a novelist.

The strongest continuity between *Pierre* and *Moby-Dick* lies in Melville's examination of the figure of the hero. The Pierre who walks through deserted city streets defying the "storm-admiral," pressing himself with grim joy against its "vindictive peltings of hail-stones" (340), is recognizably an urban version of Ahab on the deck. The vision of Pierre as Enceladus, the armless Titan who springs up to assault the precipice anew, particularly recalls the poignant image of Ahab, in the moment of losing his leg, "blindly seeking with a six inch blade to reach the fathom-deep life of the whale" (*MD* 181). Both Pierre and Ahab are heroes in a full-scale tragedy of aspiration, trying to act out a desire that is infinite with the limited means available to them as mortal men; and for both of them aspiration inevitably takes the form of defiance. They see themselves as living in a world governed by hostile powers, and they define and express themselves by aggressively asserting themselves against those powers. Their sense of the nature of their world compels them to live their lives as "deadly feuds with things invisible" (41).

In pursuing his inquiry from *Moby-Dick* to *Pierre* Melville shifts his attention backward in this figure's life, studying the origin and development of his condition of aggressive estrangement. Thus *Pierre* begins as a song of innocence. In his life at Saddle Meadows wherever Pierre looks he loves and feels loved in return. When he and Lucy "eye" each other they behold "mutual reflections of a boundless admiration and love" (4). His relation to his mother, for whom he feels the combined affections of son, suitor, and brother, seems like an earthly realization of an enthusiast's dream of paradise. There is no sharp differentiation of human and nonhuman at Saddle Meadows, so that this loving reciprocity holds between man and lower orders of nature as well. Pierre's horses are family cousins, so thoroughly humanized by their hereditary association with their masters that they are all but capable of speech; "never fear, pretty lady," they can seem to say to Lucy, "why, bless your delicious little heart, we played with Pierre before you ever did" (22). And the landscape of the Glendinning estate is so laden with ancestral memories that the earth itself is a "love-token" and the horizon a "memorial ring" (8) to Pierre.

Pierre inhabits the sort of world Ishmael perceives in "The Gilder" and Ahab in "The Symphony." His is, in each of its manifestations, a world formed in love, calling forth a sense of joyous oneness and sustaining a confident, comfortable feeling of human identity. At the same time, the nature of this Eden is from the first somewhat questionable. When cattle become "brindled kine . . . followed, not driven, by ruddy-cheeked, white-footed boys" (3), the golden haze is, we must feel, being laid on rather thick; when horses are "kind as kittens" (22) we can suspect that nature has been too thoroughly domesticated, too easily humanized. This place is too soft a pastoral; like the paradise of Blake's *Book of Thel*, it seems overripe, its very lushness a symptom of unresolved and unrecognized problems.

Indeed the collapse of this world formed in love has already begun when the book opens. Pierre has seen a face which, with its combination of "Tartarean misery and Paradisaic beauty" (43), gives him a glimpse of heaven married with hell. Even before he hears Isabel's story her face gives him a presentiment that grief and gloom, which he has never known, may be realities profounder than pleasure. And even before he learns, through her, of his enshrined father's concealed sins he recognizes her face as having the power to call into question all the gentle beliefs that his loving existence has sanctioned. The face whose "fearful gospel" can thus "overthrow ... all foregone persuasions" (43) begins to overthrow, as well, his sense of selfhood. He feels something pushing up in himself to respond to Isabel. "Bannered armies of hooded phantoms" (49) disembark in his soul. He discovers "infernal catacombs" (51) beneath the calm surface of his conscious mind. The vision energizes his own unconscious, forcing him to see in himself what Ishmael calls "the horrors of the half, known life."

Pierre struggles to resist his experience of revelation. He vows to be Lucy's protector, and to fit himself for this role he undertakes a strenuous program of physical exercise. By this instinctive tactic of self-preservation he attempts to work off the terrific psychic energy Isabel has awakened in him and to channel that energy back into the relationships that compose his familiar world. But this tactic can be only temporarily successful. Isabel's letter, with its revelation of her identity and of Pierre's father's sexual transgressions, breaks down his defenses and completes the process of estrangement from his earlier life that his first sight of her had initiated. The letter uncovers for him the evils on which the apparent goods of his world have been based, and in its light he rejects all natural and familial pieties to embrace a darker faith:

> "Thou Black Knight, that with visor down, thus confrontest me, and mockest at me; Lo! I strike through thy helm, and will see thy face, be it Gorgon!—Let me go, ye fond affections; all piety leave me; I will be impious, for piety hath juggled me, and taught me to revere, where I should spurn. From all idols, I tear all veils; henceforth I will see the hidden things, and live right out in my own hidden life!"
>
> (65-66)

In this speech the heroic Pierre is born. He discovers his own inscrutable foe and resolves to strike through its mask. He sees himself now not as at one with his world but as separate from it and in opposition to it. He exchanges reverence for the right worship of defiance and chooses as his true self the potentially infernal power in him that he had previously attempted to shun.

The accession of consciousness that leads Pierre to see the falsity of the human relations and values on which his youth's pastoral is based also leads him to perceive the natural world in a new way. Pausing on his way to Isabel's cottage he sees the pasture elms as shivering "in a world inhospitable" (109). The mountain masses that formerly inspired him with lyrical thoughts now seem to him "black with dread and gloom"; the slidings and crashings of their rocks suggest the "infinite inhumanities" (110) of raw natural processes. The lake reflects the sky, but this is no longer evidence of joyful reciprocity: "only in sunshine did that lake catch gay, green images; and these but displaced the imaged muteness of the unfeatured heavens" (109). He is discovering the alienness of nature that obsesses Ahab, and the final blankness that fills Ishmael with dread.

Isabel's tale reinforces these insights. In her autobiography she recalls not the memorial ring of Pierre's horizon but a ring of stunted pines whose shadows seemed to snatch at her and a ruinous house containing no tokens of a human past, no "memorial speaking" (115). The differentiation of human and nonhuman is as minimal in her world as it is in Pierre's, but for the opposite reason: nothing in it helps her to define her own human identity by offering a reciprocation of her love. In place of Pierre's fiancée and mother she remembers two grim figures who would not speak to her and who seemed "just like the green foundation stones of the house to me" (116). In place of horses kind as kittens she remembers a cat that responded to her tendered sympathy with a terrifying hiss. This figure of a consciousness stranded in a totally alien world does come to experience love and to recognize herself as different from her environment, but this increases, not alleviates, her sense of isolation and dread; she is left with the perpetual feeling of "my humanness among the inhumanities" (123). And her tale extends for Pierre the vision that her letter had opened up for him; in *Moby-Dick*'s terms, it inducts him into a world whose spheres are formed in fright.

The terrifying inhumanity and indifference of nature is only one aspect of the new vision Isabel gives Pierre access to. She leads him, as well, from the reality of a "visible world" that has seemed "all too common and prosaic to him; and but too intelligible" to a reality whose every facet is "steeped a million fathoms in a mysteriousness wholly hopeless of solution'' (128). Since she cannot give an objective location to the scenes in her tale or an objective account of how and why she was moved from one to another, the course of her life's history admits of no external explanation. And even if it did, this would tell nothing essential about who or what she is. Her ''vague tale of terribleness'' (121) can tell only how she experienced and became conscious of the strangeness of her being; it renders mystery as a permanent condition of existence.

The realm of mystery she inhabits is also one of magic. Her tale, unfolding according to the urgings of her unconscious mind, has the dreamlike organization of romance, and since it has no independent reality-principle it freely includes apparently supernatural events—a guitar comes to her with her own name written in it, and when she whispers to it, it responds with the voice of her mother. Her own mode of being in the novel is that of a creature of wild romance. She scarcely seems to exist within the contexts of manners, dress, family, and social station in which the ''all-understood'' (129) Lucy has her being; her appearance and position as a dairymaid are an incongruous disguise through which the electrical power of her ''dark, regal being'' (152) occasionally flashes forth. Nor is she bound by the laws of ordinary causality. In the weird rituals in which she conjures voices from her guitar and glows with phosphorescent light she operates, in effect, as a witch. In her presence Pierre is literally ''enchanted,'' sitting motionless as a ''tree-transformed and mystery-laden visitant, caught and fast bound in some necromancer's garden'' (128). She is his passport to a spirit-ridden realm, to the invisible spheres that elude comprehension but arouse powerful emotions of wonder and terror.

Pierre's discovery that what he has taken to be ''the solid land of veritable reality'' (49) is a surface concealing a deeper reality, one that is inhuman, inscrutable, and supernatural, marks his initiation into an Ahabian sense of the world. In *Pierre* the process of discovery presented in Ahab's case in the foreshortened form of flashback is stretched out so that we can observe all its stages. It becomes not a necessary prelude to the novel's action but the novel's action itself. In addition to this difference in presentation, Pierre's initiation takes place in a context that is in important ways different from that of *Moby-Dick*. Both Ahab and Pierre receive a ''wound'' (65; cf. *MD* 182) that is, for them, a revelation of the dark, Hindoo half of things, of truth with malice in it. Pierre's learning of his father's sexual transgressions is his equivalent to Ahab's loss of his leg; in this book the cause of the hero's wound is not a natural creature but a human sin. And where Ahab generalizes from Moby Dick's cruelty by seeing a principle of evil within the beauty of nature,

Pierre generalizes from the specific sin by seeing such a principle within the beauty of conventional social morality and religion. The evil he perceives is not natural but moral.

For both Ahab and Pierre this insight yields a new condition of selfhood. They find their identities now in a resolution, an unwavering determination to perform an act that will assert once and for all the primacy of benevolent human values against a malevolent world. In this respect Pierre's upholding of a Christlike ethic of sacrificial love in his acknowledgment and rescue of Isabel is akin to Ahab's assertion of personality against the impersonal in his hunt for Moby Dick; certainly the spirit of aggressive idealism and energetic absolutism that informs their quests is the most striking bond between them. But again, the dimension and direction of Pierre's quest are in important ways different from Ahab's. Ahab's adversary is in nature, Pierre's in society. Where Ahab seeks to achieve metaphysical justice through a physical act, Pierre aims at a much more specifically human and moral justice, to be achieved through an act of pure ethical choice.

This crucial shift in focus helps to explain Melville's change of fictional genre from *Moby-Dick* to *Pierre*. The action of the latter requires a social, not a natural setting. The form of sentimental romance enables Melville to create such a setting, to unfold a world of parents, sisters, fiancées, and clergymen. Further, in a way that no other genre Melville has worked in does, this one emphasizes human interaction: it establishes its characters' experience as lived within a complex web of loves and duties. Thus in *Pierre* the hero's wound is given concrete embodiment as a product of his specific relationships to others and to the framework of value he has inherited from them. He makes his discovery and works out his resolution in terms of these relations. His vision of evil is particularized as a discovery of his father's true nature, of his mother's pride and propriety, of Reverend Falsgrave's ethical trimming; his commitment to the cause of Holy Right is particularized as a choice to go to Isabel's aid, and the specific form that his aid takes proceeds from his sifting of his conflicting bonds of emotion and obligation to his sister, to Lucy, to his mother, and to his dead father. However unsuited they may seem to his talents, the characteristic figures and conflicts of this literary genre serve Melville as the means he needs to deal with what most interests him in Pierre. They enable him to construct a dramatic action in which he can explore the operations of good and evil in a social and moral context.

There is, then, a serious purpose behind Melville's adoption of this fictional form. This fact needs to be stressed; but as soon as it is admitted, we must add that his use of the form is anything but straightforward. In a provocative essay R. P. Blackmur writes:

The deadest convention was meant for life—to take its place.
. . . [But] Melville either refused or was unable to resort to the available conventions of his time as if they were real; he either preferred or was compelled to resort to most of the conventions he used for dramatic purposes not only as if they were unreal but also as if they were artificial.[5]

In relation to the rest of Melville's novels this contention is highly debatable, but *Pierre* illustrates Blackmur's point. The materials that sentimental romance offers Melville for the construction of a dramatic action never get fully realized or dramatized. The pairings of genteel hero and genteel heroine, or of light and dark lady, are not transmuted into living relations among the characters but remain visible as stylized formulas. A close look at *Pierre* indicates that Melville's emphasis on the conventionality of the conventions he resorts to may be the product not of his disabilities but of conscious preference on his part.

His presentation of Lucy in "Love, Delight, and Alarm" demonstrates this most clearly. What is finally noteworthy about his description of her is how little complexity of individual being it confers on her. Melville shows her as an exemplum of "lovely woman," a "visible semblance of the heavens" (24), and instead of becoming more specific as he proceeds he simply reiterates in increasingly vigorous hyperbole the fact of her angelic loveliness. But there are also odd dissonances here. To the reader who quibbles with his paean to beauties Melville replies: "By immemorial usage, am I not bound to celebrate this Lucy Tartan? Who shall stay me? Is she not my hero's own affianced?" (25). This sounds like Ishmaelean mock-heroic puffing, but taken at face value it is, really, a declaration that his celebration is an obligatory performance, that his idealization of his heroine meets the strictures of a generic requirement. Other passages reinforce this suggestion. "It is needless to say that she was a beauty" (23), the narrator tells us, because handsome, well-bred youths always fall in love with beautiful girls—as every novel reader knows. Lucy's "eyes some god brought down from heaven; her hair was Danae's, spangled with Jove's shower; her teeth were dived for in the Persian Sea" (24). If we want to know who Lucy is we must find such descriptions as this increasingly frustrating, and this seems to be their point. The narrator is dramatizing his inability to present her as anything but a compendium of all the idealizing clichés that the "immemorial usage" of sentimental romance forces him to perpetuate.

Melville's irony here is directed not at Lucy but at the literary form that engenders such pallid heroines and at the readers whose demands make it the "proper province" of novelists to deal exclusively with the "angelical part" (25) of their female characters. As the chapter continues, he hints that the problems involved here extend beyond the realm of literature, that the procedures of such fiction are themselves symptoms of a more fundamental difficulty in the relations of the sexes in America. His wildly chauvinistic hymn to American chivalry ends on a surprising note:

> Our Salique Law provides that universal homage shall be paid all beautiful women. No man's most solid rights shall weigh against her airiest whims. If you buy the best seat in the coach, to go and consult a doctor on a matter of life and death, you shall cheerfully abdicate that best seat, and limp away on foot, if a pretty woman, traveling, shake one feather from the stage-house door.

(25)

This is what the idealization of women means in practice, and the extremity of the passage's hyperbole makes the basic cruelty of this situation all the more apparent. The novelist compelled to idealize his heroine is only a special case of man subjected to the whims of women, trapped in a ritual of deferential worship that works to deny the complex personal natures and needs of both parties.

Melville's description of Lucy both involves us with and distances us from her. He presents her as a character who can figure in his dramatic action, but at the same time he asks us to recognize her as a stock figure from a certain sort of fiction, covertly inviting us to see as well the emotional problems that underlie this fiction's idealizations. His scenic art complicates our perception in a similar way. The scene in which Lucy and Pierre become engaged is as charged with exemplary sweetness and innocent love as any popular lady novelist could wish. The narrator dilates on the heavenly origin of earthly matches; he decks out his setting with all the paraphernalia of idealized courtship—copies of Moore's Melodies, swatches of bridal veils, the sheet music to "Love was once a little boy." But as the scene unfolds, it becomes clear that its sentimental setting is a cunning contrivance. Mrs. Tartan has made Lucy into a heavenly creature and surrounded her with props alluding to love's consummation in order to seduce Pierre's imagination. Lucy is simultaneously "angel" and "bait," and she is keenly humiliated at the prospect of being "tasted in the trap" (28). Lucy and Pierre are in effect victims of Mrs. Tartan's sentimental art; she constructs a scene that arouses and plays upon sexual desire without, however, letting it be frankly acknowledged or fully expressed.

In this respect she is not unlike Mrs. Glendinning, and in showing Pierre's relation to his mother Melville again presents his scenic action in such a way that a concealed sexual drama can be discerned beneath a sentimental surface. Describing how Pierre helps his mother complete her morning toilet, he insists on the wonderful tenderness of their relationship; Pierre's courtly bow, he says, shows how "sweetly and religiously was the familiarity of his affections bottomed on the profoundest filial respect" (14). But later in his narration he makes it clear that this scene too is a product of manipulation, noting Mrs. Glendinning's cunning in using such "merest appearances" as her becoming state of "dishabille" to play upon "the closest ties of the heart" (15). And then he steps back still further to indicate the unconscious needs that motivate her manipulations, to show how her "subtlest vanity" and her emotional condition as she nears her "grand climacteric" (16) make her son's adoration necessary to her.

At the end of this chapter the narrator readopts the voice of a bright celebrant:

> this softened spell which still wheeled the mother and son in one orbit of joy, seemed a glimpse of the glorious possibility, that the divinest of those emotions, which are incident to the sweetest season of love, is capable of an indefinite translation into many of the less signal relations of our many chequered life. In a detached and individual way, it seemed almost to realize here below the sweet dreams of those religious enthusiasts, who paint to us a Paradise to come, when etherealized from all drosses and stains, the holiest passion of man shall unite all kindreds and climes in one circle of pure and unimpairable delight.
>
> (16)

He sees Pierre and his mother as proof that the kind of tender affection felt in courtship can spread out from an individual object into other relations, thus raising all modes of relationship to the level of its own purity. But in light of the rest of the chapter this blissful conclusion is somewhat ironic. After all, it is not that Pierre's feelings for Lucy have been translated into his feelings for his mother. He *is* his mother's suitor; she has ensnared him into a courtship that allows her to feel as gratified as "the most conquering virgin" (16). And to say that in their relationship love is "etherealized from all drosses and stains" tells only half the story. It is not that there is no sexuality in their relation, as Mrs. Glendinning's use of a becoming dishabille shows, but rather that it is based on a sexual attraction that can never be consummated or even recognized as such. In these terms the etherealization of Pierre's love is less a glorious possibility than a psychological problem.

Melville's language in this passage is calculatingly deceptive, and the nature of its deception is appropriate to its occasion. Like much of the style of *Pierre*, it conspicuously idealizes what it represents. It hints at sexuality only obliquely and euphemistically, pointedly averting its eyes from the elements of sexual cunning Melville has previously alluded to. The rhetoric here is sentimental, and in a sense the nature of sentimentality is the real subject of the passage. The etherealized passion of reverential affection purged of sexual dross is what the sentimental religion of love worships. But what Melville's concealed analysis of Pierre suggests is that this passion not only ignores sexuality but is itself energized by a sexual interest that has been suppressed and that the idealizing fiction that subscribes to this sweet vision operates in the same way.

The separation of sex and sentiment, and the way in which sentiment is exaggerated by the suppression of sexual awareness, is the essence of Pierre's predicament. The sight of Lucy's bedroom kindles an almost fetishistic impulse in him, and the stronger his wish to see her "secret thing" (40), the more he feels her room to be a sacred place, a saint's holy shrine. His "extreme loyalty to the piety of love" (39) here, like his "reverentialness" toward his mother earlier, is made all the more extreme because the energy of his suppressed desire is transferred into it. Lucy is an "invoking angel" to Pierre *because* he feels masculine desire to be "profane" (4). Every bridegroom leading his bride to the marriage bed is, to him, a new Pluto leading Proserpine to hell. And however much he may come to see the falsities on which his life at Saddle Meadows is based, Pierre cannot escape from the cycle of repression and idealization that he has learned in that life. When, for example, he considers Isabel's avoidance of his embraces and realizes that it will never be possible for them to express affection as brothers and sisters customarily do, Melville writes that the thought of other than brotherly embraces "never consciously intruded" in his mind; instead at this impasse "Isabel wholly soared out of the realms of mortalness, and for him became transfigured in the highest heaven of uncorrupted Love" (142). He is making angels again, and in the same old way. Because he remains committed to this cycle of repression and idealization he is compelled to see himself as living in a world divided between good and evil, heaven and hell, without realizing that his own images of the heavenly are fueled by what he considers hellish in himself.

Melville's sentimental mode creates and responds to its fictional world in the same way that Pierre does to his actual one. Like Pierre in Lucy's bedroom the book's style surges with exaggerated reverence and holy awe whenever it presents a scene with a sexual dimension. Its consistent use of the word "nameless" to refer to sexual feelings parallels Pierre's inability to recognize such feelings in himself. Its light and dark ladies, its angelic Lucies and potentially demonic Isabels, are its own versions of Pierre's emotional projections of the heavenly and the hellish. The sentimental romance of *Pierre* allows Melville to re-create in the texture of his own fiction the processes of seeing and feeling that are its subjects at the dramatic level. This mode repeatedly calls attention to itself as a kind of fiction in *Pierre,* but it does this, finally, not to discredit its own worth, but rather to engage us in a consideration of the psychological dynamics out of which this kind of fiction is created—in novels and in life.

Melville's use of sentimental romance in *Pierre* is thus strikingly similar to Hawthorne's use of gothic romance in his major novels. His machinery of light and dark ladies has the same status as Hawthorne's machinery of family curses or magical letters. Both authors employ fictional means that they know at one level are ridiculous and shopworn but that they see at another level as providing them access to the treatment of certain sorts of psychic experience. They use these means to construct their works' dramas, but they avoid becoming prisoners of them or forcing us to accept them literally by making us conscious of them as means, as fictive artifices, and inviting us to consider the nature of the imagination that informs them.

Considering *Pierre* as a whole, this remarkable resemblance becomes less surprising. This novel is saturated with evidence of Melville's close study of *The Scarlet Letter* and *The House of the Seven Gables.* However much *Moby-Dick* may have in common with Hawthorne's work, it is in *Pierre* that Melville sets himself to the school of Hawthorne's craft. In his letter in praise of *The House* Melville had commented on the kind of symbolic details in its furnishings—the "rich hangings, wherein are braided scenes from tragedies," the "old china with rare devices"[6]—that reflect upon its present action and suggest that action's meaning. In *Pierre* he adds such momentarily revealed symbols to his own novel's furnishings. The way he interrupts, for instance, the scene of Pierre's revelation of his "marriage" to his mother to show the statue of the Laocoön group on the landing—"the temple-polluting Laocoön and his two innocent children, caught in inextricable snarls of snakes" (184–85) —is strictly analogous to the way Hawthorne allows the tapestry of the adulterous David and Bathsheba and her husband Uriah to come into momentary focus during Dimmesdale's interview with Chillingworth. Certainly Melville's use of the two portraits of Pierre's father to suggest the antithetical relation between his socially presented self and his secret character must remind us of Hawthorne's use of portraits of the Pyncheon family. He imitates, as well, Hawthorne's way of building a fourth dimension of historical time into his presented world. The ghosts of Grand Old Pierre and his horses are seen as present when Pierre takes Lucy for a ride in the ancestral carriage; the camp bed designed to support the bulk of his grandfather dwarfs Pierre, creating an explicitly Haw-thornesque vision of physical decline from generation to generation.

But what is most like Hawthorne in *Pierre*—and, really, least like *Moby-Dick*—is the way Melville goes about presenting the interior lives of his characters. He has mastered Hawthorne's art of psychic close-up. His extended description of Pierre's alternating impulsive resolutions and strong reactions against his own thoughts after he first sees Isabel closely resembles Hawthorne's description of Dimmesdale's responses to the townspeople after he returns from the forest. His account of how Pierre compulsively half-destroys Isabel's letter and then recoils with shock both from his deed and from the involuntary wish it reveals is equally similar to Hawthorne's account of Dimmesdale's urges to laugh and shout during his midnight vigil. Like Hawthorne here Melville follows each twist and turn in the course of a character's consciousness during a psychic emergency in such a way as to reveal without commenting on them the subterranean pressures of wish and fear that are determining that course's shape. Melville has mastered, as well, Hawthorne's delicately meticulous art of analysis. When Pierre awakens on the first day of his woe he finds himself "almost without bodily consciousness, but his soul unobtrusively alert" (93); by being careful not to move his body he keeps himself in a trancelike state in which he can contemplate the full dimensions of his grief without feeling it as his own. This passage recalls Hawthorne's description of how Hester, on the scaffold, absents herself in reverie, seeing the origins and consequences of her situation without feeling the direct pain of her actual punishment. This minutely discriminating dissection of the phases of a character's feelings is something new in Melville's work, as is his fine attentiveness to the secret resources of mind that enable his character to endure his suffering.

Melville's creative imitations of Hawthorne in *Pierre* illustrate a permanent feature of his genius, the remarkable responsiveness with which he goes out to another's art, intuitively comprehends its pro-cedures, and makes them his own. But he has not just mastered a body of techniques; he has internalized the vision of experience and the defini-tion of fiction's subject matter implicit in those techniques. His presenta-tion of the present in relation to patterns of continuity and change through time, for instance, demonstrates a new sensitivity on his part to the persistence of the past. Much more than Ahab, Pierre has a history; in this book Melville understands his hero's life as a function of his own and his family's past experience. Similarly his local debts to Hawthorne's ways of recording inner experience point toward a larger change of focus. He takes as his scene what Hawthorne calls the interior of the heart. Motives and modes of passion, the texture and dynamics of consciousness, become his novel's central subject. When Melville steps out from behind the mask of sentimentality in *Pierre* he emerges as an analytic psychological realist; and certainly what is most excitingly new in his art here, as well as what is most genuinely valuable in this novel, is the work of the author who, as James says of Hawthorne, "cared for the deeper psychology."[7] Hawthorne's study of the mind has afforded Melville a new possibility for his fiction.

Pierre is the first of Melville's novels in which he adopts the narrative stance of an omniscient outsider instead of a first-person speaker-participant. His new commitment to psychological investigation accounts for this major change in procedure. In this book he needs a narrator who can know all the important determinants of his characters' lives, one who can both follow the involutions of their feelings and comment from without on the quality of their experience and on the inner processes that, unknown to them, give shape to their experience. He needs a narrator who can see where—and why—his characters are blind, one who can understand the workings of their minds even when they are most confused or self-deluded.

The narrator of *Pierre* is not totally omniscient, and he insists that he cannot be so.

> In their precise tracings-out and subtile causations, the strongest and fieriest emotions of life defy all analytical insight. . . . Idle then would it be to attempt by any winding way so to penetrate into the heart, and memory, and inmost life, and nature of Pierre [as to show why he responds so strongly to Isabel's letter].
> (67)

His words here recall Ishmael's, who concludes his depth analysis of Ahab by alluding to continuing mysteries that "to explain, would be to dive deeper than Ishmael can go" (*MD* 184). Like Ishmael, this narrator is careful to keep his fiction from seeming to make an inscrutable reality too comfortably comprehensible. But, given this as a final qualification, he does affirm the possibility of presenting a suggestively adequate account of the "subtile causations" of his characters' feelings. He can, thus, select the items in the inventory of Pierre's memory—his father's deathbed ravings, Aunt Dorothea's tale of the chair portrait, his repressed reflections on his mother's aversion to this portrait, and so on—that show how his life had prepared him to accept Isabel's revelation as being true. The narrator can reveal elliptically, if not totally, the past that determines this response in the present. Pierre resolves to go to Isabel's aid, and only afterward realizes that this choice entails his abandonment of Lucy. But the narrator can observe a causal relation at work, can note the way in which the conscious choice of Isabel is also an unconscious choice to reject Lucy, so that "in the more secret chambers of his unsuspecting soul" Pierre willingly binds Lucy over as "a ransom for Isabel's salvation." While Pierre can only become conscious of the "subtler elements" at work in him "in their ultimate resolvings and results," the narrator can see at least in part the "concocting act" (105), the interaction of hidden psychic forces by which what is "foetally forming" (106) in Pierre develops. And by emphasizing that his method does not make mental reality totally knowable he guarantees the validity of the kind of knowledge he can possess and communicate.

As his handling of the sentimental mode prepares us to expect, what Melville most often uses his qualified omniscience to show is the relation between Pierre's conscious idealizings and his unconscious sexuality. As Pierre debates whether or not to destroy the mysterious letter without reading it his antagonistic impulses appear before him as two angels, a bad one urging selfish self-protection and a good one appealing to his unselfish magnanimity. When he rejects the counsels of the bad angel

> the good one defined itself clearer and more clear, and came
> nigher and more nigh to him, smiling sadly but benignantly;
> while forth from the infinite distances wonderful harmonies
> stole into his heart; so that every vein in him pulsed to some
> heavenly swell.
>
> (63)

In this moment of ethical ecstasy the good angel takes on the mournful beauty that is Isabel's, and she awakens in Pierre the sense of supernatural music that Isabel always arouses in him. This strange metamorphosis suggests the existence of an antagonism besides that of selfishness and altruism. It hints that his inner conflict is also between his powerful dread of the possibilities Isabel offers and his even more powerful attraction to her dark beauty. An ethical and a sexual logic are inextricably entwined in his decision, but he masks this ambiguity by presenting his sexual ambivalence to himself solely in ethical terms.

What is hinted in this episode is made explicit later. When Pierre makes his final resolution to go to Isabel he experiences a "Christ-like feeling" (106) and he urgently prays to be sustained in this exalted condition, to be bound "in bonds I cannot break" to "the inflexible rule of holy right" (106-7). But when his rhapsodic prayer is over, the narrator steps forward to "show how this heavenly fire was helped to be contained in him, by mere contingent things, and things he knew not"—by his attraction to Isabel's "womanly beauty" (107). The point here is not that his holy feeling is simply a sexual desire in disguise but that it is, unknown to Pierre, amplified by such a desire and that it is his suppression of his awareness of this desire that causes him to exalt his own ethical intentions into holy crusades. His feelings are both genuinely disinterestedly noble and genuinely sexual, but because he cannot recognize this doubleness he is bound to think of his sexual desires in terms of ethical imperatives, to conceive of his private wishes in the language of public duties, and to do so in such a way that the stronger his desire is, the more idealized his sense of his mission must be.

In uncovering the sexual logic that is hidden to Pierre the narrator becomes extremely self-conscious about his own role. He dramatizes himself as an intrepid psychic explorer: "I shall follow the endless, winding way,—the flowing river in the cave of man; careless whither I be led, reckless where I land" (107). And he insists that we understand his revelations as evidence of his special commitment as a novelist, his commitment to write nothing less than a "book of sacred truth."

> So let no censorious word be here hinted of mortal Pierre. Easy for me to slyly hide these things, and always put him before the eye as immaculate; unsusceptible to the inevitable nature and the lot of common men. I am more frank with Pierre than the best men are with themselves. I am all unguarded and magnanimous with Pierre; therefore you see his weakness, and therefore only. In reserves men build imposing characters; not in revelations.
>
> (108)

His exposure of his character requires from us a delicate respect, and also, he suggests, a measure of self-recognition. Pierre's condition, we are asked to see, is the human condition, the inevitable and common lot—"men are jailers all; jailers of themselves" (91). In affording us the privilege of seeing through his character's self-deceptions he asks us not to judge him but to see ourselves as *hypocrites lecteurs.* His psychological analyses, he implies, are an act of honesty designed to create a community of candor. They work against the habitual concealments of ordinary fiction and of the human mind itself, ours as well as Pierre's, for the sake of releasing a recognition of the real nature of human character.

I said before that in moving from *Moby-Dick* to *Pierre* Melville shifts his attention backward in the hero's life. It will be obvious by now that he also shifts his attention downward and inward. The psychological interests of this book's omniscient narrator produce a narrative that focuses less on the action and object of the hero's quest than on the inner processes through which he comes to define and act on his conception of his quest. *Moby-Dick* presents Ahab in something like the terms in which he sees himself. When Ahab addresses the gods in "The Candles" we too feel their presence, and we respect his act of defiance accordingly. Pierre is a youthful Ahab in his ranting addresses to powers beyond, but when these moments are over in *Pierre* the narrator steps forth to make us hark to a lower layer, to make us see the forces that fuel his moods of exaltation and defiance. This book has its own version of the tension in *Moby-Dick* between Ahabian absolutism and Ishmaelean relativism. Pierre, like Ahab, sees his acts as deriving fixed meaning and value from a larger spiritual order. His choice to help Isabel is, to him, less a personal decision than a heaven-sanctioned enactment of holy right. But the narrator of *Pierre* refuses to confirm or deny Pierre's conception of his quest's meaning. Instead he makes sense of it in terms of the processes of mental experience that inform it, recognizing his own account as being truthful only to the extent that it faithfully reflects the full complexity of that experience. And in this book the hero's vision is held firmly within that of the narrator, perpetually surrounded and qualified by the more open-ended and humanistic sense that the narrator makes.

To understand why Melville tells his story as he does, and indeed why he tells a story in *Pierre* at all, we need to turn to the long narrative essay that precedes Plinlimmon's pamphlet. The subject of this essay is the apparent incompatibility of the precepts which the human heart recognizes as coming from God and those implicitly obeyed in actual human behavior. The discovery of this discrepancy allows an enthusiastic youth three choices: to prove recreant and ignore the problem, to prove gullible and accept a facile solution to it, or to search for a "talismanic secret" that can "reconcile this world with his own soul." Melville continues:

> Now without doubt this Talismanic Secret has never yet been found; and in the nature of human things it seems as though it never can be. Certain philosophers have time and again pretended to have found it; but if they do not in the end discover their own delusion, other people soon discover it for themselves, and so those philosophers and their vain philosophy are let glide away into practical oblivion.... That profound Silence, that only Voice of our God, which I before spoke of; from that divine thing

without a name, those impostor philosophers pretend somehow
to have got an answer; which is as absurd, as though they should
say they had got water out of stone; for how can a man get a
Voice out of Silence?

(208)

Reconciling the soul and the world, the divine and the earthly, is a problem
that preoccupies the narrator as much as his hero. But he knows in addition
that this problem admits of no solution. And because he knows that to
obtain a voice from the silent heavens is to dupe oneself, there is only one
use to which he can put his own voice. That is to tell the story of the search
for final truths, the story of how this problematic state of being is entered
into and endured. He cannot, he knows, announce any answer, but he can
tell of the insights and impostures that cause and attend a search for one.
He must make the human mind, not the spheres beyond, the haunt and
the main region of his song, scrupulously attending to his character's
unfolding experience and at the same time maintaining a continual ironic
distance from which to observe and disentangle the self-deceptions that
that experience involves. His irony toward Pierre is, like Hawthorne's
toward Hester, itself a vehicle for genuine sympathy, but it represents as
well his only weapon against the evil deity of this novel's cosmos—
Juggularius, the juggler. The maximal lucidity with which he can
understand the mixed nature of the web of life is the only truthfulness
possible for him in a world in which Truth is eternally elusive.

But as soon as we admit the genuineness of Melville's effort to write such
a psychological novel in *Pierre*, we must recognize at once that the second
half of the book has little to do with the sort of literary endeavor I have been
describing. If Melville's essay on the soul and the world clarifies his
position and purpose as narrator, it also marks a crucial change in the
emphasis of his narration. Involving himself here directly in a consideration of the metaphysics of morals, he emerges once more as a seeker; and in
the chapters that follow he leaves the story of Pierre's unfolding experience
to explore the antinomies of heavenly virtue and worldly behavior for
himself.

As he does so the structure of his narrative becomes looser. Its chapters
take on the status of self-contained blocks rather than parts in a
continuous action as he carries his exploration into arena after arena.
"Chronometricals and Horologicals" addresses the contradictions of
"Heaven's own Truth" and "things provisional" philosophically. Plotinus Plinlimmon, the author of this pamphlet, does not pretend to have
found a talismanic secret by which to reconcile "so-called intuitions of

right and wrong" with "mere local standards" (211). His message is that dualism is itself the answer; God's and man's moral truth are "by their very contradictions . . . made to correspond" (212). What he argues for is not just a morality of virtuous expediency but a principled ignoring of the gap between heavenly and earthly. In his pamphlet's terms it is the preoccupation with this discrepancy that causes all unique and original sins, all real moral evil.

In "Young America in Literature" Melville shifts to topical satire, presenting the hurly-burly of a literary marketplace in which a new set of Augustan dunces, having taken control of the machinery of artistic production and distribution, use their business skills to deck out a trivial literature with the full regalia of high art.[8] This chapter's version of the divine soul is the genius of the earnest artist, whose spiritual gift is ensnared into this system of trivialization and debased into accepting its inverted standards of success.

The mode of urban realism through which Melville describes the changing uses of a building in "The Church of the Apostles" shows the division of worldly and spiritual as a function of social history. In a tableau worthy of James or Howells Melville evokes, through a particular place, a vision of a congregation that, having grown prosperous, grows secular as well and moves uptown, leaving their desacralized church to be subdivided into law offices. The concern for things of the spirit that society thus abandons becomes the legacy of the counterculture of crackpot intellectuals that the church slowly recruits as the tenants of its upper floors. But the new apostles seem more like society's victims than its conscience; deprived of access to actual application, their spirituality can exist only inside the solipsistic tangles of faddist systems. Very much as Hawthorne does, Melville here sees the spiritual and the practical, the imaginative and crass common sense, as hopelessly split apart in contemporary life, divided and opposed in a way that impoverishes both parts.

Melville was wise not to let a foolish consistency keep him from exploring the subjects and methods he does in these chapters; they are among the most interesting in *Pierre*. But their inclusion has a curious effect on the book's narration. The novel *Pierre* becomes, in effect, *The Ambiguities*. Instead of studying the interactions of divine and earthly as his hero comes to perceive them, or as he himself can perceive them going on within Pierre's mind, Melville turns to consider them directly in the world. By doing so he enormously expands his book's frame of reference; each chapter here provides a new context and a new order of meaning in terms of which to make sense of the enthusiastic youth's crusade. But as a result of the proliferation of these orders Pierre himself becomes something of a generalized blur. Instead of steadily unfolding the drama of Pierre's individual personal experience Melville converts his experience into a parabolic exemplum of a philosophical and cultural problem. And as these new orders of meaning begin to pile up, we come to suspect that they may be designed less to enrich than to replace the sense that his psychological narrative has made. Melville pointedly ignores the "mere contingent things" in Pierre now, and he collapses the distance from his character that his awareness of these psychic complexities had required of him. Increasingly he comes to see his hero in the terms in which his hero sees himself. Pierre becomes artistic Earnestness and Grandeur assailed by Mediocrity and Commonplace, Christlike moral man besieged by immoral society; "the wide world is banded against him; for lo you! he holds up the standard of Right, and swears by the Eternal and True!" (270). By shifting his attention from conflicts of sexual and ethical impulses within the self to conflicts between virtuous self and external evil Melville dispenses with his need for irony, moving to resuscitate as an absolute value the idealism that he had previously shown to be at least partially a product of sexual repression and self-deception.

When a sexual drama does surface in the second half of *Pierre,* it does so with the luridness of a return of the repressed. The movement from the early dissections of Pierre's hidden feelings to the scenes of the *ménage à quatre* at the Apostles' is a movement from finely controlled psychological analysis to wildly compulsive fantasy. Isabel's "am I not enough for thee?" (312) and her intense sexual rivalry with Lucy—"she shall not get the start of me! ... I will sell this hair; have these teeth pulled out; but some way I will earn money for thee!" (333)—threaten to inaugurate a new genre of hilarious, maniacal pornography. In its alternations of metaphysical and cultural philosophizing and such fantastic melodrama *Pierre* itself comes to act out the dynamic split between urgent abstraction and sexual wish that it had begun by taking as its dramatic subject.

Toward the end of *Pierre* Melville gives his own reason for refusing to engage in the sort of analysis that gave the first half of the novel its strength. Discussing Pierre's reception of disastrous tidings from Saddle Meadows he writes:

> Deep, deep, and still deep and deeper must we go, if we would
> find out the heart of a man; descending into which is as descending a spiral stair in a shaft, without any end, and where that
> endlessness is only concealed by the spiralness of the stair, and
> the blackness of the shaft.
>
> (288-89)

Both the mind and the world, he now feels, are "nothing but surface stratified on surface": "appallingly vacant as vast is the soul of a man!" (285). These statements should remind us of his earlier insistence that no final account of the mind's movings is possible: "in their precise tracings-out and subtle causations, the strongest and fieriest emotions of life defy all analytical insight" (67). But at that point he had felt that a suggestive partial account could be made, and he had resolved to follow the "endless, winding way" (107). Now he declares that way to be a dead end. If the self is a winding stair leading nowhere, or a succession of surfaces concealing a void, then no effort can possibly succeed at yielding any sort of valid explanation of the self's mysteries. Accordingly Melville resolves from now on to write a fiction of the absurd, presenting character as a series of inconsistent appearances and making no attempt to uncover a hidden logic to bind them together:

> look for no invariableness in Pierre. Nor does any canting showman here stand by to announce his phases as he revolves. Catch his phases as your insight may.
>
> (337)

Related to Melville's refusal to explain his characters is his refusal to give their experience the significant shape of a coherent plot. Early in the book he writes: "This history goes forward and goes backward, as occasion calls. Nimble center, circumference elastic you must have" (54). He implies that the structure of his narrative is flexible to the point of chaos, but in fact this is not so. He interrupts the sequence of present events to unearth the spots of time in Pierre's past that determine his feelings in the present. His plot goes forward and backward, then, because he is trying to give his novel's time-scheme a more psychologically meaningful order than that of linear chronology. In "Young America in Literature" he expands on this earlier comment, drawing a Fieldingesque distinction between the narrative organizations of history and chronicle, which he concludes: "I elect neither of these; I am careless of either; both are well enough in their way; I write precisely as I please" (244). In regard to his book's second half this is a true confession. Its massive digressions show how slight the occasions have become that can call him away from his dramatic action. When he does return to carry that action forward he is, above all, careless. He introduces details that are utterly unprepared for and that scarcely fit together with what he has already told us. How does Pierre, the author of a half-dozen sonnets and anagrams, suddenly become a literary genius? Who writes to tell him that his mother has died, and how do they know where to find him? How does Lucy, "a girl of seventeen" (56) six months ago, become legally of age so quickly, and what on earth impels her to move in with Pierre and his supposed wife Isabel? Strange! All of these can be explained as results of authorial oversights, but in the spirit of *Pierre*'s conclusion such oversights seem to be pointed and purposeful. Melville is flaunting the narrative contract, refusing even to pretend to tell a plausible story.

The absurdity of the dramatic action in *Pierre* is not just a function of its author's new metaphysical nihilism. From *Mardi* on, Melville's relation to what he calls straightforward narrative has always been a problematic one. *Moby-Dick*'s action is the hunt for the white whale, but, characteristically, Melville wants his story to be much more than this; he wants it to be about the nature of nature. However, *Moby-Dick* succeeds in raising so large a question because it is, in the first place, a quest narrative. The controlling design of Ahab's pursuit of Moby Dick gives shape to the novel's inquiry, and it gives it definite content as well. Since the question whether a principle of malicious evil exists in nature is practically embodied in the question of Moby Dick's nature and intentions, as the narrative action goes forward it is always moving toward a potential resolution of its more metaphysical queries. The story of Pierre's rejection of Saddle Meadows and his acknowledgment of his illegitimate sister similarly interests Melville less for its concrete dramatic potential than for the issues it raises. It enables him to explore the origins and value of an ethic of self-sacrificing love, and the relation of such an ethic to prevailing worldly forms. But here the specific action and the larger inquiry split apart. Pierre sorely lacks a Moby Dick. Having taken Isabel to New York, his quest no longer has a definite object to move toward. As a result, the continuing actions and interactions of the book's characters become effectively irrelevant; they no longer serve the author as a means for investigating moral problems. The middle of *Pierre* is like that of *Moby-Dick* in its digressiveness and its inclusion of all sorts of new materials and points of view, but its final function is quite different. Instead of enlarging the scope of a story that is still going on, its fragments serve to replace a story that now has little point of its own. All the novels I have discussed strive to create orders of significance independent of the dramatic one of the characters' lived experience, but in *Pierre* alone that order simply collapses. *Pierre* is the other side of Melville's artistic coin, illustrating the possibility for disaster inherent in the attempt to transcend the dimensions of ordinary narrative that succeeds so magnificently in *Moby-Dick*.

The breakdown of *Pierre* is also a function of a change in its narrator's attitude. "Nor does any canting showman here stand by to announce [Pierre's] phases as he revolves. Catch his phases as your insight may." These lines bear a direct resemblance to Ishmael's conclusion to "The Prairie": "I but put that brow before you. Read it if you can" (*MD* 345). The difference between them is one of tone. The lines from *Pierre* are really truculent; and throughout the second half of this book Melville addresses us with deliberate mockery and calculated hostility. His discussion of the position of authors before their audience—"only hired to appear on the stage, not voluntarily claiming the public attention; their utmost life-redness and glow is but rouge, washed off in private with bitterest tears" (258)—finally becomes explicitly personal:

> Still, it is pleasant to chat; for it passes the time ere we go to our beds; and speech is further incited, when like strolling improvisatores of Italy, we are paid for our breath. And we are only too thankful when the gapes of the audience dismiss us with the few ducats we earn.
>
> (259)

We are no longer trusted confidants; we are the paying public whose coins minimally support the author and whose demands also force him into a shameful self-prostitution. Instead of seeing his fiction as a means by which he can enlist us in a community of candor it becomes for Melville the medium of exchange through which we exploit and debase his gifts. And however much his careless art may proceed from a discovery of voids beneath the world's surfaces, that art must also be understood as a self-defensive and revengeful response to this felt exploitation. In making his own novel absurd he forestalls our disapproval and taunts us for having demanded a story from him in the first place.

As Melville comes to see himself as trapped within the debased fictional means by which he had initially hoped to open up new dimensions of psychic experience, his "book of sacred truth" becomes increasingly conscious of itself as a lie. The author learns what Pierre learns: that all books pack the deck, and that he is "but packing one set the more" (339). The way of presenting experience that he established in the book's first part is not a means to truth but an engendered deception. To make any kind of fiction is to pretend to make sense of what defies comprehension, and to do this is to engage in conscious falsehood. Accordingly when Melville's novel calls attention to itself as a fiction in its second part it does so in order to expose itself as a hollow cheat. As a writer of mysteries Pierre becomes "skeptical of all tendered profundities" (354) as being suspiciously similar to his own cheap concoctions, and this comment invites us to see the tendered profundities of *Pierre* itself as a novelist's sham invention.

In the charred wreckage of this book's conclusion there is a final moment of extreme beauty and power. This is Pierre's dream vision of the Mount of Titans. Like a drowning man's, Pierre's exhausted mind returns to its origins and relives, in brief symbolic form, his life's whole course. He begins on the piazza of Saddle Meadows, from which the Mount seems to offer the "purple promise" (343) of its first name, the Delectable Mountain. He has reentered the world formed in love. But as he approaches the Mount its purple haze is transformed into the verdure of a hanging forest, and "coming still more nigh" he sees through the rents in this lovely surface the inhuman and hideously repulsive landscape of a de-created place: "stark desolation; ruin, merciless and ceaseless; chills and gloom,—all here lived a hidden life, curtained by that cunning purpleness" (344). He has discovered once again the world Isabel initiates him into, the world formed in fright; and in his perception, now, of a previously concealed palisade, he reencounters something like the arbitrarily imposed but insurmountable incest barrier that bars him from her. At this point, corresponding in Pierre's life to the birth of his sense of Christlike mission, the vision becomes more frankly allegorical: in the contest of the catnip, "that dear farmhouse herb," and the sterile but immortal amaranth the narrator sees a conflict of "man's earthly household peace, and the ever-encroaching appetite for God." And now Pierre sees the rocky form of Enceladus, who, as he watches, springs to life and all armless assails the heavens. "Enceladus! it is Enceladus!" (346), Pierre cries, and as he sees the Titan take on his own facial features his cry becomes one of self-recognition: it is Enceladus that I am.

Pierre has had his moment of tragic self-discovery. When it is over, the narrator speaks around his character one last time.

> Old Titan's self was the son of incestuous Coelus and Terra, the son of incestuous Heaven and Earth. And Titan married his mother Terra, another and accumulatively incestuous match. And thereof Enceladus was one issue. So Enceladus was both the son and grandson of an incest; and even thus, there had been born from the organic blended heavenliness and earthliness of Pierre, another mixed, uncertain, heaven-aspiring, but still not wholly earth-emancipated mood; which again, by its terrestrial taint held down to its terrestrial mother, generated there the present doubly incestuous Enceladus within him; so that the present mood of Pierre—that reckless, sky-assaulting mood of his, was nevertheless on one side the grandson of the sky.
> (347)

This explication makes the myth of Enceladus figure forth the dynamics of Pierre's moral agony, the repeated binding of his heavenly ethical impulses to earthly forms and his own earthly desires. It provides as well the book's clearest explanation of the dynamics of his psychological experience, showing how his relation to his mother breeds in him an ambiguous mixture of sexual desire and reverential love that, doubled and compounded in his relation to Isabel, produces the aggressive idealism of his titanic self. The passage shouts the words "incest" and "incestuous" five times, and the hopefulness of its conclusion seems carried over from its author's exultation at finally being able to utter his book's secret password. But instead of collapsing Pierre's predicament into a merely personal psychological problem, or generalizing him into a simple figure of beleaguered virtue, Melville's explication reconciles the two. In it the book's conflicts of sexuality and idealism within the self and its conflicts between spiritual self and worldly society become figures for each other. The vision of Enceladus is as much a moment of self-comprehension for the novel as it is for its hero. Melville is not embarrassed by the feeling that he is packing a deck; in a burst of resilience he returns to the task of finding out what his story has meant and of communicating, through that story, a vision of the complexity of experience.

But this expanded moment of lucidity cannot last. Having learned who he is, Pierre must go on to act out that grim identity in a suicidal assault; and having discovered what it has been about, Melville must go on to complete his story. He returns to the enterprise he so loathes and distrusts, hurrying on to create for his work the "mutilated stump" that is the emblem of Enceladus's woe and grandeur and that symbolizes, for him, fiction's only proper ending. The only words he can find with which to conclude his last scene are these: "All's o'er, and ye know him not!" (362).

"Ye know him not!" The last line of *Pierre* leads us back to the ending of *Moby-Dick*; it reminds us that finally we know no more about who Pierre is or what his life has meant than we do about the white whale that surfaces, destroys, and vanishes. The line leads us back still further, to Ishmael's cetological conclusion: "I know him not, and never will" (*MD* 376). As it does in *Moby-Dick*, and as it always must in the work of an author who believes that reality, like its creator, passes understanding, our adventure in knowledge culminates in a discovery of the permanence of our ignorance.

But in *Pierre* this discovery is more devastating. As Ishmael's mind plays across its objects they come to seem more and more real, if less and less knowable; whatever else we may be left to wonder about at the end of his tale, we do not doubt the actuality of the whale. It is just this that becomes questionable at the end of *Pierre*. The actuality it presents comes to seem like a chimera, or an imposture, or like the insubstantial fabric of its creator's nightmare. It gives us the feeling Pierre describes to Isabel: "it is all a dream—we dream that we dreamed we dream" (274). Reader and author have dreamed a world in which others dream other worlds, and as we realize that they have become trapped in their dream we see that this is our own condition as well. In *Pierre* reality becomes not just unknowable but finally unreal.

The intuition that fiction packs the deck by purporting to make experience comprehensible is not new to Melville in *Pierre*. Ishmael is continually conscious that he is attempting "the classification of the constituents of a chaos" (*MD* 129), that the sense he makes of his world is created by his own mind rather than discovered in the world itself. But this recognition, rather than inhibiting it, is the very basis for his own art. By passing on to us his own awareness that the orders he makes are imaginative constructs, he can keep using his imagination to make a tentative and temporary sense of something that eludes final knowledge. What is new in *Pierre* is Melville's feeling that such constructs are not excellent falsehoods but out-and-out lies.[9] The philosophers who bring forth a voice from the Silence are either deluded or impostors; Pierre himself is both by turns, a fool to his own theory of virtue and a knave as author of a "coiner's book" (357); even the Tale of Isabel is finally suspected to have been "forged for her, in her childhood" (354); and as if this spirit were infectious, Melville's own book reveals itself as a deception and a fraud. *Pierre* comes to allude to its own fictionality, not, as *Moby-Dick* does and as it started by doing, to extend the validity of imaginative art as a means to qualified truth, but to demonstrate the illusoriness and invalidity of all imaginative creations.

Because reality remains in place and imagination self-assured in *Moby-Dick*, Ishmael's "I know him not" leaves open for him the possibility of vital encounter. His mind can keep moving out, releasing its own resources in the presence of things, rolling on through the series of provisional positions that make up his draught of a draught. Because reality collapses into dreamlike fantasy in *Pierre* all that its author has left as material and occasion is the contents of his own mind, and by the end of the book he has already discredited the possibility that what he makes out of what he imagines can have any sort of value. He sees thought not only as not reaching its objects but as insincere in its own terms; and having arrived at this point, he had better turn his mind off. *Pierre* is a draught of a draught in a more desperate sense: it traces its author's discovery of the impossibility of his own creative project, and the moral of its story rules out even the minimal faith in his own work that the task of revision would require of him.

Melville's movement from a sense of literary and mental fictions as means to a tentative truth in *Moby-Dick* to a sense of them as means to deception and delusion in *Pierre* recapitulates Hawthorne's movement from *The Scarlet Letter* to *The Blithedale Romance. Blithedale* is the exact contemporary of *Pierre*—both were completed in April 1852—and the resemblances between them are astonishing. Both books are fascinated with the phenomenon of involuntary self-deception, and specifically with the ways in which buried sexual desires become displaced into the social and ethical idealism espoused by the conscious mind. Pierre's Christlike crusade is energized by exactly the same process of transference that energizes Zenobia's feminism, Hollingsworth's reform movement, and Coverdale's commitment to his role as dutiful observer. But having presented a strikingly ironic vision of the permanent gap between ideals as they are consciously entertained and their true psychic origins, both Hawthorne and Melville become extremely uncomfortable with what they have shown, and accordingly their books become contorted and chaotic. Their dramatic plots become a source of embarrassment to them—the number of overlooked or unexplained events in *Pierre* is no larger than that in *Blithedale;* they take flight from these plots, steering their work in new directions.

One of these is cultural satire. "Young America in Literature" and "The Church of the Apostles" are Melville's equivalents to Hawthorne's scenes in the urban barroom and the village hall. Both of them turn their fiction outward toward contemporary society, and what they find there is remarkably similar—a world in which art is changed into artifice, form takes the place of substance, and a spiritual past gives way to a secularism without valid alternatives (the community of the Apostles is, if anything, even more effete than the Blithedale community). Another new direction is evident in such chapters as "Fauntleroy" and "Chronometricals and Horologicals," interpolated forms in which Hawthorne and Melville use a new method of articulation to translate thier characters' actual relationships into more conceptual terms.

All these developments have the function of distracting us from and attempting to reverse the implications of the books' psychological dramas. Their satires work to make the degradation of the spiritual seem like a problem of culture, not of character. The conceptual schemata they introduce strive to resuscitate ideals that their own psychological analyses have undermined. Melville's image of Pierre as chronometrical, a heavenly soul assaulted by the world, tries to make him a genuine repository of spiritual purity in exactly the same way that Hawthorne's tale of the veiled lady and the evil wizard tries to restore the value of Priscilla.

Finally both authors return to their dramatic actions, resolving them with strongly imagined tragic endings. But both books have another ending as well, one that carries the weight of their authors' confusion and uneasiness. "All's o'er, and ye know him not!" is *Pierre's* version of "I—I myself—was in love—with—PRISCILLA!" It stands the rest of the book on its head, casting into doubt all the sense it has made; and as such it sums up a powerful streak in both books suggesting that there is nothing but deception and self-deception, in fiction or in life.

Melville's pain at his novel's internal failure is more extravagantly displayed than Hawthorne's, but it takes a similar shape. Like Hawthorne in the preface to *Blithedale,* he feels that the fictional means he has employed have backfired. Having set out to use the conventions of sentimental romance for his own purposes, he finds that they have used him. They have trapped him into having to complete a story he does not wish to tell, and trapped him too into presuming an authority he cannot believe in; an omniscient analytic narrator becomes, to him, the same as a "canting showman" (337). And because they have failed to serve him, he takes on as Hawthorne does an exacerbated sensitivity to his means *as* means, to fiction as a set of conventional procedures. Finally Melville's brutal assaults on his readers and on American literary culture are his versions of Hawthorne's more politely restrained complaints about the failure of American readers to grant him the conventional privileges available to romancers in the Old World. They blame the hardship of their lot as novelists on the forms available to them, on their audience, and even on their country.

Clearly the sense of fiction as deception and delusion that they express in *Blithedale* and *Pierre* is not simply a newly adopted philosophical position or artistic premise. They arrive at this sense by discovering new implications in the methods and themes that have characterized their work with the novel all along. This sense is also the expression of their despair at a specific failure, a failure that many factors have joined to produce—their relation to their public, their relation to their literary tools, as well as confusions and tensions within their visions themselves.

In writing *Pierre* Melville inaugurates his own age of suspicion; but what he does not realize here is that the age of suspicion has pleasures and possibilities of its own. This is what makes room for his later work. The declarations that signal the defeat of his fictional endeavor in *Pierre* can themselves be seen as indicating what is left for him. That the heart of man is a spiral stair leading down to no discoverable bottom is a cause for despair only to an author who had all along secretly counted on his ability finally to decipher the riddle of the self. A world knowable only as surface stratified on surface is an impossible situation only to an author who has always secretly hoped that he could discover its essential nature. Melville learns that he must accept more unequivocally the finality of the mysteries that have been his subject. When he stops using it to search for solutions, he finds the multiplicity of uses to which his fiction can be put in creating an "excellently illustrated re-statement of a problem" (210).

The results of this can be seen in works like "Bartleby" and *Benito Cereno*. In these we see into an enigma through a mirror:[10] the author has absconded with himself, leaving in his place an account of the progress of someone else's consciousness down the spiral stair into the mystery of another's being. Because Melville represses his own desire to dive here he can write a strictly controlled narrative fiction that at the same time continually illuminates the gap between the mind's fictions and the nature of its objects. What he has learned about the deceptions implicit in fictional conventions in *Pierre* gives him one subject for *The Confidence-Man*, and what he has discovered about the disjunctions between endorsed values and the real nature of the mind's and the world's behavior gives him another; and in both cases, rather than outraging him as they did in *Pierre*, these insights serve as the basis for spirited play. The vision of surface stratified on surface in *Pierre* suggests, as well, the method of *The Confidence-Man*; in its presented world every certainty at one level proves to be a deception at another, and we are led from level to level in such a way as to realize that there is no final layer.

John Seelye accounts for these later developments by saying that as Melville came to terms with mystery, he "celebrated that final acquiescence by withdrawing behind mysteries of his own."[11] His later works whet our desire for meaning only to make us conscious of meaning's masquerade. And the author no longer accompanies us on the expedition of sense-making; he leaves us alone in the labyrinth. Melville realizes now that in seeking "to evolve the inscrutable" (*M* 352) his art's fictiveness, not its truth, is its only means to truth, and that the only truth it can enact is that of deception.

Moby-Dick and *Pierre* are written before Melville makes his withdrawal into mysteries of his own, although both of them indicate why that withdrawal is necessary. In them he is still trying to "probe the circle's center" (*M* 352). His acquiescence to the mystery is equivocal here; or rather he is engaged, both as a thinker and as an artist, in a dialectic of acquiescence and resistance. He could not have prolonged the pause within which this dialectic operates forever. The search for final truth has been defeated too many times, the mind has discovered the fictiveness of its representations of the real too often. But it is out of this dialectic that the lively and self-exploring forms of *Moby-Dick* and *Pierre* are born; and however much we may respect the intellectual consistency of his final withdrawal, we must still admire these forms as tokens of the earnestness, the inventiveness, and the honesty with which Melville endured and enriched the pause.

IV |
Conclusion

The relation of art to life is of the
first importance especially in a
skeptical age since, in the absence
of a belief in God, the mind turns
to its own creations and examines
them, not alone from the aesthetic
point of view, but for what they
reveal, for what they validate and
invalidate, for the support that
they give.

Wallace Stevens, "Adagia"

9 | The Unencumbered Travelers

On 20 November 1856 Hawthorne wrote in his English notebook:

> A week ago last Monday, Herman Melville came to see me at the Consulate, looking much as he used to do (a little paler, and perhaps a little sadder), in a rough outside coat, and with his characteristic gravity and reserve of manner.... I felt rather awkward at first; because this is the first time I have met him since my ineffectual attempt to get him a consular appointment from General Pierce. However, I failed only from real lack of power to serve him; so there was no reason to be ashamed, and we soon found ourselves on pretty much our former terms of sociability and confidence. Melville has not been well, of late; he has been affected with neuralgic complaints in his head and limbs, and no doubt has suffered from too constant literary preoccupation, pursued without much success, latterly; and his writings, for a long while past, have indicated a morbid state of mind....
>
> He stayed with us from Tuesday till Thursday; and, on the intervening day, we took a pretty long walk together, and sat down in a hollow among the sand hills (sheltering ourselves from a high, cool wind) and smoked a cigar. Melville, as he always does, began to reason of Providence and futurity, and of everything that lies beyond human ken, and informed me that he had "pretty much made up his mind to be annihilated"; but still he does not seem to rest in that anticipation; and, I think, will never rest until he gets hold of a definite belief. It is strange how he persists—and has persisted ever since I knew him, and probably long before—in wandering to-and-fro over these deserts, as dismal and monotonous as the sand hills amid which we were sitting. He can neither believe, nor be comfortable in his disbelief; and he is too honest and courageous not to try to do one or the other. If he were a religious man, he would be one of the most truly religious and reverential; he has a very high and noble nature, and better worth immortality than most of us.[1]

This is in many repects a somber passage. Two old friends meet and discuss annihilation in a cold and arid landscape. Five years earlier Melville had written: "Whence come you, Hawthorne? By what right do you drink from my flagon of life? And when I put it to my lips—lo, they are yours and not mine. I feel that the Godhead is broken up like the bread at the Supper, and that we are the pieces."[2] But by 1856 he and Hawthorne had lost touch with each other for four years, and their "infinite fraternity of feeling" is replaced, here, by an initial sense of distance and a hint of failures of mutual aid; the passage has the added pathos of recording their last meeting. Melville had written in 1851, "when the big hearts strike together, the concussion is a little stunning."[3] This remark measures another heavy change: if the continuing intimacy of their relationship is now past, so is the period of stunning artistic achievement that accompanied their personal encounter. The Hawthorne whom Melville calls on is not an author but a United States consul; and Melville himself is a convalescent tourist, driven to this, as Hawthorne suggests, at least partly by the strains and accumulated frustrations of his literary preoccupations. The passage reads like an epitaph on their creative encounter as men and as artists.

But if these figures seem a little paler and sadder, in other ways they look much as they used to. Melville is still the man who dives, obsessively steering the talk toward ontological mysteries; and having enunciated a position toward these, he does not rest but gets ready to press off in search of another. By a beautiful twist Hawthorne converts the actual seting into a metaphorical expanse onto which he projects the figure of Melville, an outcast Cain doomed to wander without rest through the deserts of metaphysical speculation. Characteristically, Hawthorne obscures his own presence, both in the passage and apparently in the conversation as well. Instead of asserting himself he records the life of another, sensitively analyzing the conditions of soul that lead this other to think and feel as he does. He is exhibiting the same gift he displays in his novels, and here as in his novels this act of imaginative penetration itself expresses not cold detachment but genuine sympathy and even admiration. If the passage reads in one sense like an epitaph, in another it records the persistence of the mental powers that distinguish Hawthorne and Melville as men and that justify their claims to our attention as authors.

When Hawthorne and Melville meet in Liverpool they have passed out of the chronological period and the phase of artistic creation that have been the subjects of my study; the meeting recorded in the *English Notebooks,* with the backward glance it affords on their relations and achievements, is as good a place as any for this book to stop. There is no point, here, in rehearsing the shared features that, I have argued, give their achievement its peculiar identity, or in retracing the parallel patterns that I have tried to demonstrate in their works' development; indeed if anything needs emphasis at this point it is not their work's unity but its prodigious diversity of method and concern. But some tantalizing questions remain: Where does their particular kind of art come from? Why does it take the form it does? If Hawthorne and Melville have anything to teach, it is a wariness about assuming that such matters are susceptible of final explanations. But they also believe in trying; and in their spirit we might look again at Hawthorne's passage, not for the answers it yields to these questions but for the hints it provides.

"He can neither believe, nor be comfortable in his unbelief"—this is perhaps the most important and accurate assessment ever made of Melville. Certainly the expansiveness of his novels is the product of an imagination impelled to ask questions about the order of the world that require answers taking the form of religious assertions: What talismanic secret can reconcile the world's observed behavior with the injunctions of the Sermon on the Mount? "Where is the final harbor, whence we unmoor no more?" His insistence on asking such questions is matched by his refusal to accept answers to them, to moor in the final harbor of any absolute belief.

Melville reciprocates Hawthorne's assessment in a letter we have already looked at:

> There is a certain tragic phase of humanity which, in our opinion, was never more powerfully embodied than by Hawthorne. We mean the tragicalness of human thought in its own unbiassed, native, and profounder workings. We think that in no recorded mind has the intense feeling of the visable truth ever entered more deeply than into this man's. By visable truth, we mean the apprehension of the absolute condition of present things as they strike the eye of the man who fears them not, though they do their worst to him,—the man who, like Russia or the British Empire, declares himself a sovereign nature (in himself) amid the powers of heaven, hell, and earth. He may perish; but so long as he exists he insists upon treating with all Powers upon an equal basis.[4]

For all his efforts to explain what he means Melville remains rather obscure here, but what he seems to be asserting is something that does genuinely characterize Hawthorne's art. We can see this in Hawthorne's meticulous analyses and in his authoritative narrative stance: he asserts his own right to try to account for and evaluate experience, organizing it and presenting it as it strikes the impassive and penetrating eye of a human observer.

Hawthorne never says NO! in thunder. He does not, as Melville does, see himself as locked in a contest with Powers, and in any case thundering is not his way. But he does tacitly refuse to pledge allegiance to the visions of absolute orders; the sense he makes in his novels is a human sense. Whatever he considered himself in his life, in his fiction Hawthorne is no more a believer than Melville is.

In fact both Hawthorne and Melville are remarkably detached from the doctrines and dogmas of any transcendent system of order or value. The experience that most interests them is exactly that which lies outside of accepted frameworks of evaluation, and they have no moral preconceptions to short-circuit their access to this experience or to prematurely determine their attitudes toward it—to convert Hester Prynne into a mere adulteress, for instance, or Captain Ahab into a mere blasphemer. In Melville's terms they belong to the band of "unincumbered travellers." They resist acceptance of any code of final belief, religious, cosmological, ethical, or aesthetic; and as a result they can easily pass through the gates at which the "*yes*-gentry," loaded down with the heavy baggage of their own affirmations, get halted.[5]

Melville's discussion of a tragic phase of humanity describes a nineteenth-century phenomenon that includes his own and Hawthorne's work and extends beyond it. This is, in the largest terms, a movement from a vision of the world as governed from above by a divine order to a vision of it as governed from within by its own inherent laws, a movement from a world that makes sense in terms of higher causes to one to be understood, in John Stuart Mill's words, through "our experience, and what can be inferred from our experience by the analogies of experience itself."[6] Specifically in terms of American fiction the phase that Hawthorne and Melville help to inaugurate stretches forward into the work of realists like James, Twain, and Howells. The "visable truth" is what these authors address themselves to. Transcendence is banished as a presence from their fictional worlds, and it is also banished as a moral sanction. They are all intensely ethical in their concern, but they express this concern by observing their characters' attempts to discover an adequate system of value for themselves on the basis of their own experience; as authors they refuse to entertain moral ideals more absolute than those their characters have achieved or expressed in their lives. They present a complex actuality, and they give to it only as much order, significance, and value as they can see emerging from that actuality itself. They know that their own accounts are not final truth but only what strikes the eye of a human observer—Melville's phrase looks forward to their own emphases on point of view and center of consciousness—but this is, for them, the only kind of truth worth possessing or believing in.

Invoking this later generation of novelists helps to show where Hawthorne's and Melville's work is tending; but there are also important differences between their art and that of the American realists. In particular, they do not so easily confine themselves to a world whose only dimension is the experiential one. Some comparisons will make this clear. Arthur Dimmesdale and Huck Finn make an incongruous couple, but their dramas have interesting similarities. They share as their central experience a moment of choice, and both see the alternatives before them—fleeing with Hester or confessing, traveling on with Jim or returning him to his owner—as leading to damnation or salvation. The cycle of guilt, self-scrutiny, repentance, and cleansing action that Huck's conscience puts him through as he resolves to write his letter is exactly the same as the cycle that leads Dimmesdale to his public self-exposure. But the way that this orthodox theological vision is presented in the two scenes is quite different, and the difference is not just that Huck finally decides to go to hell. Twain's scene keeps us firmly rooted in the human plane. His character thinks in terms of a larger spiritual order, but we do not see that order; we see his heaven and hell as psychological images internalized from the deformed conscience of his society. Dimmesdale's orthodoxy is also seen as the product of the interaction of his inner nature and his society's frame of belief, but Hawthorne does not simply reduce it to the level of sociopsychology. The mysterious scarlet letter that he uncovers is a dreadful witness that a supernatural order might really exist and act on human sinners. As a result, although Hawthorne does not endorse his theological conception of sin, he does not make it as easy to dismiss as Twain does; its validity remains a real possibility in *The Scarlet Letter.*

Howells's *A Hazard of New Fortunes* is, like *Pierre,* a study of the impulse to loving self-sacrifice in conflict with personal selfishness and the institutionalized self-interest of capitalist society. Howells too embodies this impulse in characters devoted with incandescent single-mindedness to pure spiritual principles; the revolutionary Lindau and the Christian socialist Conrad Dryfoos are his Pierres. But it is telling that these figures are on the margins of Howells's action, not, as with Melville, at its center. He presents such spirituality obliquely, as it is seen and understood by the more normative human consciousness of Basil March. And he is much more willing than Melville is to rest in uncertainty about its final meaning and value. Melville cannot say what heaven's own truth is, but the desire to uncover such a truth and to see his character under its aspect is urgent in *Pierre* in a way that it is not in Howells's novel. As with *The Scarlet Letter,* the reality of a transcendent order is powerfully present as a possibility in Melville's book.

What this suggests is that if Hawthorne and Melville do not believe, they are also not comfortable in their unbelief. They are not so much at home in a demystified world as these later novelists are; they do not find it so easy to disregard the possibility that the condition of present things may have a more absolute meaning than what strikes the human eye. Melville's image of the artist as one who "declares himself a sovereign nature (in himself) amid the powers of heaven, hell, and earth" fits himself and Hawthorne as it does not fit a Twain or a Howells. The powers are still vital presences to them. The "visable truth" of their experiential accounts is forged in the face of a strong sense that there is or may be another order than that of the visible, and a more essential order of truth.

The tension between their refusals to affirm such an order and their refusals to deny it helps to explain the sorts of subjects they choose for their fiction. Hawthorne's novel of adultery is a study of passionate desire at odds with the restrictions of conscience and society, but it is also more than that. On the basis of these conflicts he erects a larger one, between a humanistic art and morality achieved in response to the complex needs of the self and an orthodox art and morality that claims to have a divine sanction. The whole thrust of *Moby-Dick* is toward determining whether an invisible intelligence governs the visible spheres, and if so, what its nature is. In pairing Ahab and Ishmael Melville engenders a conflict between two approaches to this endeavor similar to the one Hawthorne establishes in another context—between an outlook that sees the world as ruled by and as making fixed sense in terms of a supernatural design and an outlook that forges models of the world on the basis of its own actual experience, flexibly modifying these to fit the full complexity and variety of that experience. *Blithedale* and *Pierre* are about characters who oppose a secular society by establishing systems of relationship that they believe to be endowed with genuine spiritual value; the antithesis to their conceptions is expressed in a strain of narrative irony that shows their spiritual ideals as indexes to a psychological problem. Hawthorne and Melville trace the same pattern of opposition in a rich variety of contexts in their novels, the opposition between a transcendent and an experiential vision. Instead of believing in the one or accepting the secure skepticism of the other they imagine situations in which the two are placed in dramatic conflict; and their fiction's actions, rather than moving toward a resolution of their differences, open out onto a full-scale exploration of them in their opposition.

Hawthorne's and Melville's distance from the later novelists' demystified sense of reality also involves a distance from their artistic methods.

James's *The Bostonians* shows the difference most clearly. His satire of New England social crusaders draws heavily on *The Blithedale Romance,* but he carefully suppresses Hawthorne's evil wizards and clairvoyant maidens —he lops off the romance. From the hands of these later authors we might expect a *Scarlet Letter* without magical letters, or a *Moby-Dick* without spirit spouts or strange fatalities. To think of these novels deprived of these features illuminates what they serve to accomplish. It is the romance magic of diabolical villains and supernatural signs that gives the Puritans' divine order of good and evil a vital presence in *The Scarlet Letter.* It is the romance suggestions attached to Moby Dick that give Ahab's vision of a purposeful spiritual order plausibility and imaginative urgency in *Moby-Dick.* Romance is the fictional method through which Hawthorne and Melville make a transcendent order a real possibility in their novels. But if they do not suppress romance, they do not succumb to it either. Its enchanted vision is always balanced against another one— Ahab's plot against the naturalistic narrative of ordinary whaling, *The Scarlet Letter*'s diabolism against its analytic psychological realism, *Blithedale*'s war of spirits against its complex dramatic presentation. As a result their novels act out a conflict of fictional modes parallel to their dramatic ones—a conflict between an account that arranges experience in the context of a spiritual system and an account that discovers its order within the processes of actual life. And in their fiction's form as in its action, rather than committing themselves to the one or the other of these accounts they engender an encounter between them, an encounter through which they can explore the sort of significance that each of them achieves.

Poised between the yes-gentry's affirmations of a larger order and later unencumbered travelers' confident disregard of such an order, Hawthorne and Melville occupy a precarious perch. The confusions resulting from their embrace of and resistance to irony in *Blithedale* and *Pierre* demonstrate clearly enough how difficult the balancing act required of them is. But their failures in these novels illuminate the conditions on which their successes have also been achieved. In their best work they master this position, taking its very ambiguities as their subject and evolving a form adequate to the open-ended examination of these ambiguities. In doing so they produce a fiction that is less interesting for the system of human values it has to present than for its study of the nature of such systems, a fiction less important for the vision of reality it re-creates than for its examination of the operations and implications of such visions.

In "Hawthorne and His Mosses" Melville presents the truth-seeker of

Hawthorne's "Intelligence Office" as an embodiment of "that lasting temper of all true, candid men—a seeker, not a finder yet."[7] He identifies this figure as Hawthorne; compounding his generous fallacy, we might see it as reflecting himself as well. Their commitment as novelists is to the process of exploration. In its method and its openness of view theirs is in the fullest sense an experimental art; and remarkable as it is for its discoveries and its perfections of achievement, it is to be admired even more for the lively inventiveness and the strict seriousness with which it keeps reformulating and pursuing its concerns. If Hawthorne and Melville are better worth immortality than most of us, it is for the record their work provides of their own active seeking, and for the vision it offers us of the possibilities and values of the search itself.

Notes

INTRODUCTION

1. For a more extensive chronological listing of novels produced in the first half of this period see Kathleen Tillotson, *Novels of the Eighteen-Forties* (Oxford: Clarendon Press, 1954), pp. 2-6.

2. Journal entry for 4 November 1849, in Eleanor Melville Metcalf, ed., *Journal of a Visit to London and the Continent by Herman Melville, 1849-1850* (Cambridge, Mass.: Harvard University Press, 1948), p. 18.

3. Herman Melville to John Murray, 25 March 1848, in Merrell R. Davis and William H. Gilman, eds., *The Letters of Herman Melville* (New Haven: Yale University Press, 1960), pp. 70-71.

4. Ibid., p. 71.

CHAPTER ONE

1. See R. S. Crane, "The Concept of Plot and the Plot of *Tom Jones*," in *Critics and Criticism: Ancient and Modern,* ed. R. S. Crane (Chicago: University of Chicago Press, 1952), pp. 616-47 and especially pp. 620-23.

2. Northrop Frye, "The Road of Excess," in *Myth and Symbol: Critical Approaches and Applications,* ed. Bernice Slote (Lincoln, Neb.: University of Nebraska Press, 1963), p. 7. See also Joseph Frank, "Spatial Form in Modern Literature," *The Widening Gyre: Crisis and Mastery in Modern Literature* (New Brunswick, N.J.: Rutgers University Press, 1963), pp. 3-62.

3. For a judicious discussion of different kinds of interest that fiction creates and of conflicts of interest in fiction see Wayne C. Booth, *The Rhetoric of Fiction* (Chicago: University of Chicago Press, 1961), pp. 125-36.

4. W. J. Harvey, *Character and the Novel* (Ithaca, N.Y.: Cornell University Press, 1965), p. 28. See also Henry James, "Preface to *The American*," in *The Art of the Novel,* ed. R. P. Blackmur (New York: Charles Scribner's Sons, 1934), pp. 20-39, and Georg Lukács's discussion of the relation of novel and epic forms to "the extensive totality of life" (p. 46) in *The Theory of the Novel,* trans. Anna Bostock (Cambridge, Mass.: M.I.T. Press, 1971), especially pp. 40-69.

5. William Butler Yeats, "Emotion of Multitude," *Essays and Introductions* (New York: Macmillan, 1961), pp. 215-16.

6. Henry James's description of Donatello's status in *The Marble Faun*

perfectly catches the effect such characters create: "He is of a different substance from them; it is as if a painter, in composing a picture, should try to give you an impression of one of his figures by a strain of music." *Hawthorne* (1879; rpt. New York: Collier Books, 1966), p. 144.

7. Barbara Hardy, *The Novels of George Eliot* (New York: Oxford University Press, 1967), p. 29.

8. Kathleen Tillotson discusses character modes in *Dombey and Son* in *Novels of the Eighteen-Forties,* pp. 163-75. On the overlapping of realistic and romantic traditions in nineteenth-century fiction see Leslie Fiedler, *Love and Death in the American Novel,* rev. ed. (1966; rpt. New York: Dell, 1969), pp. 128-29, 440, and passim; and Donald Fanger, *Dostoyevsky and Romantic Realism: A Study of Dostoyevsky in Relation to Balzac, Dickens, and Gogol* (Chicago: University of Chicago Press, 1965), pp. 3-27.

9. Richard Chase, *The American Novel and Its Tradition* (Garden City, N.Y.: Doubleday Anchor Books, 1957), p. ix. On romance and the American novel see, in addition to Chase's book, Fiedler, *Love and Death,* and Joel Porte, *The Romance in America: Studies in Cooper, Poe, Hawthorne, Melville, and James* (Middletown, Conn.: Wesleyan University Press, 1969). In *American and English Fiction in the Nineteenth Century: An Antigenre Critique and Comparison* (Bloomington: Indiana University Press, 1973) Nicolaus Mills mounts a spirited attack on the opposing of English and American fiction as novelistic and romantic.

10. See Northrop Frye, *Anatomy of Criticism* (1957; rpt. New York: Atheneum, 1966), pp. 33-35, 131-40, and "Myth, Fiction, and Displacement," *Fables of Identity: Studies in Poetic Mythology* (New York: Harcourt, Brace, and World, 1963), pp. 21-38.

11. Chase, *American Novel and Its Tradition,* p. viii.

12. The classic discussion of this kind of form in Shakespeare's plays is the chapter "Planes of Reality" in S. L. Bethell's *Shakespeare and the Popular Dramatic Tradition* (London: Staples Press, 1944), pp. 31-41. See also Harry Berger, Jr., "The *Mutabilitie Cantos:* Archaism and Evolution in Retrospect," in *Spenser: A Collection of Critical Essays, Twentieth Century Views,* ed. Harry Berger, Jr. (Englewood Cliffs, N.J.: Prentice-Hall, 1968), pp. 146-76.

13. Melville to Hawthorne, 17? November 1851, *Letters,* p. 143.

CHAPTER TWO

1. James, *Hawthorne,* pp. 15-16.

2. The entry is apparently from 1845. See Nathaniel Hawthorne, *The American Notebooks,* ed. Claude M. Simpson (Columbus: Ohio State University Press, 1972), *Centenary Edition,* 8:254.

3. For more extensive discussions of Hawthorne's process of creation see Arlin Turner, "Hawthorne's Method of Using His Source Materials," in *Studies for William A. Read,* ed. Nathaniel M. Caffee and Thomas A. Kirby (University: Louisiana State University Press, 1940), pp. 301-12, and Edward H. Davidson, *Hawthorne's Last Phase* (New Haven: Yale University Press, 1949).

4. Albert Béguin, *Balzac lu et relu,* cited and translated by Donald Fanger, *Dostoyevsky and Romantic Realism,* p. 15.

5. Charles Feidelson, Jr., *Symbolism and American Literature* (Chicago: University of Chicago Press, 1953), p. 6.

6. This oscillation is most fully described in Edgar A. Dryden, "Hawthorne's Castle in the Air: Form and Theme in *The House of the Seven Gables,*" *ELH* 38 (June 1971): 294-317.

7. Hawthorne to James T. Fields, undated letter, in Fields, *Hawthorne* (Boston: James R. Osgood, 1876), pp. 40-41.

8. Hawthorne's major exercise in generic definition is in the preface to *The House of the Seven Gables;* my formulations link his comments here to those in his other prefaces. The fullest discussion of the critical background to Hawthorne's distinction between novel and romance is in John Caldwell Stubbs, *The Pursuit of Form: A Study of Hawthorne and the Romance* (Urbana: University of Illinois Press, 1970), pp. 3-36.

CHAPTER THREE

1. On the novel's accuracy of historical detail see Charles Ryskamp, "The New England Sources of *The Scarlet Letter,*" *American Literature* 31 (November 1959): 257-72.

2. See Feidelson, *Symbolism and American Literature,* p. 10: "Every character, in effect, re-enacts the 'Custom House' scene in which Hawthorne himself contemplated the letter, so that the entire 'romance' becomes a kind of exposition of the nature of symbolic perception. Hawthorne's subject is not only the meaning of adultery but also meaning in general; not only *what* the focal symbol means but also *how* it gains significance." For a reading of *The Scarlet Letter* in terms of the characters' relationships to their author as creators see Porte, *Romance in America,* pp. 98-114.

3. James, *Hawthorne,* p. 99.

4. See Mills, *American and English Fiction,* pp. 52-73.

5. Hawthorne to James T. Fields, January 1850, in Fields, *Hawthorne,* p. 21.

6. Harry Berger, Jr., "Spenser's *Faerie Queene,* Book I: Prelude to Interpretation," *Southern Review* 2 (1966): 31.

7. For Freud "overdetermined" describes the process in dream whereby "not only are the elements of a dream determined by the dream-thoughts many times over, but the individual dream thoughts are represented in the dream by several elements." *The Interpretation of Dreams,* trans. James Strachey (New York: Avon Books, 1965), p. 318. Joseph C. Pattison argues that "conscious dream" is the experience Hawthorne tries to make us enter into in his works in "Point of View in Hawthorne," *PMLA* 82 (1967): 363-69.

8. For an illuminating discussion of Dimmesdale's guilt see Frederick Crews, *The Sins of the Fathers: Hawthorne's Psychological Themes* (New York: Oxford University Press, 1966), pp. 136-53.

9. Geoffrey H. Hartman, "False Themes and Gentle Minds," *Beyond Formalism: Literary Essays, 1958-70* (New Haven: Yale University Press, 1970), p. 285.

It is such a "freer attitude" that Henry James is describing in his famous assertion that the sense of sin in Hawthorne has an *"imported* character'': "it seems to exist there merely for an artistic or literary purpose." *Hawthorne,* p. 59.

10. Hartman, p. 288.

11. Crews, *Sins of the Fathers,* p. 150.

12. In connection with Chillingworth's rigidification of being and meaning see Angus Fletcher's discussion of the allegorical hero's possession by a daimonic energy in *Allegory: The Theory of a Symbolic Mode* (Ithaca, N.Y.: Cornell University Press, 1964), pp. 25–69.

13. Fiedler, *Love and Death,* p. 440.

14. See Charles Feidelson, Jr., *"The Scarlet Letter,"* in *Hawthorne Centenary Essays,* ed. Roy Harvey Pearce (Columbus: Ohio State University Press, 1964), pp. 31–77.

15. John C. Stubbs makes a parallel claim in *The Pursuit of Form,* p. 7: "Hawthorne used romance distance as a means to engage the reader in a debate about human experience."

CHAPTER FOUR

1. Hawthorne to James T. Fields, November 1850, in Fields, *Hawthorne,* p. 29.

2. The whole passage, from the seventeenth chapter of *Adam Bede,* is relevant to my discussion:

> It is for this rare, precious quality of truthfulness that I delight in many Dutch paintings, which lofty-minded people despise. I find a source of delicious sympathy in these faithful pictures of a monotonous homely existence, which has been the fate of so many more among my fellow-mortals than a life of pomp or of absolute indigence, of tragic suffering or of world-stirring actions. I turn, without shrinking, from cloud-borne angels, from prophets, sibyls, and heroic warriors, to an old woman bending over her flower-pot, or eating her solitary dinner, while the noonday light, softened perhaps by a screen of leaves, falls on her mobcap.

The opposition of Dutch realism to the sublime and its association with the vision of loving fellowship go back to eighteenth-century discussions of the sublime and the picturesque. For a more extended discussion of Hawthorne's method of humanizing his scenes see Leo B. Levy, "Picturesque Style in *The House of the Seven Gables,"* *New England Quarterly* 39 (June 1966): 147–60.

3. Georg Lukács, *Studies in European Realism* (New York: Grosset and Dunlap, 1964), p. 9.

4. Ibid., p. 6.

5. For a fuller treatment of social themes in *The House of the Seven Gables* see F. O. Matthiessen, *American Renaissance: Art and Expression in the Age of Emerson and Whitman* (New York: Oxford University Press, 1941), pp. 316–37. This should be supplemented with the subtly reasoned comments on the same

theme in Edgar Dryden's "Hawthorne's Castle in the Air: Form and Theme in *The House of the Seven Gables.*"

6. Hawthorne to Horatio Bridge, 15 March 1851, in Bridge, *Personal Recollections of Nathaniel Hawthorne* (New York: Harper and Brothers, 1893), p. 125.

7. Fiedler, *Love and Death*, p. 223.

8. Clark Griffith, "Substance and Shadow: Language and Meaning in *The House of the Seven Gables,*" *Modern Philology* 51 (February 1954): 192.

9. D. H. Lawrence, *Studies in Classic American Literature* (1923; rpt. New York: Viking Press, 1964), p. 104.

10. In "Who Killed Judge Pyncheon? The Role of the Imagination in *The House of the Seven Gables,*" *PMLA* 71 (1956): 355–69, Alfred H. Marks ingeniously argues that as he sits in the ancestral chair Jaffrey sees a ghost—Clifford, who is so many times said to look like a ghost; thus the imagination he has spurned precipitates his own death.

CHAPTER FIVE

1. Hawthorne to Edwin P. Whipple, 2 May 1852, cited by Roy Harvey Pearce in his introduction to the *Centenary Edition* of *The Blithedale Romance and Fanshawe*, p. xix.

2. Chase, *American Novel and Its Tradition*, p. 14.

3. See Nathalie Sarraute, "Conversation et sous-conversation," *L'Ère du soupçon* (Paris: Editions Gallimard, 1956), pp. 97–147.

4. On veils and veiling see Frank Davidson, "Toward a Re-evaluation of *The Blithedale Romance,*" *New England Quarterly* 25 (September 1952): 374–83.

5. William Dean Howells, *Heroines of Fiction* (New York: Harper and Brothers, 1901), 1:175. Howells also discusses *Blithedale* in "My Literary Passions," and in "My First Visit to New England" he records the pleasure Hawthorne took in hearing him cite *Blithedale* as his favorite of Hawthorne's works. Howells, *Literary Friends' and Acquaintance*, ed. David F. Hiatt and Edwin H. Cady (Bloomington: Indiana University Press, 1968), pp. 50–51. James discusses the novel in *Hawthorne*, pp. 115–20, and his own *The Bostonians* is in important ways a revision of this novel.

6. Howells, *Heroines of Fiction*, 1:175; James, *Hawthorne*, p. 116.

7. For a discussion of artifice and incoherence in particular, and, in general, the creative responses to contemporary social and intellectual issues in *Blithedale*, see James H. McIntosh, "Flickering Fires in a Waste of Chaos: An Essay on the Instability of Belief in *The Blithedale Romance*" (unpublished essay).

8. A suggestive discussion of Coverdale as observer and of his hermitage is in Richard Poirier, *A World Elsewhere: The Place of Style in American Literature* (New York: Oxford University Press, 1966), pp. 115–24.

9. *Blithedale* thus provides an excellent illustration of Irving Howe's contention that "in those 19th-century American novels that do deal with politics, ideology or what passes for it in this country is seen in a far more intimate relation to personal experience than in the European political novel; in fact, ideology is sometimes treated by American novelists as if it were merely a form of

private experience." *Politics and the Novel* (New York: Meridian Books, 1957), p. 162. Howe discusses this novel acutely on pp. 163–75.

10. Two particularly interesting discussions of the relation of Coverdale to Hawthorne's art, both quite different from each other and both different again from my own, can be found in Porte, *Romance in America,* pp. 125–37, and Frederick C. Crews, "A New Reading of *The Blithedale Romance,*" *American Literature* 29 (May 1957): 147–70.

11. Marius Bewley, *The Eccentric Design: Form in the Classic American Novel* (New York: Columbia University Press, 1963), p. 148.

12. Hawthorne to Edwin P. Whipple, 2 May 1852, cited in Pearce's introduction to the *Centenary Edition,* p. xix.

13. "Wrote the last page (199th manuscript) of the Blithedale Romance, April 30th. 1852. Wrote Preface, May 1st. Afterwards modified the conclusion, and lengthened to 201 pages." Hawthorne, *American Notebooks,* p. 314.

CHAPTER SIX

1. Warner Berthoff, *The Example of Melville* (1962; rpt. New York: W. W. Norton, 1972), p. 5.

2. Melville to Hawthorne, 17? November 1851, *Letters,* p. 142.

3. Melville to Evert A. Duyckinck, 3 March 1849, *Letters,* p. 79.

4. Melville to Hawthorne, 16? April? 1851, *Letters,* pp. 124–25.

5. Melville to Evert A. Duyckinck, 13 December 1850, *Letters,* p. 117.

6. Melville to Hawthorne, 29 June 1851, *Letters,* p. 133.

7. E. M. Forster, *Aspects of the Novel* (1927; rpt. Harmondsworth: Penguin Books, 1962). Forster discusses the prophetic imagination most acutely on pp. 136–38; he discusses Melville on pp. 141–46.

8. Melville to Richard Bentley, 5 June 1849, *Letters,* p. 86. "Hawthorne and His Mosses," reprinted in Jay Leyda, ed., *The Portable Melville* (New York: Viking Press, 1952), p. 407.

9. Melville to Hawthorne, 1? June 1851, *Letters,* p. 130.

10. Melville to Hawthorne, 17? November 1851, *Letters,* p. 143.

11. Melville to John Murray, 25 March 1848, *Letters,* pp. 70–71.

12. Walter E. Bezanson, "*Moby-Dick:* Work of Art," in *Moby-Dick Centennial Essays,* ed. Tyrus Hillway and Luther S. Mansfield (Dallas: Southern Methodist University Press, 1953), p. 56.

13. Babbalanja's comments show how exactly Melville shares Keats's feeling that "that which is creative must create itself." John Keats to James Augustus Hessey, 8 October 1818, in Hyder E. Rollins, ed., *The Letters of John Keats* (Cambridge, Mass.: Harvard University Press, 1958), 1:374.

14. Melville to John Murray, 25 March 1848, *Letters,* p. 71.

15. Fiedler, *Love and Death,* p. 126.

16. James, "Preface to *Roderick Hudson,*" *Art of the Novel,* p. 5.

17. Harvey, *Character and the Novel,* p. 89.

18. Melville, *Billy Budd, Sailor* (*An Inside Narrative*), ed. Harrison Hayford and Merton M. Sealts, Jr. (Chicago: University of Chicago Press, 1962), p. 128.

19. Allen Hayman notes this resemblance in "The Real and the Original: Herman Melville's Theory of Prose Fiction," *MFS* 8 (1962): 220. His essay is a useful collection and discussion of Melville's comments on fiction.

CHAPTER SEVEN

1. Lawrence, *Studies in Classic American Literature*, p. 2.

2. Paul Brodtkorb, Jr., provides a full phenomenology of the strangeness of things in *Moby-Dick* and discusses the interactions of strangeness and human meditation in *Ishmael's White World: A Phenomenological Reading of Moby Dick* (New Haven: Yale University Press, 1965).

3. Forster, *Aspects of the Novel*, p. 137.

4. Aristotle, *Poetics*, cited in Fletcher, *Allegory*, p. 148.

5. Lawrence, *Studies in Classic American Literature*, p. 152.

6. Susanne K. Langer, *Feeling and Form* (New York: Charles Scribner's Sons, 1953), p. 331.

7. Alfred Kazin, "Introduction," *Moby-Dick* (Boston: Riverside Press, 1956), p. vii.

8. See Leo Marx, *The Machine in the Garden: Technology and the Pastoral Ideal in America* (New York: Oxford University Press, 1964), pp. 301–2.

9. The fullest and most illuminating discussion of this pattern and of self-conscious form in *Moby-Dick* is in Edgar A. Dryden, *Melville's Thematics of Form: The Great Art of Telling the Truth* (Baltimore: Johns Hopkins Press, 1968), pp. 83–104.

10. Although he does not mention Melville, D. W. Jefferson provides an excellent summary of one of the traditions this book belongs to in "*Tristram Shandy* and the Tradition of Learned Wit," *Essays in Criticism* 1 (1951): 225–48.

11. Victor Brombert, *Stendhal: Fiction and the Themes of Freedom* (New York: Random House, 1968), p. 69.

12. Brodtkorb says of *Moby-Dick*'s irony: "by so frequently seeming to offer us no firm standpoint, Ishmael forces the reader back upon his own resources and prevents any direct relationship: the reader cannot appropriate the Ishmaelean ironist's positive attitude in order to be a follower of or a dissenter from it because the ironist offers him none to appropriate." *Ishmael's White World*, p. 3.

13. James Guetti works out this comparison at the level of Ahab and Ishmael's attitude toward language and metaphor in *The Limits of Metaphor: A Study of Melville, Conrad, and Faulkner* (Ithaca, N.Y.: Cornell University Press, 1967), pp. 33–37.

14. Frank Kermode, *The Sense of an Ending: Studies in the Theory of Fiction* (New York: Oxford University Press, 1966), p. 47.

15. Ibid., pp. 46–47.

CHAPTER EIGHT

1. See Raymond J. Nelson, "The Art of Herman Melville: The Author of *Pierre*," *Yale Review* n.s. 59 (Winter 1970): 197–214.

2. Melville to Richard Bentley, 16 April 1852, *Letters,* p. 150.

3. Melville to Hawthorne, 1? June 1851, *Letters,* p. 128.

4. Melville, "Hawthorne and His Mosses," *Portable Melville,* p. 418. The interesting and difficult subject of Melville's attempts to mediate between popular forms and his own ambition is sensitively discussed by William Charvat in *The Profession of Authorship in America, 1800–1870: The Papers of William Charvat,* ed. Matthew J. Bruccoli (Columbus: Ohio State University Press, 1968), pp. 204–82.

5. R. P. Blackmur, "The Craft of Herman Melville: A Putative Statement," *The Lion and the Honeycomb: Essays in Solicitude and Critique* (New York: Harcourt, Brace, and World, 1955), pp. 127–28.

6. Melville to Hawthorne, 16? April? 1851, *Letters,* p. 124.

7. James, *Hawthorne,* p. 64.

8. Perry Miller provides a lively description of the actual literary world that Melville satirizes in "Young America in Literature," in *The Raven and the Whale: The War of Words and Wits in the Era of Poe and Melville* (New York: Harcourt, Brace, and World, 1956).

9. On Melville's changed understanding of the nature of fictive constructs in *Pierre* see Dryden, *Melville's Thematics of Form,* pp. 117–41.

10. Jorge Luis Borges recommends this translation of 1 Corinthians 13:12, "videmus nunc per speculum in aenigmate," in "The Mirror of Enigmas," *Other Inquisitions, 1937–1952,* trans. Ruth L. C. Simms (New York: Washington Square Press, 1966), pp. 131–34.

11. John Seelye, *Melville: The Ironic Diagram* (Evanston, Ill.: Northwestern University Press, 1970), p. 10.

CHAPTER NINE

1. Nathaniel Hawthorne, *The English Notebooks,* ed. Randall Stewart (London: Oxford University Press, 1941), pp. 432–33.

2. Melville to Hawthorne, 17? November 1851, *Letters,* p. 142.

3. Ibid., p. 143.

4. Melville to Hawthorne, 16? April? 1851, *Letters,* pp. 124–25.

5. Ibid., p. 125.

6. John Stuart Mill, *On Bentham and Coleridge,* cited in Harold H. Kolb, Jr., *The Illusion of Life: American Realism as a Literary Form* (Charlottesville: University Press of Virginia, 1969), p. 38. My thinking throughout this paragraph has been shaped by Kolb's discussion of American realism.

7. Melville, "Hawthorne and His Mosses," *Portable Melville,* p. 416.

Index